Competitive Semiconductor Product Management

Navigating the Future of Semiconductor Technology in the AI Era

Sultana Begum
Faiyaz Chowdary

Apress®

Competitive Semiconductor Product Management: Navigating the Future of Semiconductor Technology in the AI Era

Sultana Begum
Folsom, CA, USA

Faiyaz Chowdary
Folsom, CA, USA

ISBN-13 (pbk): 979-8-8688-0919-4
https://doi.org/10.1007/979-8-8688-0920-0

ISBN-13 (electronic): 979-8-8688-0920-0

Copyright © 2024 by Sultana Begum and Faiyaz Chowdary

This work is subject to copyright. All rights are reserved by the Publisher, whether the whole or part of the material is concerned, specifically the rights of translation, reprinting, reuse of illustrations, recitation, broadcasting, reproduction on microfilms or in any other physical way, and transmission or information storage and retrieval, electronic adaptation, computer software, or by similar or dissimilar methodology now known or hereafter developed.

Trademarked names, logos, and images may appear in this book. Rather than use a trademark symbol with every occurrence of a trademarked name, logo, or image we use the names, logos, and images only in an editorial fashion and to the benefit of the trademark owner, with no intention of infringement of the trademark.

The use in this publication of trade names, trademarks, service marks, and similar terms, even if they are not identified as such, is not to be taken as an expression of opinion as to whether or not they are subject to proprietary rights.

While the advice and information in this book are believed to be true and accurate at the date of publication, neither the authors nor the editors nor the publisher can accept any legal responsibility for any errors or omissions that may be made. The publisher makes no warranty, express or implied, with respect to the material contained herein.

    Managing Director, Apress Media LLC: Welmoed Spahr
    Acquisitions Editor: Susan McDermott
    Desk Editor: Laura Berendson
    Editorial Project Manager: Jessica Vakili
    Copy Editor: Kim Burton

Distributed to the book trade worldwide by Springer Science+Business Media New York, 1 New York Plaza, Suite 4600, New York, NY 10004-1562, USA. Phone 1-800-SPRINGER, fax (201) 348-4505, e-mail orders-ny@springer-sbm.com, or visit www.springeronline.com. Apress Media, LLC is a California LLC and the sole member (owner) is Springer Science + Business Media Finance Inc (SSBM Finance Inc). SSBM Finance Inc is a **Delaware** corporation.

For information on translations, please e-mail booktranslations@springernature.com; for reprint, paperback, or audio rights, please e-mail bookpermissions@springernature.com.

Apress titles may be purchased in bulk for academic, corporate, or promotional use. eBook versions and licenses are also available for most titles. For more information, reference our Print and eBook Bulk Sales web page at http://www.apress.com/bulk-sales.

Any source code or other supplementary material referenced by the author in this book is available to readers on GitHub. For more detailed information, please visit https://www.apress.com/gp/services/source-code.

If disposing of this product, please recycle the paper

I dedicate this book to my husband, Faiyaz, a divine presence and a source of unconditional support and strength; my parents, Farzana and Mansoor Ali; my sister, Sameena, for her unconditional support and continuous inspiration; and my godparents, Alma and Alex, for being my pillars of strength

—Sultana Begum

Table of Contents

About the Authors xi

About the Technical Reviewers xiii

Acknowledgments xv

Introduction xvii

Chapter 1: Competition and Its Significance 1
    Competition in the PC Industry 5
        Competition Categories 12
    Challenges and Opportunities 27
    Competitive Landscape 29
    Summary 33

Chapter 2: Semiconductor Product Management Life Cycle 37
    Significance of Product Management Life Cycle 39
        Planning Stage 43
        Design and Development 50
        Semiconductor Manufacturing 57
        Regulatory Compliance 58
        Go-to-Market Plans and Product Launch 58
        Maintenance, Support, and End of Life 59
    Summary 59

TABLE OF CONTENTS

Chapter 3: Competitive Semiconductor Product Strategy 61
Significance of Competitive Semiconductor Product Strategy 63
Competitive Semiconductor Strategy Development Framework............67
Semiconductor Products Strategy Execution 87
Summary............88

Chapter 4: SoC Architecture and Power Management............91
CPU Architecture 95
Instruction Set Architecture (ISA) 97
Microarchitecture 102
Memory Hierarchy 106
CPU KPIs 107
CPU AI 112
GPU Architecture 114
Memory Hierarchy 118
GPU KPIs 120
GPU Programmability............123
NPU Architecture 126
Media 131
SoC Integration 131
Power Management 133
Transistor Threshold Voltage 138
Operating Voltage and Frequency............142
Thermal Design Power (TDP) 143
IP Power Management 145
SoC Power Supply and Delivery Management 147
Implementing Power Management from IP to Device 149
Performance per Watt............152
Summary 155

TABLE OF CONTENTS

Chapter 5: Semiconductor Manufacturing 157
Transistor Technology 159
Manufacturing 161
    Monolithic and Desegregated Dies 166
    OSAT 171
Semiconductor Manufacturing Leaders 173
Semiconductor Manufacturing Pricing 175
    TSMC 175
    Intel 176
Performance Per Dollar 179
Security 181
Summary 183

Chapter 6: The CHIPS Act of 2022 185
The Impact of the CHIPS Act 186
    Technological Impacts 187
    Economic Impacts 188
    Other Impacts and Challenges 190
    Role of Product Managers and Management 190
Just-in-Time Manufacturing 192
Summary 194

Chapter 7: OEMs and Channel Partners 195
OEMs 196
    Motherboard Assembly 198
    Final Product Assembly and Testing 198
    Operating System, Drivers, and Other Software Installation 199
    Quality Inspection, Performance Testing and Tuning, and Packaging 199

TABLE OF CONTENTS

   Channel Partners 200

   Summary 200

Chapter 8: Performance Management 203

   Product Performance Management Strategy 206

   Implementing a Product Performance Management Strategy 207

      SoC-Level Performance Management Strategy 208

      System-Level Performance Management Strategy 214

   Product Performance Management 218

      Stages in Performance Management 220

      Go-to-Market Strategy 254

      Support and EOL 256

   Summary 257

Chapter 9: Competitive Semiconductor Product Roadmaps 259

   Defining Competitive Semiconductor Product Roadmaps 260

      Roadmap KPIs 261

      Organizing Product Roadmaps 263

   A Path to Achieve Product Roadmap KPIs 265

      Process Technology 266

      Design and Microarchitecture 268

      HW-SW Co-Design 273

      System Co-Design 277

      Programmability and Developer Tools 279

      Competitive Intelligence 285

      Projections 287

      Product Portfolio 288

   The Secret to Strong Product Roadmaps 292

   Summary 296

Chapter 10: AI in Semiconductor Product Management 299

    AI Transformation in Semiconductor Product Management..............................300

        AI in Product Development Life cycle 301

    AI Use Cases 302

    Competition in AI..304

    Summary..306

Conclusion 307

Next Steps: Reading Pointers 314

Index..315

About the Authors

Sultana Begum is a de facto expert of competitive product management and technology enthusiast with over a decade of experience at Intel Corporation. With deep technical expertise and a keen eye for strategic thinking, her expertise spreads widely across semiconductor design development to define and execute a competitive product strategy, with hands-on experience in launching multiple software and hardware products at Intel Corp.

Sultana's career at Intel began in 2015 as a design verification engineer. It supported industry-leading compute and memory solutions while gaining a breadth of technical knowledge on complex semiconductor design methodology, with her always learning and curiousness to understand end-to-end semiconductor product development. Sultana held critical roles in technical product marketing hardware and software product management to gain a broad and deep-rooted expertise in the technology industry. She is a product manager-strategy defining artificial intelligence–based computing products at Intel.

Prior to her tenure at Intel, Sultana honed her technical skills in engineering roles at Accenture. Sultana holds both bachelor's and master's degrees in electronics, an MBA in product management, and is currently pursuing Executive Management Education at Stanford University.

ABOUT THE AUTHORS

Sultana is a proud wife, daughter, and sister of a beautiful, loving family and feels lucky to be the mother of six beautiful cockatiel birds. When not working or writing, she likes to listen to music, read books on philosophy and spirituality, and write research papers.

Faiyaz Ahmed Chowdary is a technology enthusiast with over a decade of experience working at various technical industry leading companies. With deep technical expertise and a keen eye for business and technical aspects of technology, his expertise spreads widely across technology development.

Faiyaz's career began at BoFA in 2014 as a Technology Analyst and continued his journey to be a Technology and Business Product Manager. Prior to his tenure at BoFA, Faiyaz honed his technical skills in engineering roles as Wipro.

Faiyaz holds bachelor's in electronics and communication and master's degree in industrial engineering. Faiyaz is a proud Husband and Son of a beautiful, loving family.

About the Technical Reviewers

Massimo Nardone has more than 29 years of experience in security, web/mobile development, and cloud and IT/OT/IoT architecture. His true passions are security and Android. He has been programming and teaching how to program with Android, Perl, PHP, Java, VB, Python, C/C++, and MySQL for more than 30 years. He holds a Master of Science degree inComputing Science from the University of Salerno, Italy. He has worked as a chief information security officer (CISO), software engineer, chief security architect, security executive, OT/IoT/IIoT security leader, and architect for many years. He currently works as VP of OT Security for SSH Communications Security.

Anil Kumar is a seasoned principal engineer at Intel Corporation, where his zeal for transforming concepts into tangible, market-ready designs is the cornerstone of his professional journey. As a system architect with the Client Computing Group, Anil collaborates closely with Intel's partners to deliver innovative computing devices, empowering users to create and connect in meaningful ways. His prior tenure in the Internet of Things Group (IOTG) saw him spearheading the connectivity platform architecture, where he played a pivotal role in integrating essential connectivity and communication technologies. This led to diverse IoT solutions deployed across various industry verticals.

Anil's career at Intel began in 2007 as a design engineer in the Digital Home Group, where he quickly established himself as a platform architect, developing Intel architecture-based media processors for TV and set-top box applications. His expertise as the chief architect in the Intel Media Group resulted in several designs that garnered accolades at the Consumer Electronics Show (CES), including the pioneering Google TV devices based on his reference designs.

Prior to his tenure at Intel, Anil honed his technical skills in design engineering roles at global tech firms such as Fujitsu and Alcatel.

An accomplished author, Anil has contributed to the body of knowledge in his field with works like *Connecting the Internet of Things* (Apress, 2023) and *Demystifying Internet of Things Security* (Apress, 2020), sharing his insights and expertise with a broader audience.

Acknowledgments

This book covers a myriad of specialized topics and concepts. I would like to appreciate and acknowledge the contributions of many experts in both direct and indirect ways. Open source platforms have been a great source of learning, and I would like to thank the institutions for providing such vast knowledge systems with the latest industry trends. I thank Anil Kumar and Sunil Cheruvu for providing unconditional support.

A special thanks to Todd Lewellen, Charles Anyimi, Rajshree Chabukswar for being a great mentor, a strong pillar of strength and a teacher in shaping my understanding of the technology ecosystem. Kris Fleming for being an amazing mentor.

I sincerely thank my colleagues Raghunathan Sadagopan, Manu Prasad Manmathan, Manini Sharma, and for their continuous support in helping me learn the fine details of industry trends and encouraging me to formulate new strategic concepts.

Introduction

Without sales, nothing would get sold.

Without engineering, nothing would get built.

Without support, customers would leave.

Without product managers? Life would be just fine. (For a while.)

— Kenneth Norton, Google Ventures

Can we tell the presence of salt in the food you haven't cooked without tasting it? No, isn't it? Salt just dissolves and makes it difficult to find its presence without tasting it but once you have tasted it, the first thing you will notice is the absence of the salt if not added. In product management, product managers are similar to salt in a product served as a dish to its customers. It is not easy to detect their absence during the journey, but it will make a huge difference.

The secret to a successful product in any industry is its ability to continuously create and capture value in the market. Product managers play a key role in defining a product's value creation and capturing strategy along with its execution path by guiding products from concept, design, and go-to-market plans for product success. The role of product managers can be further extended as a bridge that connects various teams, aligns product development with strategic goals, and ensures that the product meets customer needs and market demands. Driving innovation, managing risks, and maintaining a customer-focused product design approach, the role of product managers can be pivotal in the product's and

INTRODUCTION

the company's overall success. Depending on the industry, the roles and functions of the product managers vary. But in the technology industry, the role of a product manager is much larger than in other industries.

In the semiconductor product management life cycle, which is usually longer than a typical product management life cycle, the execution demands a meticulous process. The long life cycle, paired with research and development innovations and collaboration involving broader teams and other external stakeholders in the ecosystem, makes semiconductor product management a complex task with huge risks. A systematic approach to planning and developing product design, manufacturing in fabrication facilities, positioning across various customer segments, and launching with an effective go-to-market plan to manage products until their end of life (EOL) is critical to the success of semiconductor products.

The technology industry is growing at an unprecedented speed to shape an advanced future. Competitors with fast-paced research and development in hardware and software platforms continuously challenge the product features and capabilities. The technology trends and innovations are changing within weeks, while hardware products take time to catch up to them. For example, recently, transformers large language models disrupted the technology industry. But within a short time, with the help of the open source community, transformer models have seen numerous innovations and optimization methodologies like quantization, 1-bit LLM, and so forth, and we already have a rival Mamba/State space models(SSM) or Hybrid(SSM+attention) large language model. With such faster growth, semiconductor hardware companies must develop hardware faster and catch up to the disruption to shape an advanced future. Unlike other industries, these faster changes drive technological innovations, help in advanced problem-solving capabilities, and set a vision for the future. A product manager in the technology industry holds the steering wheel of the advanced future influenced by innovation, effectively realizing those as products by creating and capturing value in the marketplace.

INTRODUCTION

Therefore, semiconductor product managers can play a crucial role in systematically pulling product management phases together and ensuring the product targets are met with a customer-centric approach while embracing cutting-edge technological innovations. To successfully execute these roles, product managers must clearly understand the strategic and technical aspects of semiconductor products and the product ecosystem, which this book aims to provide. In simple terms, as we know, product managers are the CEO of the products. This book provides frameworks, strategic approaches, technical deep dive information, and secrets for long-term roadmap planning to ensure product managers can be successful CEOs of semiconductor products. And an approach to plan and execute semiconductor products for sustained long-term success in the ever-growing competitive semiconductor landscape that can deliver software solutions to shape an advanced future.

CHAPTER 1

Competition and Its Significance

Without competition, the spectacular development of technology that we have seen in the last one hundred years in this country would not have happened.

—Lee R. Raymond

We live in a modern world of technology powered by semiconductor products such as smartphones in our pockets, wearables, personal computers in our backpacks, cars we drive, home appliances we use for our daily needs, medical equipment, cameras, and many other products and services as shown in the Figure 1-1. Everyone is motivated to have semiconductor products to reap the benefits of technology in making their everyday life easier, secure, and safer. The semiconductor industry has been and will be the foundation to continuously shape the future. With the emerging benefits of artificial intelligence, the semiconductor industry is at a crossroads of unprecedented demand, generating billions of dollars in revenue annually, fueling not just technology companies but the world economies. With such economic and developmental opportunities, this industry has been the center of innovation, with strong competition pushing the boundaries of possibilities.

CHAPTER 1   COMPETITION AND ITS SIGNIFICANCE

Figure 1-1. Cloud services connecting various electronic device segments

This chapter discusses the significance of competition in the semiconductor industry and its evolution from a basic transistor to advanced semiconductor products. The categories of competition and the methodology of economic and social value created by various companies operating in the semiconductor industry. The significance of competition in delivering customer-centric products and product managers' role in developing a strategy for long-term competitive semiconductor product management. We shall navigate through the current competitive landscape, trends, and insights into the personal computer (PC) industry as an example to discuss the key areas of focus in strategic semiconductor product management.

There are numerous products and services in the modern semiconductor industry and the foundational elements of these products are semiconductor hardware and software as a combination. Both hardware and software depend on each other to deliver a user-accessible application that can provide value to the customer. With the physical semiconductor hardware as the foundation, several other products are designed as software applications that execute on this hardware.

CHAPTER 1   COMPETITION AND ITS SIGNIFICANCE

Both hardware and software products work hand in hand to execute the intended functionality and deliver value to its users. As a result, the technology industry is divided into hardware and software products in which hardware is the physical product to realize the software product's value by the customer. For example, to access our emails on Gmail, a software product provided by Google, we need a physical hardware device like a computer, a phone, or a tablet. Therefore, hardware and software are critical to technological innovation and advancements.

Today's computing technology industry can be broadly divided into cloud, enterprise, and client solutions, offering various products and services per the needs with a high degree of flexibility, besides on-device computing and application services specific to client devices. The cloud-client network-based solutions provide a connected and coherent user experience. Let's take the same Gmail example. We can access our Gmail using any client device based on our needs and preferences. The Gmail application service is hosted from the cloud via an Internet network. With account authentication, we can login to our Gmail account using any compatible client device with a network connection or installing an app. Another way to think of it is when we use a watch to monitor our health. Although the health is tracked through a watch sensor, the cloud-client service flexibility allows you to access the same data through a phone or a PC as all our data is managed and stored in the cloud. Therefore, combining the cloud or enterprise client creates a flexible, need-based solution environment in today's world as our data is managed on the cloud, and endpoint devices can be PCs, tablets, watches, or phones.

With the technology revolution and continuous innovations in this industry, there is increased competition in almost all technological space. Multiple products offer great user experience for the users to choose from in almost all categories, as shown in Table 1-1.

CHAPTER 1   COMPETITION AND ITS SIGNIFICANCE

Table 1-1. Some Products in the Client and Cloud Space

Client Products	Client Product Competition includes	Cloud Service Competition includes
Television and services	Samsung, Sony/ LG/ Panasonic, and more	Netflix, Amazon Prime, Apple TV
Smartwatches and services	Apple, Pixel watch, Samsung Galaxy, Fitbit	Apple, Google, Fitbit
Home security and services	Google, Ring, Arlo, Roku, Blink	Google, Arlo, Roku, Blink storage and services
PC/tablet/phones and services	Dell, Apple, HP, Samsung, Lenovo, Microsoft	Amazon, Google, Microsoft

In each of the categories shown in Table 1-1, multiple product choices are offered by various companies competing against each other to provide a great customer experience. Each company tries to outperform other companies' product solutions, increasing the competitive rivalry. As Lee R. Raymond said, without competition, technology wouldn't have advanced to where we are today. Competition is crucial to keep pushing the boundaries of possibilities and innovation in any industry. In the world of multiple choices, products that can create and capture value with differentiation and maintain it for a longer period with continuous updates will be successful—making the role of product managers more critical and demanding with aggressive competition everywhere. The key is to not just think about competition but keep competition as one key input in all the product management phases to improve product quality by continuous innovation and scalability to provide great customer service at a great price while maintaining product differentiation.

The Microsoft Windows phone is a good example of the impact of missing competitive product management. Microsoft-designed Windows phones had a tragic failure, and the reason was mainly due to a lack of product competitiveness compared to Android phones and iPhones offered at that time. Android and iOS phones at that time offered better value and leadership in price, social value, and ease of use features with a clear differentiation. The Windows phone at that time lacked differentiation to position itself uniquely against Android and iOS-based phones. It had the same, if not low, features to offer and failed to attract customers. Moreover, it was late to the market, and the customers were already used to the better value provided by the iOS and Android phones. The key insight from the Windows phone failure is that competitive product management is a way to develop successful products in a highly competitive landscape. Therefore, in today's world of advanced technology and severe competition, product management must evolve to competitive product management to deliver successful products.

Let's get into the details of competitive product management. This book covers the client semiconductor products in the personal computing space, focusing on competitive *system on a chip* or *system-on-chip* (SoC) product management, which can be applied to most semiconductor products and solutions.

Competition in the PC Industry

All failed companies are the same. They failed to escape competition.

—Peter Theil

CHAPTER 1   COMPETITION AND ITS SIGNIFICANCE

In the case of Windows phones, it was simple to identify competition as Android and iOS based on the product positioning at that time. Today, general-purpose computing devices are differentiated into multiple layers to create unique customer value. It is important that product managers know the various layers of differentiation there can be to aim for a tailored and personalized customer product. The hardware and software organization of general-purpose computing devices like PCs, tablets, and phones are shown in Figure 1-2. The system is broadly organized using SoC, operating system, and user application software. The competitive advantage can be gained by owning one or more layers besides hardware in this hierarchy to deliver a unique or higher product value to beat the competition or by providing unmatched product value beyond competitors.

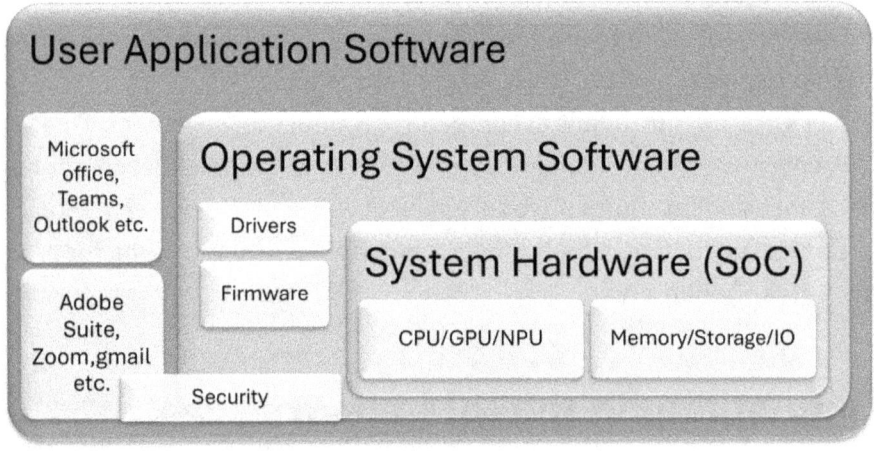

***Figure 1-2.** System hardware and software organization*

In the personal computing space, there are multiple-user application software like Microsoft Outlook, Gmail, Microsoft Office, Microsoft Teams, Zoom, Adobe Creative Suite, FaceTime, Final Cut Pro, and so on. The PC user can utilize any application software as long as it is available through the operating system. Operating system software is the bridge

CHAPTER 1   COMPETITION AND ITS SIGNIFICANCE

that connects the user application with hardware. Typically, it has application programming interface (API) drivers firmware built-in, so the user application software runs on compatible hardware consisting of a central processing unit (CPU), a graphics processing unit (GPU), a neural processing unit (NPU), memory, and storage. On the other hand, security can either be provided as part of the operating system or as an individual user application software or both. For example, Windows Defender is a security solution for Windows OS. McAfee is an add-on third-party security solution for users to install for additional security.

The hardware is the last layer required to run these user applications with the operating system's help. There are many common user applications compatible with multiple hardware devices. The popular proprietary operating systems available as personal computers are Microsoft Windows, Google ChromeOS, and Apple macOS. Linux and Ubuntu are other open source operating system options. However, the user base is higher on Windows and macOS in the personal computers segment. Apple macOS and iOS are compatible only with Apple proprietary hardware, while the Windows operating system is compatible with Intel, AMD, Qualcomm, and NVIDIA hardware. So far, it has been established that software applications need hardware to operate with the help of operating systems, and hardware defines the limitations of software applications and their capabilities. In simple terms, hardware is critical in the technology industry as it is the foundation for building technological solutions.

Hardware is categorized into multiple variant types depending on its usage. The typical hardware differentiation can be based on input, output device hardware, compute and memory hardware, networking, and other specialized hardware capabilities and configurations designed to implement specific functionalities. In personal computing devices such as PCs and tablets, the hardware component types are combined to form SoCs capable of handling general-purpose computing use cases. These

CHAPTER 1   COMPETITION AND ITS SIGNIFICANCE

hardware products are manufactured using semiconductor material, usually called *semiconductor products*. Table 1-2 shows some examples of the current companies offering solutions in personal computing.

Table 1-2. *Examples of Hardware and Software Solutions in PCs*

User Applications		Operating System Software	Hardware SoC
	iMessage, Pages, Safari Final cut Pro, Logic Pro	macOS, iOS, iPadOS, Linux, Ubuntu	Apple M1/M2/M3/M4 SoCs
Microsoft Office, Games, Zoom, BlackMagic, OneNote, Google Chrome			Intel 12th, 13th, 14th Gen SoCs and Intel+ NVIDIA Graphics Cards
	Edge, Notepad	Linux, Windows, Android, Ubuntu	
			AMD Zen3, Zen4, Zen 5 SoCs and AMD+ NVIDIA Graphics cards
			Qualcomm Snapdragon SoCs

The basic building block of semiconductor hardware is transistors, which are made of silicon material. Silicon is a hard, brittle, crystalline, solid chemical element with a blue-gray metallic luster. Its chemical symbol is Si, and the atomic number is 14. It is the second most abundant element in the earth's crust, after oxygen. It has the ideal electrical properties for semiconductors as it can act as an insulator at low temperatures and as a conductor at higher temperatures. Overall, silicon's chemical characteristics, abundance, electrical properties, thermal stability, and doping versatility with established manufacturing infrastructure made it a cost-effective material for semiconductor mass production to deliver reliable and efficient semiconductor products.

From transistors to field programmable gate arrays (FPGA) to CPU, GPU, and NPU integrated on SoC as shown in the Figure 1-3, semiconductor products have been at the edge of any innovation by pushing the boundaries of transistor technology. Besides standard computer hardware like CPUs, this industry has developed application-specific chips, general-purpose chipsets, GPU accelerators, and incremental learning AI (artificial intelligence) chipsets in unbelievably small-sized chips utilizing advancements in semiconductor fabrication technologies and design methodologies.

Although semiconductor hardware significantly contributes to the technology, software is also essential in realizing the benefits the technology industry can offer. The operating system and user applications layers on top of the hardware layer act as a medium for users to utilize technology by converting complex hardware instructions to simple, readable human language. Therefore, hardware and software innovations make the technology industry advancements responsible for shaping the future.

CHAPTER 1   COMPETITION AND ITS SIGNIFICANCE

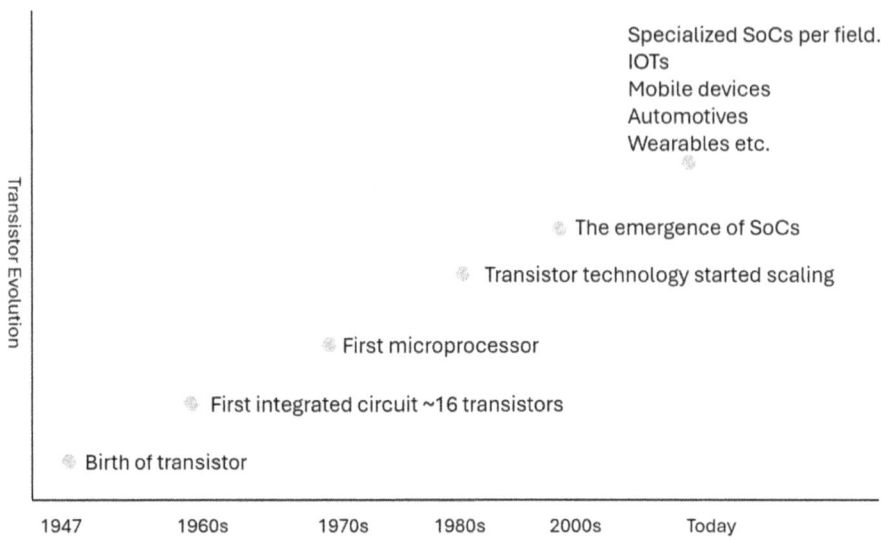

Figure 1-3. Evolution of SoCs from transistors

These continuous advancements through research and development in innovative hardware and software are a result of resilient product managers and technology enablers on a mission to develop products with long-term vision. There is also a flip side of this industry, which repeatedly iterates that many leading companies at one point in time failed eventually by pushing back on innovation and taking risks; for example, Nokia said no to Android, Yahoo dismissed Google, Blockbuster rejected Netflix, and so on. Therefore, the technology industry has tremendous potential to evolve with innovation as the backbone for hardware and software companies. The contributions of some of the companies involved in the technology industry have been phenomenal so far. for example, Apple, NVIDIA, AMD, Intel, and many others. The competitive spirit among these company leaders pushed the product's performance significantly faster with innovative features to deliver the great customer experience we see today.

Although the hardware, software applications, and operating system are basic needs for electronic devices to operate and provide value to customers. The semiconductor product customer base has increasingly

CHAPTER 1 COMPETITION AND ITS SIGNIFICANCE

become wider and denser as the modern semiconductor industry provides tailored devices crafted to provide a dedicated user experience per the needs and type of the user segment. For example, in the PC industry, tablets, laptops and desktops users are defined as two major categories: consumer and commercial as shown in the Figure 1-4.

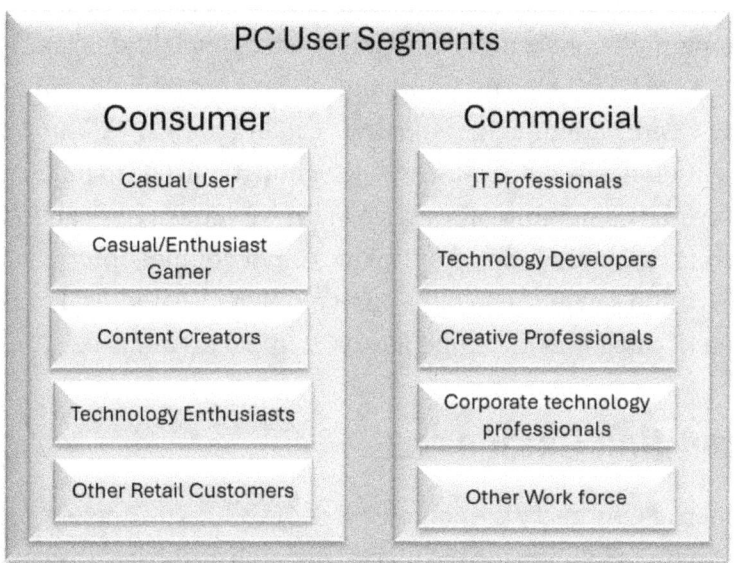

Figure 1-4. PC user segments

Within the consumer segment, there are various segments like casual users, casual/enthusiast gamers, content creators, and students who use different configurations of tablets, laptops, and desktops. As in the commercial segment, tablets, laptops, and desktops are developed for various industry professional workstreams like office workers, IT professionals and developers, creative professionals, field workers, executives and managers, healthcare professionals, and security professionals. The commercial segments add additional software manageability and asset management IT infrastructure layers to ensure safety, security, and support for the businesses.

CHAPTER 1   COMPETITION AND ITS SIGNIFICANCE

The product managers planning for a competitive PC semiconductor product should thoroughly know the various PC user segments and their compute requirements. These user segments' compute requirements, paired with other peripheral component choices can help OEMs to deliver tailored semiconductor product configurations to capture the user needs at a better value. For example, Intel positions the semiconductor products with compute differentiation, such as Intel Core i3, Intel Core i5, Intel Core i7, and Intel Core i7, to help OEMs (original equipment manufacturers) to design PCs with various choices so users can purchase the desired device based on their needs. As a result, the PC product must be manufactured with an overall competitive advantage in the PC industry by carefully considering competitive SoC features and other components such as storage, IO, and screens that make up a complete PC product. Let's discuss the different categories of competition within the PC industry.

Competition Categories

The modern PC industry is a complex web of various technology partners and competitors influencing the market dynamics. Many of the companies in partnership define, develop, and deliver competitive PC products tailored to each other's strengths as stakeholders paired with a thorough understanding of competitive factors. The modern PC industry has built a loyal customer base in this highly competitive landscape by focusing on their expertise and addressing specific market needs using various product portfolios.

The modern PC industry can be divided into Apple with iPadOS and macOS, Microsoft Windows, Google ChromeOS, and PC ecosystems competing for PC market share. But the dominant players are Apple and Microsoft. Apple offers end-to-end integrated solutions with semiconductor products, operating systems, and applications in various

CHAPTER 1   COMPETITION AND ITS SIGNIFICANCE

PC form factors like tablets, laptops, desktops, and workstations. The Windows PC ecosystem has specialized B2B (business to business) and B2C (business to customer) partners such as OEMs, operating systems vendors, and semiconductor product companies working as partners rigorously competing for the PC market share, as shown in Figure 1-5.

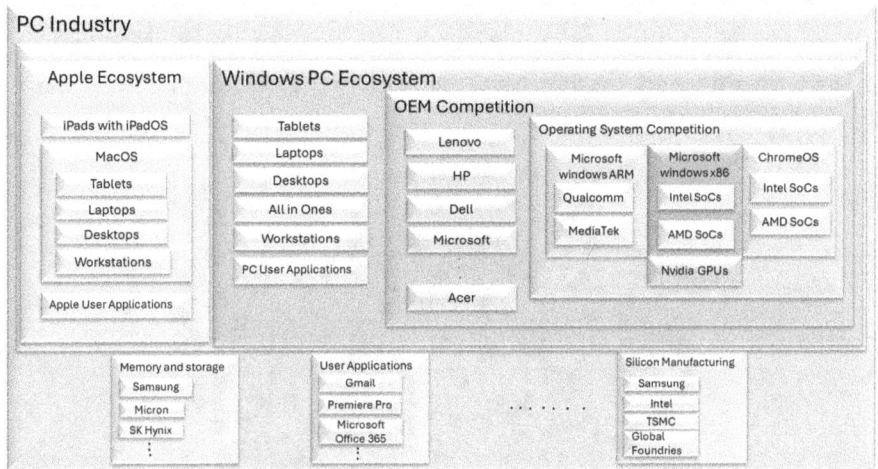

Figure 1-5. *PC industry snapshot*

In the complex Windows PC ecosystem, the semiconductor product managers should take a tiered approach to implement competitive analysis. The differentiation can be at the product level, application level, platform level, SoC level, and manufacturing level, influencing the competitive edge not just at the semiconductor definition and development for the overall success of the PC product in the market. For example, Microsoft first released Copilot+ PCs with Qualcomm semiconductor products, creating a differentiated competitive edge for Qualcomm compared to other Windows PCs. Therefore, the PC industry deals with many companies collaborating to make a single device with differentiation at multiple levels. The differentiation can be at SoC and its components, Memory support, fabrication technology and Motherboard peripherals influencing the operating systems workload scheduling methodology and performance on independent software vendors (ISVs) applications. All these components must be crafted according to the needs and willingness to pay of the different consumer and commercial segments to make the semiconductor products successful in the market. A successful PC product must lead in all these layers, such as SoC and its component capabilities, memory bandwidth and density, storage density, and applications performance with security to the customer data while offering a better value as shown in Figure 1-6.

Figure 1-6. *Various components in a PC*

With such a complex framework of PC product manufacturing by OEMs and semiconductor product management, how can product managers even get started with analyzing multifaceted competition and make sure the products can create and capture value in the market?

This complex web can be approached systematically to assess the underlying complexities by dividing it into different layers. The semiconductor product industry can be divided into design companies owning intellectual property (IP), SoC portfolios to reach multiple user segments, semiconductor fabrication manufacturing companies owning

CHAPTER 1   COMPETITION AND ITS SIGNIFICANCE

the latest process technology to manufacture the semiconductors, equipment/device manufacturing companies, independent software product companies owning operating system and software applications, and channels for product delivery as shown in Table 1-3. The semiconductor design and development company owning significant market segment share (MSS) is Intel, with design and fabrication capabilities; AMD, Apple, and NVIDIA are fabless semiconductor design companies with MSS. Intel and TSMC (Taiwan Semiconductor Manufacturing Company Ltd.) are dominant semiconductor manufacturing companies. Popular OEMs are Apple, Lenovo, HP, Dell, ASUS, Acer, and others. This layered approach can help product managers implement competitive analysis at each layer to learn the competitive dynamics and deliver a competitive PC product.

Table 1-3. Layers in PC Product Management and Competitors

Types of Layers	Competitive Rivals
design companies owning Intellectual property, SoC design and development	Intel, AMD, Apple, NVIDIA
Semiconductor fabrication manufacturing companies	Intel, TSMC, Samsung, global foundries
Equipment/device manufacturing companies	Apple, Lenovo, HP, Dell, ASUS, Acer, others
Independent software product companies	Microsoft, Apple, Google, and others
Channels for product delivery	Apple Store and other OEM websites, Amazon, Best Buy, Costco, other retail stores

The PC industry also has an ecosystem aspect with connected platforms bringing new dimensions to the user experience and customer value creation. Let's take a top-down approach to learn about the PC industry at an ecosystem level influencing PC semiconductor product management.

Apple Ecosystem

Apple is and has been a significant contributor to the technology industry; the products and services Apple offers are a great example of strategic ways to competitive semiconductor product management. Apple has evolved from a personal computer company to a global leader in technology and innovation with a diverse value-based product lineup, delivering strong financial performance. Apple continues to shape the future of technology navigating through competitive challenges with customer-centric long-term vision across their products.

Apple introduced the first personal computer, Macintosh, with a graphical user interface that set a standard for future computing back in the 1980s. Innovation and risk-taking pushed Apple to launch the iMac, known for its design and ease of use capabilities, followed by the introduction of iPods that revolutionized the music industry. Later, Apple introduced the iPhone, transforming the smartphone industry followed by a new tablet computing category of iPads. Apple then entered the wearable technology market with Apple Watch, AirPods, and Vision Pro. Apple TV followed in the entertainment industry. Figure 1-7 shows various products of Apple in both hardware and software categories. Apple used Intel SoCs earlier in their Macs. In 2020, it announced its transition from Intel processors to its custom-designed ARM-based processors for its PCs, starting with the M1 SoC.

CHAPTER 1 COMPETITION AND ITS SIGNIFICANCE

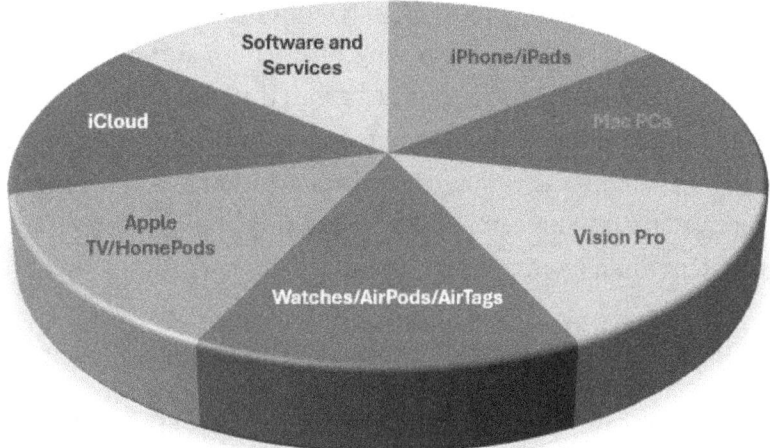

Figure 1-7. Apple product portfolio

All the products and services Apple offers are tremendous contributors to technological innovations, moreover, all products made their way into the market as revolutionary products or transformed into setting new trends. These products are a great example of creating and capturing social and economic value—the two essential requirements for product success in any industry. The social value of a product is the positive impact or service to society beyond the product's functional features, for example, environmental responsibility, health, and fitness. In contrast, economic value is the benefit a company derives from the products in terms of profits.

Social Value

Social Value helps build a strong loyal customer base reducing customer churn and increasing repeated business that contributes to the sustainable long-term success of the company. Apple's strong customer base has created a global community of users who share a common identity and support the company's innovation and sustainability efforts. Examples of social value include health and fitness, transparent privacy and security

CHAPTER 1   COMPETITION AND ITS SIGNIFICANCE

of the customer data in the products, and commitment to become carbon neutral across their entire businesses by 2030. These are some very strong social values provided by Apple products with the help of technological innovations compelling their customers to stay loyal and continuously attract new customers. The long-term product vision of Apple product managers and their management enabled them to build these values into their products while maintaining economic values.

Economic value

Economic value is the financial benefit a product can create, impacting businesses, consumers, and the broader economy. It can be defined as the difference between the cost of manufacturing products and customers' willingness to pay as shown in the Figure 1-8. The difference between the customers' willingness to pay for a product and the cost of its making should always be positive for the companies to make profits. The larger the better. In the technology industry, economic value can be derived from innovations in reducing manufacturing costs, adding innovative features and capabilities to the products, or both. Hence, the customers are willing to pay higher prices and keep the economic value high. With its research and development in technology and design choices, Apple launched social and economic value-based products, enabling it to become a successful and strong technology company.

Figure 1-8. *Economic value of a product*

Total Successful Product Value = Social Value + Economic Value

CHAPTER 1   COMPETITION AND ITS SIGNIFICANCE

Their success is not achieved in a day, Apple had quite an interesting journey into making their products successful and being a strong technology leader. Major leadership changes in the 1990s and knowing the strategic reasons for their success helped Apple develop competitive strategic plans, leading them to their success. Let's consider Apple's journey from iMacs to iPhone devices. Apple launched iTunes in 2001 as a digital media player and library application for organizing and playing music on iMacs. iTunes offered features like importing music from CDs and creating playlists, simplifying the management of digital music collections. The challenges iTunes faced were that the managed music was restricted to iMacs, limiting to a place lacking portability. During the same year, Apple launched a portable media player iPod, with iTunes integration. iTunes and the iPod created a cohesive ecosystem for digital music, making it easy for users to purchase, manage, and listen to music on the go. Soon, iTunes became a comprehensive legit media hub offering podcasts and video content, which increased the user base. The next innovation was the iPhone, which integrated iPods, iPhones, and Internet communications into one device. At this point, Apple had the iPhone in the hands of users and started innovating on services like Arcade, Apple TV+, Apple Music, and Apple News+ which helped the iPhone to become more popular for its feature offering and significantly increased its economic value. iCloud services, wearables, and other products followed later to provide a better customer experience to its users, building customer loyalty and shaping the Apple ecosystem.

Apple launched the iMac with a revolutionary, innovative, yet simple design and started looking closely at problems it could solve and shortcomings along its way. Learning from its shortcomings by taking a customer-centric approach, Apple continuously launched new products and services to stay ahead of the competition and maintain its unique platform advantage. This approach helped Apple create strategic processes for their products' long-term success and patented technological research and development innovations, making it harder for competition to catch up. Today, Apple is a leader in delivering end-to-end products and services to its customers as a single-stop shop, making it one of the most valuable companies in the world, trading at a market capitalization exceeding $3.5 trillion as of 2024.

Apple always designed their iPhone semiconductor A series SoCs and outsourced their Mac semiconductor product SoC design, development, and manufacturing to Intel. However, in 2020, Apple transitioned to its custom silicon for its Macs, terminating its long-term partnership with Intel. Apple started scaling their A series SoC IPs to design M series, M Pro series, M Max series, and M Ultra series SoCs placed in various Mac, and tablet form factors, replacing Intel SoCs. The transition to self-designed SoCs helped Apple avoid SoC supplier opportunity costs and overhead and gave them more control over designing SoCs as per their customers' computing needs. This is a huge competitive advantage Apple has today with semiconductor hardware, operating systems, applications, and iCloud data storage integrated as a single platform to offer a great user experience, as shown in Figure 1-9. The fully integrated platform and complementary products connected to each other at the hardware and software application level make Apple a walled garden of technology. Their applications' seamless performance and iCloud-based data integrity among the different product lines gave Apple an unmatched competitive advantage compared to other competitors. Therefore, Apple's approach to creating and capturing value at an ecosystem level with patented innovative features by heavily investing in research and development has been key to Apple's success.

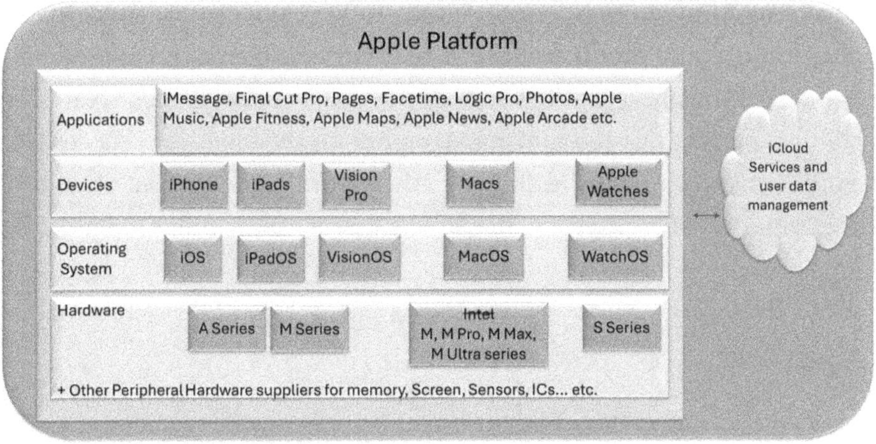

CHAPTER 1 COMPETITION AND ITS SIGNIFICANCE

Figure 1-9. *Apple platform*

The other key aspect that makes Apple unique is its brand and strong supply chain. The products are well known for their quality and innovative features, making it a well-recognized and in-demand brand in the technology industry. The supply chain with a dedicated Apple store owned by Apple is an added benefit with a strong end to end product ownership from design to product delivery to their end users. It is as if Apple product managers started with a technically innovative concept, bypassing every major dependency that might lead to any opportunity cost penalties and directly delivering the products to the hands of end customers, helping sales with higher profit margins and developing brand loyalty, a perfect recipe for success with a high long-term economic value and social value.

Understanding the Apple ecosystem can help product managers implement a competitive product management strategy where the products are defined with long-term vision paired with disruptive patented technological innovations through continuous research and development. Developing a brand image with strong product features and quality benefits users and society, making it hard for competitors to adapt to the

CHAPTER 1   COMPETITION AND ITS SIGNIFICANCE

innovations. Simultaneously, integrating design into the product delivery process with strong product marketing and bypassing major dependencies to avoid B2B (business-to-business) opportunity cost penalties creates sustained competitive product management for the long-term success of the product and company as shown in the Figure 1-10. Next, let's transition to the Windows PC ecosystem, the largest market share holder in today's PC market.[1]

Figure 1-10. *Apple revenue and stock price historic data*

Distributed Semiconductor Product Ecosystem

Apple follows a closed ecosystem of semiconductor product manufacturing, in which it owns the majority of the pieces. Another approach is the distributed semiconductor ecosystem, where high-end data centers, enterprise infrastructures, and mobile devices, including PCs, are designed and manufactured through close collaboration of individual domain-specific contributors. The journey starts with hardware vendors

---

[1] https://en.wikipedia.org/wiki/Market_share_of_personal_computer_vendors

like Intel, AMD, NVIDIA, Qualcomm, and others supplying semiconductor hardware to equipment manufacturers (OEMs) like HP and Dell in collaboration with the Microsoft Windows operating system and other independent software vendor applications to deliver a PC to the user base. This complex network is tightly coupled with partnerships to deliver PCs to customers for personal and commercial use.

Unlike Apple, the competition in the Windows OS ecosystem is high within hardware suppliers like AMD, Intel, Qualcomm, and NVIDIA and OEMs like Dell, HP, ASUS, and Lenovo, which compete on innovative features at semiconductor design at IP level, PC product level discussed earlier. The dependency on semiconductor hardware suppliers like Intel, AMD, Qualcomm, and NVIDIA applies to semiconductor-based devices and markets like phones, automobiles, Internet of Things (IoT) devices, cloud, and enterprise service providers. In the distributed semiconductor ecosystem, hardware design companies like Intel, AMD, NVIDIA, and Qualcomm have multiple product lines to supply hardware to various industry segments, like PCs, servers, IoTs, and networks. For example, Intel's Gracemont and Raptor Cove CPU IP SoCs are scaled from mobile PCs, workstations, and the Xeon W-3400 servers. Similarly, other hardware vendors like AMD scale their hardware from PCs and IoT to servers, and Qualcomm scales their hardware from phones to PCs and IoT to servers to increase the economic value of their products.

Windows PC Ecosystem

In the PC industry, hardware design companies, such as Intel and AMD, compete aggressively with each other to lead the Windows ecosystem by aiming to deliver innovative hardware features with better performance, power efficiency, and price to the OEMs. The product managers in the hardware ecosystem have a complex role to play in creating and capturing the value of their hardware in the broader ecosystem dependencies.

CHAPTER 1   COMPETITION AND ITS SIGNIFICANCE

The economic value of the product is shared among the partners, which involves buyer and supplier opportunity cost overheads along the PC product development, as shown in Figure 1-11. Each contributor is in a race to attain higher economic value with their strengths making it a highly competitive ecosystem.

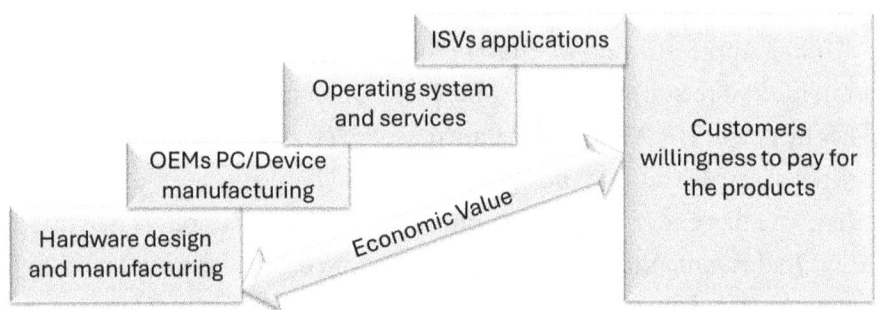

Figure 1-11. *Windows PC ecosystem economic value distribution*

Most modern PC ecosystems are divided between Windows and Apple operating systems. Apple is fully vertically integrated, as shown in Figure 1-12. At the same time, the Windows ecosystem is dependent on Microsoft for operating systems with heavy competition among various OEMs, ISVs, and hardware design manufacturing companies. ChromeOS and Linux are other available operating systems, but Windows and macOS dominate PCs just like Android and iOS for phones.

Among the Windows PC hardware vendors, Intel is a dominant semiconductor hardware design, development, and manufacturing company known for its high-performance product line across PCs, servers, IoT, and connectivity space. In contrast, AMD, NVIDIA, and Qualcomm are fabless design companies outsourcing their manufacturing to TSMC. Intel, AMD, and Qualcomm supply PC SoCs with CPU, GPU, NPU, and other peripherals to the OEMs, whereas NVIDIA supplies discrete GPUs. Intel SoCs and NVIDIA discrete GPUs based Lenovo, HP, Dell, Asus, Acer, and

CHAPTER 1   COMPETITION AND ITS SIGNIFICANCE

other PCs hold the largest[2] market share in the PC industry as shown in the Figure 1-13 compared to AMD and Apple. Being the leader, Intel is well known among PC users and has maintained its lead and popular brand positioning with continuous innovation and tailored hardware positioning approach to the PC users over the decades. For example, Intel's "good, better, best" go-to-market approach designed to segment its product offerings into three tiers, makes it easier for consumers to understand the differences and choose the right product for their PC usage needs. This differentiated strategy helped Intel become a popular brand among various user segments by simplifying the purchasing decision by offering products with different performance levels and price points.

Another reason for Intel to be the leader in the semiconductor industry is its ability to design, develop, and manufacture the hardware in their own fabrication facilities. In contrast, AMD, NVIDIA, Apple, and Qualcomm are fabless design companies outsourcing their manufacturing. Intel design innovations, patents, and advanced process node capabilities contributed to its success. However, recently, TSMC became dominant in producing advanced process node technology, giving AMD, Apple, Qualcomm, NVIDIA, and others a competitive advantage over Intel. As you go further in the book, deriving a competitive advantage from fabrication technology will be outlined.

---

[2] https://www.statista.com/statistics/735904/worldwide-x86-intel-amd-market-share/

CHAPTER 1   COMPETITION AND ITS SIGNIFICANCE

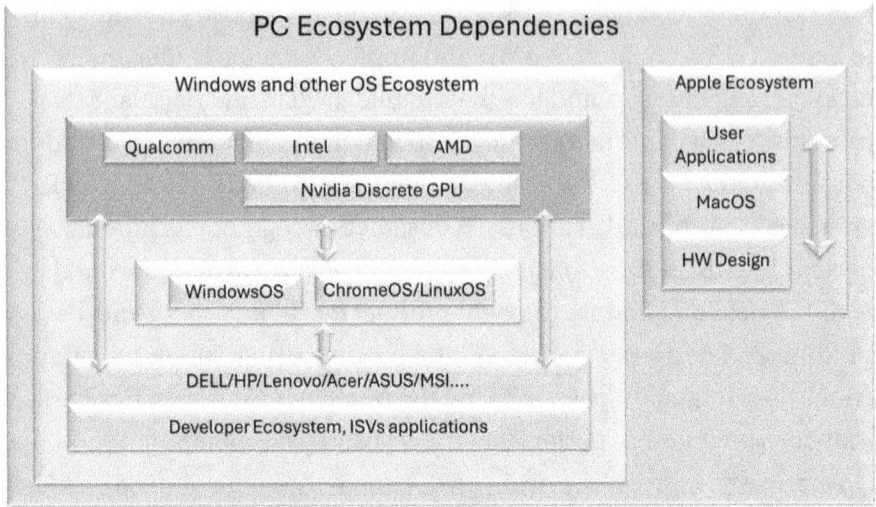

Figure 1-12. *PC ecosystem dependencies*

Competition in Windows PC

Intel and AMD go way back in competing. Both have almost the same product lines, including "good, better, best" product strategies in PC products, but Intel holds the lead in the PC industry. In recent years, AMD has delivered competitive semiconductor products utilizing advanced process nodes from TSMC to compete with Intel and NVIDIA on CPU and GPU hardware. Besides AMD, Qualcomm made a strong attempt into the PC market with custom ARM SoCs, collaborating with Microsoft and OEMs by releasing Copilot+ PCs with major semiconductor product updates compared to their older SoCs in 2024.

NVIDIA and Intel have a long history of collaboration across multiple areas, leveraging each other's strengths to drive innovation in the technology industry. Both companies have collaborated to optimize performance in data centers and the Windows PC ecosystem. Bringing the collective advantage of Intel's CPU processors with NVIDIA's discrete GPUs for high-performance computing tasks and collaborating on high-speed networking solutions. Leveraging Intel's advancements in the Ethernet and interconnect technologies with NVIDIA's expertise in GPU computing has helped the industry to shape an advanced future. However, NVIDIA recently released ARM-based CPUs and their GPUs in the data center and announced its partnership with MediaTek to design ARM-based SoCs in the Automotive and has potential to enter into windows on Arm AI PC ecosystem[3] while continuing its Intel and AMD discrete GPU partnership.

Challenges and Opportunities

The semiconductor industry's competitive landscape is growing significantly with major players such as Apple, NVIDIA, AMD, Intel, and Qualcomm, along with their deep pockets, striving to capture the entire semiconductor product market share across the product segments, as shown in Figure 1-14. In addition to the existing companies, due to the AI revolution, potential startups and major cloud service-based companies like Google, Amazon, and Microsoft started designing their own semiconductor products to offset the opportunity costs and increase their dominance in the AI-driven market. As a result of these market dynamics, semiconductor product management is at a highly competitive edge, forcing semiconductor product managers to deliver products and services tailored for numerous market opportunities with a long-term competitive advantage. Additionally, the software ecosystem is evolving rapidly with multiple AI-powered applications and services that demand high performance and innovative capabilities in semiconductor products. For example, large language models-based chatbots, AI models power conference calls through Google Meet, Microsoft Teams, Zoom, and WebEx, and improved content creation apps powered by AI.

---

[3] https://blogs.nvidia.com/blog/mediatek-intelligent-cabin-solutions/

CHAPTER 1   COMPETITION AND ITS SIGNIFICANCE

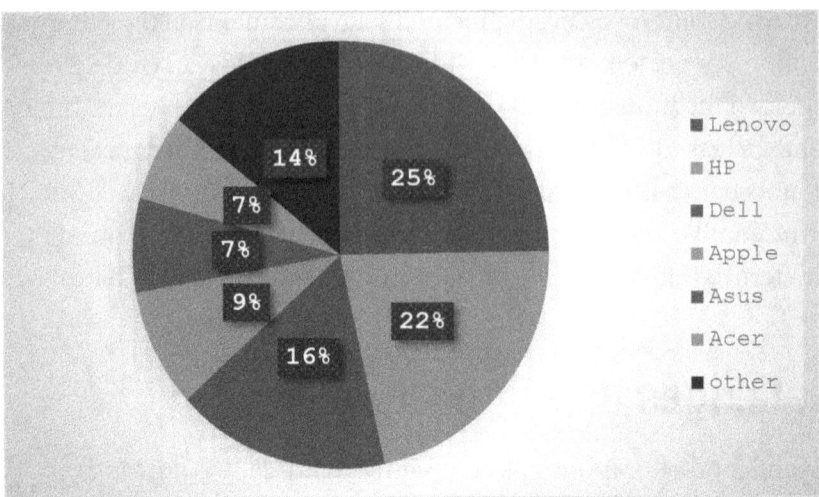

Figure 1-13. *PC vendor market share as of 2023 (source: Wikipedia)*

These innovative AI-driven technology capabilities are rapidly changing market dynamics, with many companies collaborating with academia and the open source community. This rapid growth in innovations demands increased semiconductor hardware potential for the growing needs, making competitive semiconductor product management even more critical. As a result, the aggressive competition in the hardware and software ecosystem drives the semiconductor industry into one of the largest economic business opportunities. To reap the benefits of these market opportunities, product managers must thoroughly assess the competition and the market dynamics for short- and long-term semiconductor product management to ensure sustainable product success. It helps product managers to define their team's value chain strengths and weaknesses relative to market needs, enroots new partnerships for potential product development opportunities, and build new strengths to increase the economic value of the products.

CHAPTER 1   COMPETITION AND ITS SIGNIFICANCE

Competitive Landscape

In a highly competitive environment like the semiconductor industry, the long-term success of the products demands an increased need for continuous improvements to deliver higher economic product value over competition. For every new product generation, customers expect new capabilities and features with continuously improving customer experience. To create a successful long-term semiconductor product with continuous improvements, product managers must develop a long-term product roadmap with targets for development teams and stakeholders to meet. The roadmap planning requires product managers to know about market dynamics like economic factors and technology trends, direct and indirect competitors and their strategies, and changing customer behavior.

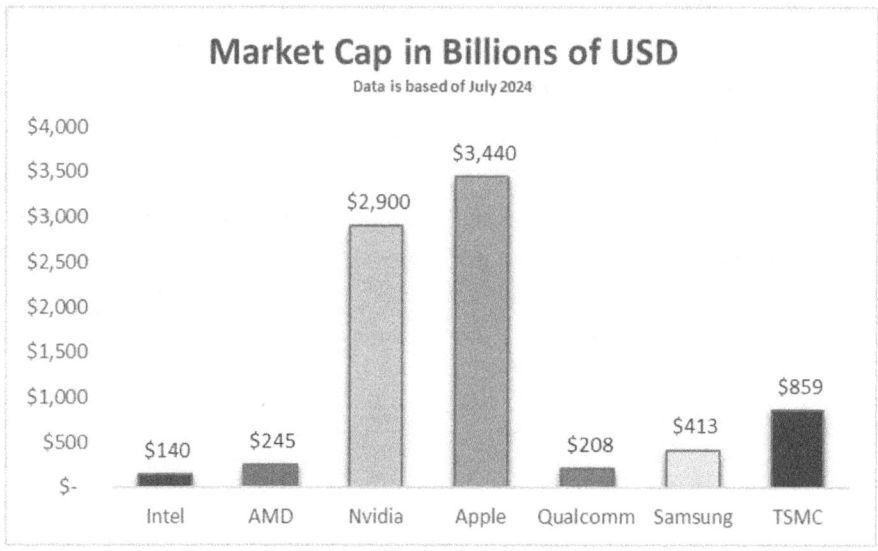

Figure 1-14. Market caps of major semiconductor companies

The approach to understanding the various factors is also crucial because it directly influences decision-making and roadmap execution. The underlying assumptions, scenarios and impacts play a key role in product managers decision-making for long-term product success.

CHAPTER 1   COMPETITION AND ITS SIGNIFICANCE

Therefore, product managers must take a systematic and strategic approach with scenario-based modeling by clearly outlining underlying assumptions to analyze the market, competitors, technological innovations, and ecosystem partners. This helps product managers make data-driven decisions required for building leadership product strategies to build strong customer relationships focusing on sustainable growth required for long-term competitiveness and success in the evolving semiconductor market.

So, how can product managers use this information to make strategic long-term decisions?

Developing a competitive landscape assessment approach to capture strengths, weaknesses, threats and opportunities for each partner and competitor to learn industry insights and dynamics. Product managers can implement a data-driven competitive landscape using a SWOT (strengths, weaknesses, opportunities, and threats) analysis approach to understand the different long-term dynamics and opportunities in the semiconductor industry as shown in the Figure 1-15. Knowing the ecosystem and strengths to build on, weaknesses to improve, and opportunities to increase business is a great approach. It helps identify potential threats to plan for risk mitigation for long-term success.

CHAPTER 1 COMPETITION AND ITS SIGNIFICANCE

Figure 1-15. *SWOT analysis*

The data-driven competitive landscape analysis often reveals insights like new opportunities and possible additional strengths to build to reduce opportunity costs. For example, AMDs acquisition of Xilinx added AI compute unit expertise into all of AMD's semiconductor product portfolio tremendously increasing their strength in AI accelerator computing. Google's lack of healthcare integration into their Android wearable products revealed the opportunity to acquire Fitbit. The acquisition enhanced Google's Android electronic watch product line, giving Google Health and Fitness a competitive advantage over other Android electronic watch providers. Apple A series phone semiconductor design and development strength enabled Apple to successfully design PC semiconductor SoCs for Macs and reduced the opportunity costs from semiconductor product partners like Intel. Many such examples reveal successful insights for long-term product strategies.

CHAPTER 1   COMPETITION AND ITS SIGNIFICANCE

Semiconductor product managers can implement current and futuristic competitive landscape SWOT analysis on the market dynamics, allowing them to implement long-term competitive product strategies that can help to create and capture value, as shown in the Figure 1-16. The product value can be created by delivering a unique value proposition in collaboration with partners; for example, Microsoft, OEM, and semiconductor design companies collaborated to deliver Microsoft Copilot+ PCs for AI-centric PC devices differentiation over Apple Macs. To stay competitive, Apple developed its own Apple intelligence for differentiation. On the other hand, AMD implemented block FP16 (floating-point 16 precision data type) on the neural compute unit (NPU) for enhanced AI performance and being Microsoft Copilot+ PCs advantage. The next generation of these products should have new or improved capabilities than block FP16, Apple Intelligence, and Microsoft Copilot+ PCs capabilities, respectively. Therefore, competitive landscape analysis helps semiconductor product managers formulate a unique value proposition leveraging strengths and opportunities. In addition to knowing the competitive landscape, product managers must implement a competitive product strategy involving various other dependencies, as discussed in the next chapter.

CHAPTER 1 COMPETITION AND ITS SIGNIFICANCE

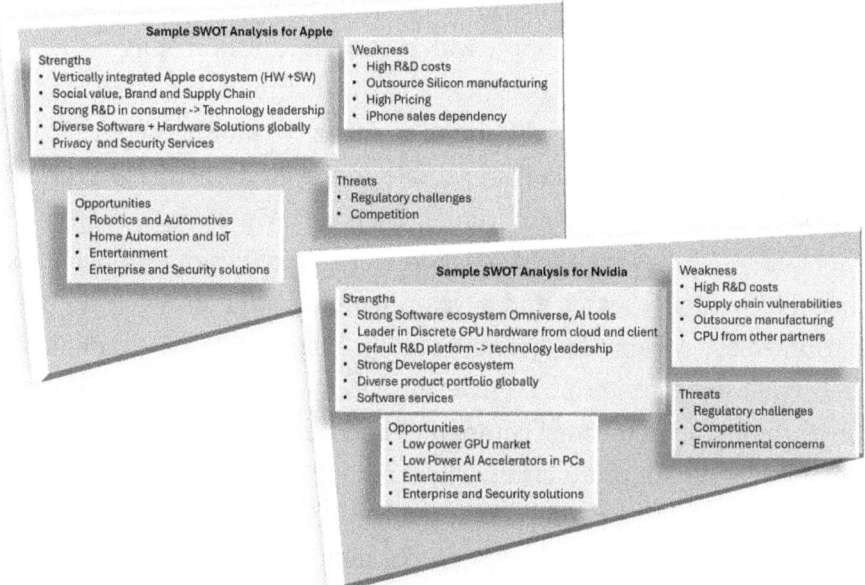

Figure 1-16. Examples of SWOT Analysis

Summary

The semiconductor industry is the key to shaping the advanced future with innovations in hardware and software, making the industry one of the largest economy businesses with aggressive competition. Various supplementary product choices are offered in the market, and companies compete directly and indirectly in the semiconductor industry. The competitive dynamics in the industry demand that semiconductor product managers to embrace a competitive semiconductor product management approach to drive long-term product success with a sustainable competitive advantage.

CHAPTER 1   COMPETITION AND ITS SIGNIFICANCE

The semiconductor industry can be approached as ecosystem competitiveness similar to Apple with vertical integration or as a distributed semiconductor ecosystem. In the distributed ecosystem, multiple partners work closely to create innovative products with distributed economic value. For example, in the PC industry the product economic value is distributed by Intel, Microsoft Windows, Dell, HP, and other OEMs. A fully integrated ecosystem needs continuous innovations backed with huge research and development investments, while a distributed ecosystem can drive innovation at an individual stakeholder level with faster turnarounds. However, with the potential of AI and market growth, many service-based companies and startups are developing their own semiconductor products to deliver competitive solutions.

In addition to these companies, academia, and the open ecosystems are stretching the limits of possibilities in semiconductor products and solutions through continuous research and development. This highly opportunistic yet challenging market dynamics needs a systematic approach to implement competitive semiconductor product management to deliver products that can create and capture value in the market for sustained long-term success. The first step is to assess the competitive landscape with a detailed SWOT analysis of the target market, such as client, enterprise, or cloud. The competitive landscape must be paired with thoroughly comprehending the semiconductor product life cycle to plan a competitive product roadmap based on the team's value chain and possible partnerships to implement a competitive product strategy.

Further in this book, the ways product managers should systematically approach competitive product management are discussed. The next chapters dive into the critical competitive product management metrics and areas required to maintain leadership in the complex and highly competitive semiconductor industry. The analysis includes a methodology to develop a semiconductor product development strategy for long-term success, a framework for implementing long-term strategic product roadmap execution, semiconductor product development life

CHAPTER 1   COMPETITION AND ITS SIGNIFICANCE

cycle, semiconductor design methodology and architecture, power and performance management, critical information on semiconductor manufacturing, OEMs, and channel partners and how AI can be used in semiconductor product management for efficiency. These metrics and areas are imperative to help product managers understand Besides technological and business concept dependencies, political factors like the CHIPS and Science Act of 2022 also play a key role in semiconductor product management due to the risks involved in differences in regional laws and regulations. This book explains potential impacts to the fabless semiconductor hardware design companies with the CHIPS Act.

CHAPTER 2

Semiconductor Product Management Life Cycle

Design is not just what it looks like. Design is how it works.

—Steve Jobs

This chapter explains the semiconductor product management life cycle from a product manager's point of view. The aim is to provide technical and operational information to help product managers manage the products effectively and understand the dependencies in each stage for successful product implementation.

The semiconductor product management life cycle refers to the complete process involved in electronic device manufacturing, like PCs and smartphones involving multiple stages. The journey starts from idea to product planning, design, manufacturing, testing, and placing the semiconductor chips into the electronic devices with required end-user software applications and maintaining it until the device reaches its end of life. Each stage is critical to plan and deliver the intended semiconductor product to the next external partners or internal teams so the product creates and captures its value in the market.

CHAPTER 2   SEMICONDUCTOR PRODUCT MANAGEMENT LIFE CYCLE

Semiconductor product management is a complex web with many B2B companies like fabless design companies, fabrication manufacturing companies, memory vendors, other peripheral hardware vendors, and software vendors working with OEMs to deliver an end-customer product, as shown in the Figure 2-1. As a result, the stakes and risk for mistakes are higher in this life cycle making the role of semiconductor product managers a tough one. However, the consumer electronics total addressable market (TAM) worldwide is expected to have an annual growth of 2.9% from 2024 to 2029,[1] 2029 with a potential of 147B US dollars, making this risk worth taking.

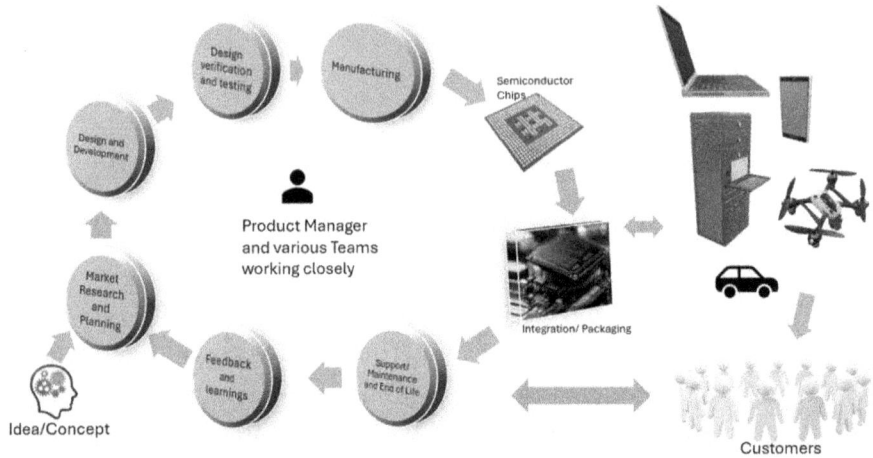

Figure 2-1. *Semiconductor product management life cycle (images generated using AI)*

In the case of Apple, as it is a closed ecosystem, efficiently managing the product life cycle is comparatively less complex, with fewer dependencies. On the other hand, the distributed semiconductor ecosystem needs semiconductor hardware design companies to work

---

[1] Outlook derived from https://www.statista.com/outlook/cmo/consumer-electronics/worldwide.

closely with other partners and OEMs to make their products successful in the market. With growing complexity of semiconductor hardware design and manufacturing combined with product assembly strategies like Just-in-Time manufacturing by the OEMs is making the quality and reliability of the electronic devices increasingly difficult to achieve. With increased competition and multiple product choices to the customers, there is less tolerance for performance degradation. As a result, semiconductor product managers must own and manage the end-to-end product management life cycle to meet the product's performance, safety, reliability, and security requirements until it reaches its end of life. This requires product managers to have a deeper knowledge of how semiconductor-based systems are developed, operated, and maintained from planning to its end of life.

Significance of Product Management Life Cycle

Semiconductor product design and development usually takes longer than any typical product development cycle and is a function of design and validation complexity and the number of IP components integrated to form a system on chip (SoC). As a result, a lot of risk is involved with product development taking longer in the modern, complex, and dynamic semiconductor industry. Some risks involved are due to implementing the innovative features for the first time, the right mix of innovation to the market demand, and dependencies associated with other ecosystem partners.

To have a competitive advantage, semiconductor companies aim to build their hardware with augmented features utilizing their research and development innovations. As these innovative features are implemented for the first time, the time for design and verification may go even longer than planned due to the uncertainties involved. These delays further increase the already longer development cycles, risking the time to market the electronic devices.

CHAPTER 2   SEMICONDUCTOR PRODUCT MANAGEMENT LIFE CYCLE

The semiconductor product manager's ability to decide the appropriate utilization of innovative features to create demand for their products defines the product's success. The new products may not be successful if the products are viewed as more advanced or lagging than the consumer market trends. The product manager should clearly define consumer response to industry trends because they may differ. The key is to place the appropriate innovations in the market at the right time to increase products' economic value and demand. For example, Google Glass failed despite its innovative technology and potential. The product managers should thoroughly do a comprehensive market and consumer analysis and strategic planning for new hardware products' success.

Additionally, the semiconductor product managers should look ahead and define the future electronic device computing needs and plan the semiconductor product roadmap accordingly. This becomes more complex in the Windows ecosystems as many independent layers operate simultaneously. Product managers should target computing needs that can reach maximum customer segments while listing semiconductor hardware specifications. Like semiconductor product managers, ISVs and other partners continuously implement innovative features on their software applications to stay competitive and improve user experience. If these new features in the ISVs (independent software vendors) applications demand more hardware resources than available, or if the hardware is defined independent of ISVs, innovations may result in unwanted results on the semiconductor products' performance impacting user experience.

Moreover, the application updates are not in the control of the semiconductor product managers; any application update can be downloaded by the users at will as long as they have a network connection. For example, Popular video streaming applications may plan to change the content resolution to 4K from 1080p, which impacts the device's battery life if the go-to-market advocacy is providing ten hours of video streaming to customers measured at 1080p resolution. When the device hits the

CHAPTER 2 SEMICONDUCTOR PRODUCT MANAGEMENT LIFE CYCLE

market, the content gets upgraded to 4K by ISVs. The launched device can no longer provide ten hours of battery life as 4K resolution needs more power than 1080p, impacting the customer experience and brand image.

To avoid such unwanted results, semiconductor product managers should collaborate with the ecosystem partners within the appropriate time frame of hardware planning and development to gather the potential plans from ISVs and OEMs and meet their requirements. This can be possible if product managers thoroughly comprehend the stages in the semiconductor product management life cycle. The semiconductor product life cycle can be broadly divided into planning, design and development, manufacturing, go-to-market, and product launch plans in collaboration with OEMs and ISVs, and finally, providing support and maintenance until the product reaches its end of life while meeting the regulatory compliance across all these stages.

Overall, the semiconductor product management life cycle is a rigorous exercise of continuous collaboration and evaluation of trends with various ecosystem partners at all stages of the life cycle, as shown in Figure 2-2.

CHAPTER 2   SEMICONDUCTOR PRODUCT MANAGEMENT LIFE CYCLE

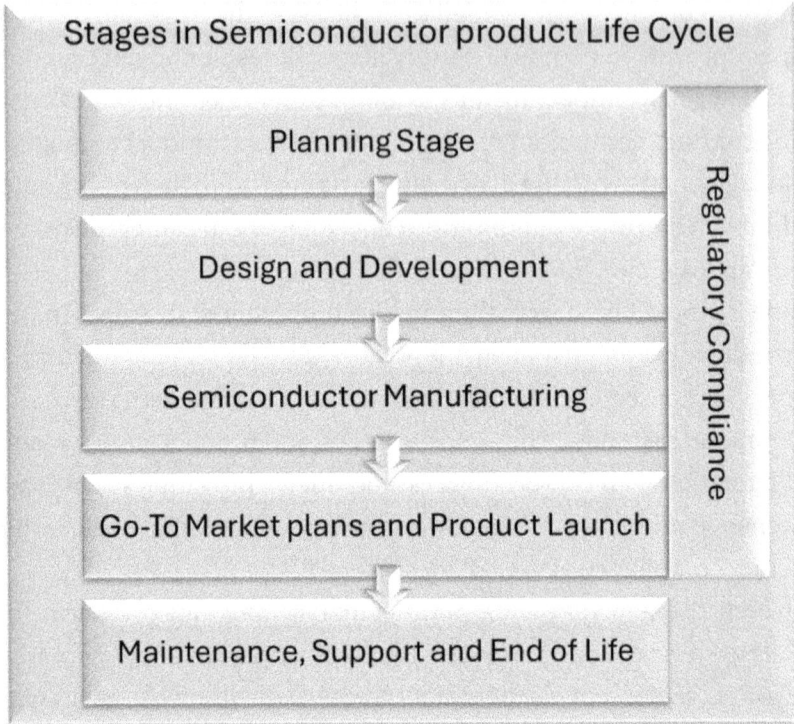

Figure 2-2. Stages in semiconductor product life cycle

The role product managers play is critical in each phase of the semiconductor management life cycle to ensure the electronic devices keep up with market needs, collaborate, and make sure the partners across all the stages keep competitive analysis as a factor so the product can maintain its economic value as planned in the early planning phase. Let's discuss the roles and responsibilities of semiconductor product managers across each of the semiconductor product life cycle stages to develop a competitive semiconductor crafted for success in the market.

Planning Stage

As in any product industry, the planning phase in semiconductor products is a critical stage. However, the stakes are even higher with rapid changes in technology, rigorous competition, strict regulatory standards, market uncertainties, and intricate supply chains. The uncertainty in all these critical pieces involved in the semiconductor planning phase requires a product manager to tie the product's vision to the organization's business objectives and make appropriate decisions. Product managers should begin with the organization's business objectives to plan products based on their technical capabilities to meet the market demands with robust risk management to overcome uncertainties.

A semiconductor product's success also depends on the company's relentless focus to continuously improve their technical capabilities to stay competitive which is only possible by extensive investments in research and development. These technical capabilities should be patented innovations for creating product value so the competition doesn't catch up easily and impact the product's value in the short and long term. Companies with successful semiconductor products are known to invest heavily in research and development, like NVIDIA and Apple with numerous patents and advanced proprietary tools making it hard for competitors to catch up. Besides technical capabilities, product managers should do a thorough market analysis to understand the industry trends and consumer behavior analysis by implementing A/B testing, reading market research reports, and so forth. This helps product managers know the likely scenarios of customers' behavior patterns and implement scenario-based modeling to predict potential demand and key dependencies in the early planning phase to plan for risk management.

A robust semiconductor planning stage should define not only the competitive semiconductor hardware features but also the key characteristics of the customer electronic device built by the OEMs to capture the economic value of the product. The semiconductor

CHAPTER 2　SEMICONDUCTOR PRODUCT MANAGEMENT LIFE CYCLE

product manager's decisions in the planning stage directly influence the willingness to pay by the customer, but semiconductor hardware is the basic enabler of user application capabilities. As a result, product managers should be aware of multiple factors that can be considered for the effective planning of a semiconductor product, as shown in Figure 2-3. A comprehensive competitive product strategy can help product managers develop a robust product plan by considering the key influencing factors shown in Figure 2-3. A methodology to develop a competitive product strategy to help product managers implement a robust product plan is discussed in the next chapter.

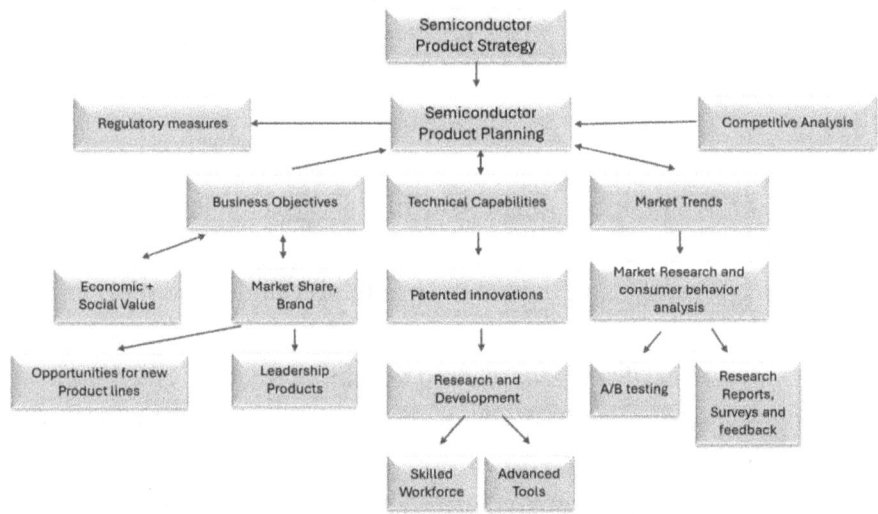

Figure 2-3. *Semiconductor product planning contributors*

The semiconductor planning phase is a comprehensive process with multiple product managers' responsibilities. It requires close collaboration of stakeholders and careful consideration of market needs, technical feasibility, and market and competitive analyses to define a product plan. Clearly document the product design definition as MRD (market requirement document) or PRD (product requirement document), resource allocation, risk management, and list of key performance indicators (KPIs) and key market indicators (KMIs). This is done so that the product management phases shown in Figure 2-4 have metrics to indicate the progress and a go-to-market plan for market awareness and demand generation. By thoroughly addressing these elements and evaluating regulatory compliance in the planning phase, product managers can set a solid foundation for the successful development and launch of a new semiconductor product.

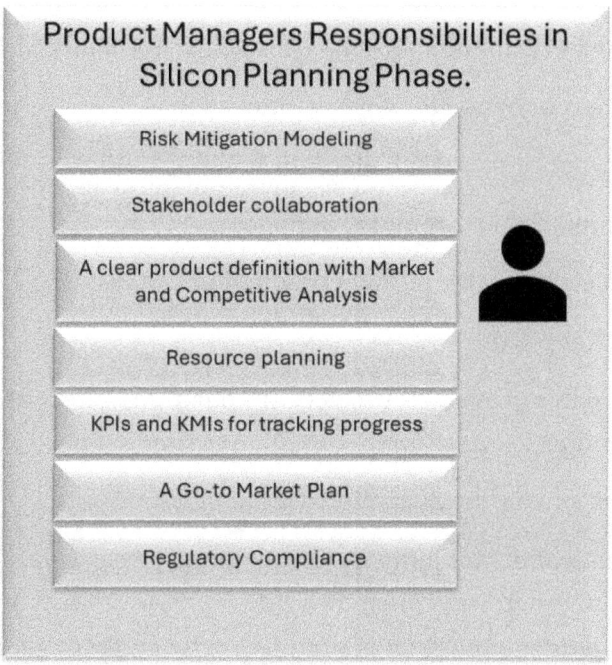

Figure 2-4. Product manager responsibilities in the semiconductor planning phase

Now that you know the influencers and contributors of a robust semiconductor planning phase, let's talk about its implementation for a product with existing competition and a new product entering the market for the first time.

CHAPTER 2 SEMICONDUCTOR PRODUCT MANAGEMENT LIFE CYCLE

Existing Competition

The key to semiconductor planning with existing competition is to define a product plan that differentiates the existing products with additional product value besides meeting the customer needs. For long-term success, patents and copyrights should protect these differentiating factors so that competitors cannot easily replicate and dismiss the differentiation. The following are some differentiating factors.

- Solves customers' existing pain points efficiently
- Incorporates technological innovations
- Outperforms available products in key metrics
- Unmatched customer experience
- Efficient/quality product production and delivery
- Better pricing
- Scalable product line to accommodate complement product lines
- Reasonable product refresh cycle

In the semiconductor industry, the planning phase usually involves defining scalable hardware integrated into multiple product lines. AMD, Intel, and others plan one type of semiconductor IP per component in a generation and scale it to multiple product lines. For example, AMD created one CPU Zen IP architecture for all its semiconductor product lines as a single generation. The product managers should plan for scalable IPs with unique features so that each product line can be differentiated to gain a competitive advantage. Besides product features, differentiation could be based on price, durability, safety, and support. However, using a price differentiator is not advised because it is a function of operational efficiency and can be easily achievable by companies with deep pockets.

The whole technical industry is lucrative because of the economic value it creates through innovative IPs and high margins. Getting into a price war is not an ideal plan for semiconductor product managers. Product managers must combine innovative features, quality, safety, and support with a brand image as key differentiators to avoid a price war. For example, Intel maintained its leads in Windows PC with feature performance, brand image, and customer support for the longest time.

The product manager in the planning phase should clearly define the targets of KPIs and KMIs of the new semiconductor hardware with the help of product roadmaps so the design phase can implement those targets. The roadmaps should also have a competitive analysis so product managers can define the pricing strategy accordingly. You will learn more about the product roadmaps, KPIs, and KMIs in upcoming chapters.

New Product Entry

Planning for a brand-new semiconductor product to enter or develop a market is very different from planning a semiconductor with existing competition. The first role of the product managers is market preparation; to prepare the market, product managers should do a market study on how and where the product can be positioned by mapping the concept against solving customer pain points efficiently with unique customer experience value or bringing a new experience altogether. The following lists some key factors of new product semiconductor planning.

- Technological innovations
- New/unique customer experience
- Privacy, safety, security, and reliability
- Strategic partnerships with other ecosystem partners for product success
- Continuous improvements to gain brand recognition

CHAPTER 2   SEMICONDUCTOR PRODUCT MANAGEMENT LIFE CYCLE

For a brand-new product, the product managers need to prepare the market for the entirely new concept of the product. If the new product solves multiple customers' problems as a single solution otherwise distributed into existing multiple products would be much easier to position its value in the market. For example, the iPhone entered a highly competitive mobile market with a new concept of integrating phone, media player, and Internet connectivity functionalities into a single device. This integration concept requires market awareness of a new product with multiple functionalities integrated into a single product. At the same time, an entirely new product concept needs market education so the customers know its value. The basis of the new product entry is innovation. Without it, there would be no means to solve the unmet needs of the customers and improve the existing solutions.

The next step is to learn the customer response to the new concept and to manage other dependencies like safety, security, privacy, and reliability. The basic human instinct says that the human reaction to new things is, by default, defensive. The aim of the product managers should be to market the new product with privacy, security, and safety as a key pillar besides the new product innovation. A product that delivers a new or unique customer experience merged with privacy, safety, and security measures ensures market acceptance, which is needed for demand generation. For example, Google Glass failed, although being a great innovative concept, as it did not manage to take the privacy and security threat it might pose to the customers using google glass.

The aim of the product manager for a brand-new semiconductor product should not only be innovation with new or unique customer experience as a key focus but also incorporate security, privacy, and safety features for its overall success. The other factors that need attention from product managers are making strategic ecosystem partnerships and managing KPIs and KMIs so the product is built as envisioned and marketed to the end customers to build a brand.

CHAPTER 2   SEMICONDUCTOR PRODUCT MANAGEMENT LIFE CYCLE

Finally, not everything is made right in the first attempt. The new semiconductor product should be part of a roadmap for continuous improvements and market penetration.

Role of Product Managers

Product managers with methodological semiconductor product planning following all the factors discussed lay a strong foundation for the success of products in the market. The product manager up for this task should have a balance of technical expertise to shape innovations into product features by having a meaningful conversation with engineering experts to scope out the resources, clearly document MRDs, PRDs, and risks associated with the product definition along with defining KPIs and KMIs to track the progress. Product managers need a broad yet comprehensive strategic vision to assess short- and long-term market trends and an eye for customer behavior patterns to plan a product with long-term competitive advantage. They also need to effectively manage the stakeholders responsible for realizing the end goal of the product. This is possible when companies support the semiconductor product managers to lead comprehensive research and development tailored to the business objectives, provide effective risk management modeling tools, great engineering and marketing teams, and teach risk-taking behavior across the organization. So, the product managers can overcome the complexities of semiconductor planning and deliver successful and innovative products to the market with continuous improvements.

There is a huge risk involved in planning a semiconductor for future market needs with multiple stakeholders involved. It is not enough to take the risk once and develop a successful product. The risk should be a norm in the electronic industry to stay ahead of the competition. Product managers doing product planning every generation should plan a product to stay ahead of the competition and continuously improve the product capabilities and customer experience. The continuous upgrades and updates to products above competition determine the success of products and organizations in the long run. For example, Nokia once was the leader in the phone market, but the company failed to keep up with the changing trends in smartphone design and continued to produce outdated devices. Nokia failed to realize the fast-moving trends of Android and lacked the appealing features offered by its competitors like Samsung, leading to its tragic downfall. From the best company at one time to a downfall in the mobile industry can be attributed to its lack of risk-taking and planning for competitive product management.

Design and Development

The semiconductor industry has one of the longest and most complex product design and development cycles compared to other products. The semiconductor design process consists of multiple stages, each with specific activities and deliverables. Starting from defining design methodology, tape-in, tape-out, samples to test and eventually getting to production design quality could take a few months to years, depending on the complexity of the design and architecture, as shown in the Figure 2-5. Successfully navigating these stages requires meticulous planning, coordination, and execution to bring a semiconductor product from concept to reality. With growing complexities in modern electronics, the design and development management phase need careful focus and a meticulous approach to deliver high-quality semiconductor design to manufacturers. Before starting the design phase, product managers should have the market and product requirements clearly documented, to begin with the design methodology.

CHAPTER 2   SEMICONDUCTOR PRODUCT MANAGEMENT LIFE CYCLE

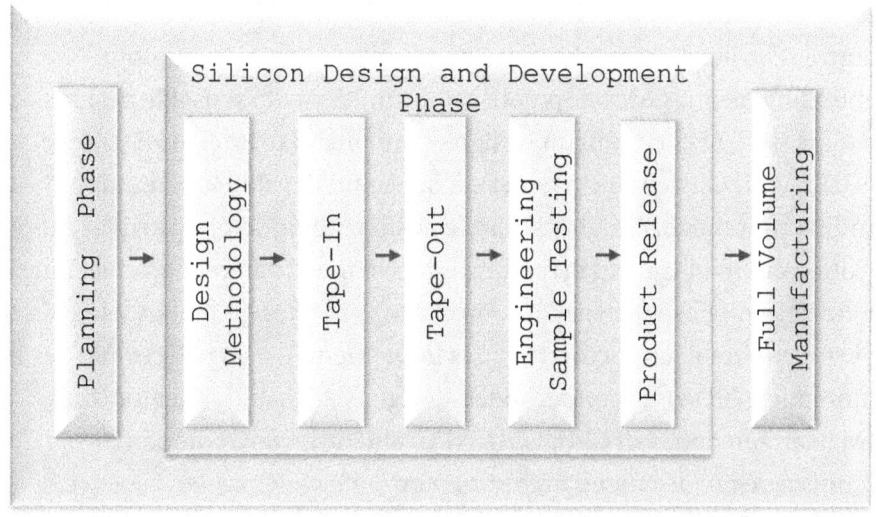

Figure 2-5. *Semiconductor design and development phase*

Semiconductor Design Methodology

Semiconductor design methodology is the first step in the semiconductor design phase that defines the systematic approach to the complex design of the semiconductor. There are different methodologies to approach semiconductor design, like top-down, bottom-up, mixed, component, and platform design. There is no right or wrong approach to design if it meets the design targets. There are multiple scenarios in the electronic design; for example, a 2-bit adder has four different logical combinations: 00,01,10,11. Today, there are 64-bit CPUs, meaning there are ~18.4 quintillion logical combinations and numerous analog circuits.

$$2^{64} = 18{,}446{,}744{,}073{,}709{,}551{,}616.$$

The complexity of dealing with such huge logical combinations demands more control over the entire design, from the smallest to the largest blocks. Therefore, regardless of the approach to the complex modern semiconductor design, product managers, in collaboration with architects, should ensure the design is flexible and scalable to have more control. The flexibility and scalability open ways for more revenue-generating business development opportunities with reusable designs. As discussed, semiconductor design companies like Intel, AMD, Apple, NVIDIA, and Qualcomm take design once and develop into multiple products approach. A highly scalable design methodology provides more flexibility to manage and meet the targets of these different product lines in the design phase with more control. Once the design methodology is chosen, the semiconductor design is implemented using electronic design automation (EDA), computer-aided design (CAD), and other tools. The design architectures of CPU, GPU, NPU, and other SoC components in architecture are discussed in the chapter.

What are these EDA and CAD tools? Why do product managers need to know their role in the design phase?

Consider an example of writing a book. Writing a book needs an idea and a planned approach to writing. The next step is to start writing on a computer with Microsoft Word and Google Docs to finalize content as chapters, as it gives more control and flow of the information. Tools like Excel, PowerPoint, and Paint come in handy for any pictures, tables, and diagrams. Finally, an actual physical layout of the book is developed and sent for printing. Similarly, tools like EDA and CAD enable engineers to create accurate and efficient designs with a streamlined development and verification process on a computer.

Tape-in

Tape-in means the logical implementation of the design and verification is complete meeting the KPIs and KMIs targets. The logic implementation implements the intended behavior of the hardware. To reach tape-in, product managers must ensure design teams follow the PRDs meeting KPIs targets with robust verification. The design optimizations with KPI targets ensure the design is functionally robust in all logical combinations.

CHAPTER 2   SEMICONDUCTOR PRODUCT MANAGEMENT LIFE CYCLE

Particularly in large and complex designs like an SoC, it marks the point where the design is considered complete from a logical and functional perspective and is ready to proceed to the next stage of physical design layout and physical verification.

Tape-out

Tape-out means the physical design layout is complete and indicates that all design work, including verification, synthesis, place and route, and physical verification, has been completed, meeting KPIs targets and is ready for the next stage. The tape-out involves meticulous physical design implementation, extensive verification, and rigorous sign-off procedures to ensure the design is robust, reliable, and manufacturable on a physical semiconductor wafer. Successful tape-out requires product managers to collaborate closely between design teams, verification engineers, and the foundry to ensure a smooth transition from design to actual semiconductor chip in the form of early engineering samples.

Engineering Sample Testing

Engineering samples are the early design prototypes sent by the manufacturing team to test the functionality and reliability of the design on a physical semiconductor chip. Engineering sample testing is a crucial phase in semiconductor product development. It needs thorough evaluation and validation to ensure the samples meet design specification KPI targets, performance standards, and reliability requirements and verify the high-scale manufacturability. The samples must also be tested to confirm compliance with industry standards before mass production and market launch.

By thoroughly testing engineering samples, validation, and design teams collaborate to identify and address potential issues early in the development process, ultimately leading to higher-quality, more reliable

CHAPTER 2   SEMICONDUCTOR PRODUCT MANAGEMENT LIFE CYCLE

products that meet market and regulatory expectations. As a result, tape-out to engineering sample testing is an iterative process that involves making multiple semiconductors stepping by updating the design and layout based on the validation results. The process continues until a fully functional and reliable semiconductor design is implemented and tested on a physical prototype semiconductor.

Product Release

Product release typically is the final stage of the semiconductor design that signifies an engineering sample has successfully passed all the tests and is ready for mass production and market release. By rigorously verifying and validating the engineering sample's performance, quality, reliability, and compliance, product release helps ensure the production semiconductor meets KPIs, customer expectations, and regulatory requirements. This process is critical for mitigating risks and ensuring customer satisfaction by delivering high-quality products.

In the complex semiconductor SoC design, each component/subsystem like CPU, GPU, and NPU are designed and verified separately with their own tape-in and tape-out stages to meet the component level KPI targets. All the required components are then integrated to form an integrated SoC by the system integration team with its own tape-in and tape-out stage, followed by SoC engineering samples and product release to meet SoC performance requirements, customer expectations, and regulatory requirements, as shown in Figure 2-6.

CHAPTER 2   SEMICONDUCTOR PRODUCT MANAGEMENT LIFE CYCLE

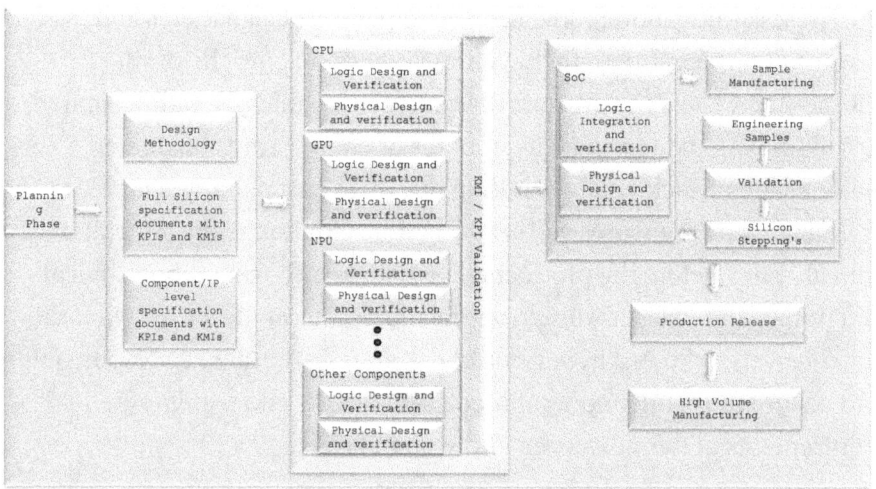

Figure 2-6. *SoC semiconductor design and development process*

Role of Product Managers

Roles and responsibilities of product managers in the design phase are critical to the overall success of semiconductor design as shown in Figure 2-7. Key roles are to ensure the risks/issues are identified and addressed at the subsystem and system level with rigorous verification and validation. Sometimes, there can be scenarios where the issues may not have the desired fixes. In these scenarios, product managers should work closely with system and component-level teams to realize the risk associated with partially fixed issues and develop a risk mitigation plan. It would be ideal if product managers implement a risk mitigation model for the issues found and assess the impact at individual subsystem and full system levels. The modeling helps reduce device behavior uncertainty by carefully considering various macro, synthetic, and real-world benchmarks, which are discussed in an upcoming chapter.

CHAPTER 2 SEMICONDUCTOR PRODUCT MANAGEMENT LIFE CYCLE

The risk mitigation model cannot help if the design issues and unwanted semiconductor behavior are identified after the product release stage. Once the product design is sent to the fabrication facility for volume manufacturing, any updates or changes are considered a major semiconductor step, resulting in a huge cost penalty. Therefore, the product manager ensures verification and validation teams find all the critical issues before the product release stage by having robust logical, functional, and physical design verification plans at the subsystem and system levels, followed by various benchmarks. Another key responsibility is to ensure the semiconductor meets KPI targets and regulatory requirements at the subsystem and system levels.

Figure 2-7. Key roles and responsibilities of product managers in the semiconductor design phase

CHAPTER 2   SEMICONDUCTOR PRODUCT MANAGEMENT LIFE CYCLE

After meticulous product planning, the design phase in semiconductor product management is critical. Product managers and engineering teams are equally important in a smooth transition from planning to design and eventually to the production phase. To achieve this, product managers should ensure the system and subsystem level design phase delivers a robust semiconductor meeting performance requirements at the system level as planned with regulatory compliance. Product managers should also work with marketing and sales teams for go-to-market plans in collaboration with stakeholders and with finance teams to develop a pricing strategy. Overall, product managers should ensure product design phase meets KPI targets with competitive advantage and is delivered on time and within the cost budget. By effectively managing requirements, coordinating cross-functional teams, mitigating risks, and driving the go-to-market strategy based on product value, the product manager helps ensure the success of the semiconductor product in a competitive semiconductor market.

Semiconductor Manufacturing

By this stage, semiconductor product management reaches high-volume manufacturing, where the design is transformed into a physical semiconductor chip for end-user product assembly by the OEMs.

Product managers in fabless design companies should ensure the fabrication facility is certified for the safety and security of the design IPs. Work closely with supply chain and sales teams to manage demand and timelines. After the manufacturing, product managers must work with OSAT (outsourced semiconductor assembly testing) and OEMs for end-user semiconductor product manufacturing. OSAT and OEMs and channel contributions in semiconductor product management are discussed in an upcoming chapter.

CHAPTER 2   SEMICONDUCTOR PRODUCT MANAGEMENT LIFE CYCLE

Intel and Samsung are major design and manufacturing companies, while AMD, Qualcomm, NVIDIA, and Apple are fabless design companies outsourcing their semiconductor design manufacturing. Due to the dependency of transistor technology in semiconductor product design and innovation, semiconductor manufacturing can be a key source of competitive advantages in electronic devices. The competitive semiconductor manufacturing process is discussed in an upcoming chapter.

Regulatory Compliance

As electronic devices deal with sensitive consumer data, voltage, current, power, heat, and batteries, meeting regulatory requirements is critical to ensure product safety, quality, and compliance with environmental and industry standards; for example, compliance with ISO 9001 quality management systems, safety and electromagnetic compatibility (EMC) standards, and WEEE (waste electrical and electronic equipment). Meeting these requirements adds social value to the product essential for its success. Product managers should add regulatory compliance requirements from the global markets as the requirements differ based on geographical location. By integrating regulatory compliance requirements into every stage of the semiconductor product management life cycle, from initial planning through design and testing, volume manufacturing product managers can mitigate risks, avoid legal penalties, and ensure successful product launches in the global markets.

Go-to-Market Plans and Product Launch

When planning the semiconductor product configurations in the planning phase, product managers should work on drafting the go-to-market plans and planning the launch in a private event or worldwide technology conferences such as Computex. Product managers should work with marketing and sales to draft a go-to-market plan that clearly outlines the product's value proposition with a competitive advantage in the market. Product positioning and brand management are key to successfully ensuring the product is accepted in the market. Because technology features are a complex subject for customers and stakeholders to grasp, product managers should work with marketing and sales to drive a simple product messaging consumable by different audiences critical for its success.

Maintenance, Support, and End of Life

Semiconductor electronic devices typically have longer refresh cycles as the investment in the devices is usually high by the consumers. Consumers expect the product to perform well for a longer period of time. Therefore, maintenance and support like warranty and repair services are critical to customer satisfaction for long-term customer loyalty and building a strong brand value. Product managers should ensure detailed support documentation, training, and guidelines for ecosystem partners to help provide customers with the best out-of-the-box user experience. Additionally, ensuring continuous support for software updates, performance monitoring, customer support documentation, and training with customer feedback helps improve semiconductor quality progressively. Finally, ensuring a semiconductor product's smooth end of life (EOL) ensures product reliability, customer satisfaction, and easy transitions to new products.

Summary

The semiconductor product management life cycle is a complex methodology involving multiple stages such as planning, design and development, manufacturing, marketing, and launch, followed by maintenance until the product reaches its EOL. Product managers play a critical role across these phases to successfully create and capture the semiconductor product's economic and social value. By knowing the different stages in the life cycle, product managers can collaborate and partner effectively with ecosystem stakeholders to deliver timely semiconductor products.

Strong semiconductor product planning requires product managers to have a balance of technical expertise to shape innovations into product features by having a meaningful conversation with engineering experts to scope out the resources, clear documentation, and risk associated with the product definition, along with defining targets to track the progress. Product managers should also aim to have a broad yet comprehensive strategic vision to be aware of short- and long-term market trends and an eye for customer behavior patterns to plan a product with long-term competitive advantage. And effectively manage the stakeholders responsible for realizing the end goal of the product effectively. The key roles of product managers in the design phase are to ensure the risks/issues are identified and addressed at the subsystem and system level with rigorous verification and validation until the engineering sample stage while choosing an appropriate design methodology. The critical design issues should be identified before the PRQ stage to generate the desired economic value of the product. The design phase is followed by manufacturing, market launch, and support until EOL while maintaining regulatory compliance.

Now that you have a better understanding of the semiconductor product management life cycle, let's get into the specific details of the semiconductor product management process starting with semiconductor product strategy development critical to begin the product management journey.

CHAPTER 3

Competitive Semiconductor Product Strategy

Every company should work hard to make their own line of products obsolete before their competition does.

—Philip Kotler

If you don't have competitive advantage, do not compete.

—Jack Walsh

Let me share one of my childhood stories. When I was in school, I was an academically low-scoring student, although I liked to study. One day, my sister asked me to answer the difference between distance and displacement. I tried to say something with my young brain at the time, but eventually, she figured out I couldn't answer. She explained what distance and displacement mean and encouraged me to measure my efforts as distance and displacement. I understood that we could walk miles in distance and still have zero displacement. I also realized that displacement is progressive only if it is in the positive direction, as shown in the Figure 3-1. This helped me assess where I am putting my efforts and what direction those efforts could lead me to. Therefore, a direction check relative to where I was with a clear goal enforced a forward moment. I eventually topped my class but the key to success starts with target setting and continuously evaluating your displacement relative to the set targets using a strategy.

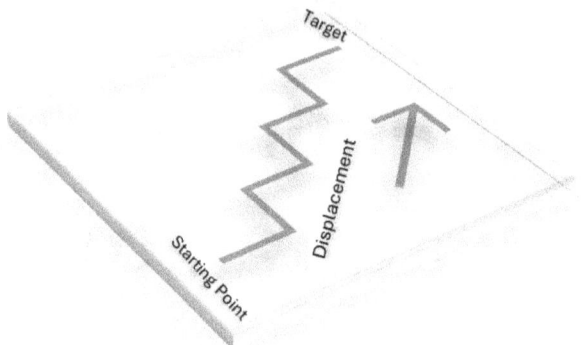

Figure 3-1. *Generic progress tracking methodology*

This chapter discusses a systematic framework approach to develop a semiconductor product strategy that helps product managers implement a robust competitive product management capable of tolerating an aggressive market dynamic.

In competitive semiconductor product management, the life cycle covers the comprehensive process of developing and managing a product from planning to end of life (EOL). It doesn't necessarily ensure that the product has a competitive advantage and market-driven product characteristics. These competitive product characteristics are required to be successful in the marketplace for the long term. There are multiple factors besides the performance and technological innovations of the products that impact long-term product competitiveness. The path to successful long-term semiconductor product management starts with a competitive product strategy-driven product management, which clearly outlines competitive advantage considering the external dependencies, opportunities, competitive product targets, and threats. Therefore, product

CHAPTER 3   COMPETITIVE SEMICONDUCTOR PRODUCT STRATEGY

managers should derive current and future product competitive advantage using a systematic competitive strategy development framework for sustainable long-term success in the modern semiconductor product industry.

Significance of Competitive Semiconductor Product Strategy

Competitive product strategy refers to the long-term approach a product manager adopts to gain and implement a competitive advantage over its rivals in the market. It involves defining how a product competes in its chosen markets, creates value for its customers, and differentiates itself from the competitors. A well-crafted competitive strategy helps product managers achieve and sustain a leadership position in the industry.

Competitive strategy is not a secret operation that requires you to spy on competitors for information to analyze their actions and prepare yours. It is more than just information gathering, which is crucial in defining long-term product targets. Enforcing product managers to have insights into market dynamics, competitor strategies, customer needs, opportunities, risk assessment, and drive innovation with emerging technologies helps provide a holistic view of the competitive landscape. Product managers with a robust competitive product strategy ensure that the product can keep pace with its competitors, anticipate market shifts, and capitalize on new opportunities. It helps product managers identify long-term and short-term competitive threats to make strategic decisions and target prioritization to help develop products with innovative features and strategic differentiation. It also helps product managers stage the go-to-market plans and identify the best time to launch their products.

Therefore, competitive product strategy ensures product managers are informed about the competitive landscape to make the right timely decisions for long-term product success. However, to be effective, the

CHAPTER 3   COMPETITIVE SEMICONDUCTOR PRODUCT STRATEGY

competitive product strategy must align with the product managers' teams' internal capabilities, such as resources, skills, competencies, external environment market conditions, and customer needs. Moreover, the competitive product strategy should be sustainable over time, allowing the product managers to maintain the product's competitive advantage even as market conditions change.

For example, BlackBerry was once well known for its phones and software services running through its servers, specializing in secure communications and mobile productivity. BlackBerry lost its dominant position in the market to its iOS and Android competitors and eventually dropped out of the phone business. From being a dominant player to exiting from the phone business is a huge downward transition, and the key reason is missing to take a competitive product strategy approach to short-term and long-term product management. Table 3-1 describes the reasons for its failure.

Table 3-1. BlackBerry Case Example

Events Happened in BlackBerry	Reasons
BlackBerry failed to adapt to the market trends like touch screens	Missed market trends Missed the potential of emerging technologies
Competitors implemented secure communications on consumer phones, dismissing BlackBerry's unique value to enterprise customers	Missed competitor strategies Late to acknowledge customer needs
Competition from iOS and Android ecosystem	
Delayed product features like touchscreen and apps	

CHAPTER 3   COMPETITIVE SEMICONDUCTOR PRODUCT STRATEGY

BlackBerry failed to have a market-driven competitive advantage and sustainable product improvements to increase its value. It failed to assess that the disruptive features could be innovated and impact the secure communication value proposition they had on the enterprise side. BlackBerry failed to understand the long-term network impact of the Android and iOS application ecosystem. It failed to acknowledge the emerging technologies like touchscreen which enhanced the customer experience significantly. The main reasons that led to the failure of BlackBerry could have been addressed by developing a competitive product strategy, as the product strategy enables product managers to assess market trends, emerging technologies, competitor strategies and customer needs. In summary, competitive product strategy greatly benefits product managers in addressing opportunities and risks from competitive threats and continuously redefining their products to stay competitive for longer.

Another aspect of using a competitive product strategy by product managers is to capture the path to product success by either delivering a differentiated semiconductor product with innovative features or delivering a similar semiconductor product value at a lower price than competitors, as shown in the Figure 3-2. With this robust product criteria, competitive strategy reveals risks and opportunities for product managers to make informed data-driven decisions. A competitive product roadmap implemented using a competitive strategy ensures the products are designed and developed with innovative improvements generation over and generation compared to the competition and adapt to the dynamic market needs. Therefore, competitive product strategy is a crucial aspect of product management for product managers to know their competition, navigate the market effectively, and make strategic decisions that enhance the competitive edge of the product in the industry. Semiconductor product managers can utilize competitive product strategy to define short- and long-term product roadmaps with clear targets. The strategy gives product managers a view of current and potential future market trajectories

CHAPTER 3   COMPETITIVE SEMICONDUCTOR PRODUCT STRATEGY

to optimize business objectives. The roadmaps implemented using competitive strategy have sustainable product KPIs that target innovative features aligned with customer market trends to ensure the product has a competitive advantage and delivers better value than competitors.

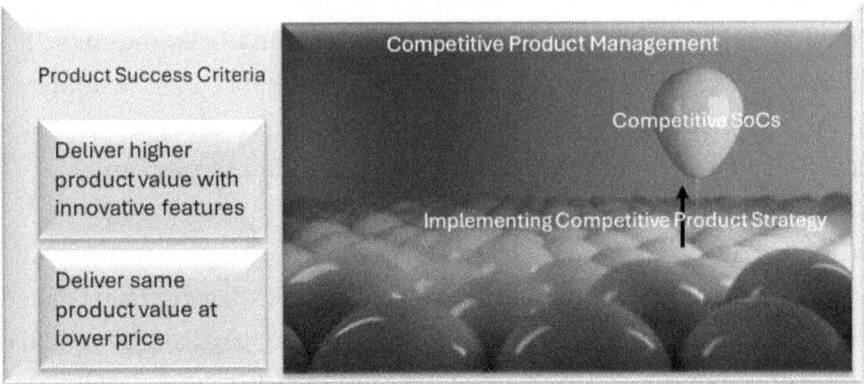

Figure 3-2. *Generic product success criteria*

The modern semiconductor industry landscape is a complex web of dependencies besides traditional competitive vectors like price and features. The industry is heavily influenced by political, geographical, economic, and technological rivalries. Product managers should utilize a competitive strategy development framework to derive and develop strategic product management for product success in a highly competitive semiconductor environment like PC and mobile. The framework addresses different aspects of decision-making, from strategic product planning and execution relevant to the market needs to external dependencies to ensure long-term product success. The strategic decisions could be based on the process technology needs, architectural improvement, and emerging technologies. Therefore, a comprehensive competitive strategy development framework helps to assess the underlying complex dependencies and their influence to help develop a robust competitive product strategy. Table 3-2 describes the advantages of the competitive strategy development framework.

Table 3-2. *Advantages of Competitive Strategy*

Advantages	Description
Informed Decision-Making	Helps product managers make decisions based on a clear understanding of the competitive landscape for short-term and long-term product execution
Risk Mitigation	Identifies potential threats and challenges from competitors, market shifts, and other geopolitical tensions, allowing product managers to take preemptive action
Opportunity Identification	Uncovers market opportunities that can be captured for growth or competitive advantage
Innovation and Differentiation	Provides insights that can lead to innovation in products, services, or processes, helping products stand out in the market

Competitive Semiconductor Strategy Development Framework

A competitive strategy development framework provides a comprehensive, systematic approach for product managers to ensure product success by carefully analyzing, developing, and implementing a sustainable semiconductor product strategy. By following this framework, as shown in Figure 3-3, product managers can systematically navigate complex, competitive environments to set and achieve their strategic goals to maintain a strong market position over the long term. Additionally, the competitive strategy development framework lets product managers create a recurring process to revise developed product strategies from time to time to continuously gain competitive advantage and stay ahead in the semiconductor industry.

CHAPTER 3   COMPETITIVE SEMICONDUCTOR PRODUCT STRATEGY

The framework execution requires product managers to thoroughly understand the competitive landscape. The landscape defines how a product positions itself in the marketplace with possible long-term opportunities to differentiate from rivals by identifying the competitive challenges from internal and external forces in the industry.

The competitive strategy development framework can be divided into three layers. Input for strategic analysis that outlines the state of the market and the company's position relative to external forces like competitors and the semiconductor industry. This input is used to formulate the second layer, which is developing a competitive product strategy with long-term and short-term objectives, and the last layer is to execute the developed product strategy using the semiconductor product life cycle. These three layers are interrelated to help make this framework a recurring and systematic methodology for product managers to ensure products have long-term success with competitive advantage. Let's discuss the three layers.

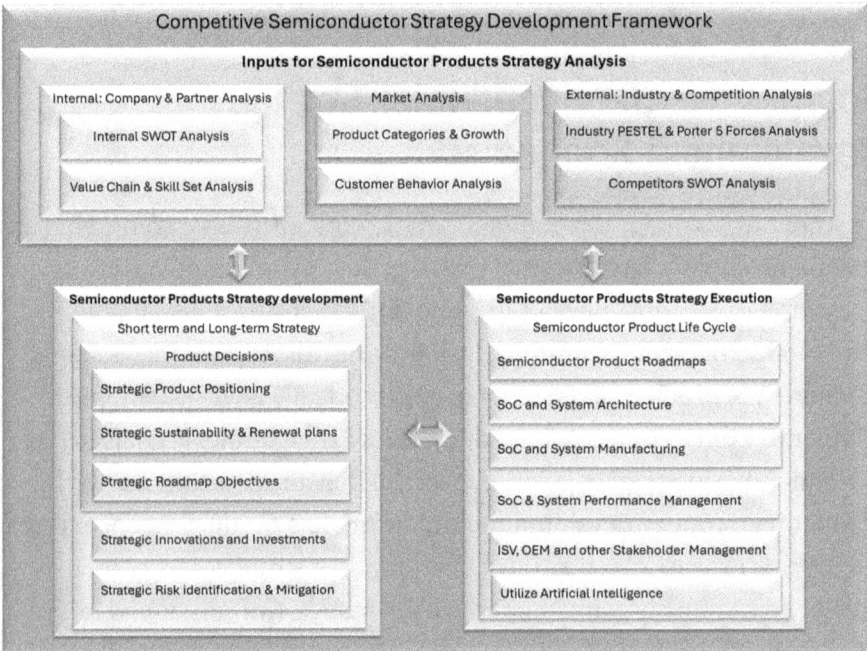

Figure 3-3. *Competitive strategy framework*

CHAPTER 3 COMPETITIVE SEMICONDUCTOR PRODUCT STRATEGY

Input for Strategic Analysis

The inputs for strategy analysis in the competitive strategy development framework can be categorized as internal, market, and external analysis. Internal analyses are specific to the product manager's internal teams and ecosystem partners as shown in the Figure 3-4. The input market analysis includes industry trends, emerging technologies, and customer behavior analysis. External inputs are the semiconductor industry and competitor analysis. The input categories are flexible and can be tailored to fit any semiconductor industry's specific needs and resources. Specific to the semiconductor PC industry, the critical inputs for developing a competitive product strategy are PC market analysis, external analysis like the semiconductor industry influencers, and available PC competitor's solution analysis.

Besides the semiconductor industry, competitors, and market analysis, product managers must clearly input their companies' value chain skill assessments and partner analysis to craft a robust competitive product strategy. These inputs must be regularly reviewed and updated to ensure the framework remains effective in a dynamic competitive environment. For example, in the case of BlackBerry, the value proposition of secure communications was a strength only until other competitors started implementing it in the consumer segment. A timely review of strategic inputs helps identify the competitor's emerging strengths and reveal other critical inputs within the industry and company.

Figure 3-4. Inputs for semiconductor products strategy analysis

69

CHAPTER 3   COMPETITIVE SEMICONDUCTOR PRODUCT STRATEGY

Internal and Ecosystem Partner Analysis

Internal Analysis of the company and its partners in the semiconductor product ecosystem provides product managers with details like the innovations secured by patents and skillsets for long-term sustainable feature development. This value chain analysis of the company can be leveraged as a competitive advantage in developing the product strategy. For example, Apple's phone silicon development expertise helped Apple to make a strong entry into PC silicon development. For example, Apple's SWOT analysis before 2020 reveals its dependency on Intel for PC silicon as a weakness. As Apple already had the necessary skillset in silicon design and development, entering the PC silicon design and development was not a hard choice. Therefore, Apple closed its weakness by leveraging its value chain strengths to enter the PC silicon design and development starting in 2020. Therefore, internal analysis helps product managers access their company's strengths using the value chain and skill set analysis to help develop a product strategy and partner strengths to try to remove their weaknesses, capture more opportunities, and mitigate threats identified using its own SWOT analysis.

Market Analysis

Market analysis is a customer-focused strategy analysis input to the competitive strategy development framework, as this input defines the limitations, opportunities, and growth potential of the customer segments. This input helps product managers understand customer needs and analyze how they are currently served by competitors. It reveals valuable insights like consumer behavior patterns, ecosystem trends like artificial intelligence, and potential growth opportunities. Product managers can implement market analysis using market research, technological research reports, seminars and conferences, customer feedback and surveys, technology trends, and forecast reports from the International Data

Corporation (IDC). The market analysis reveals customer behaviors and insights into the new opportunities to serve customers better with a new product introduction. For example, AMD introduced MI300 AI accelerator cards to capitalize on the AI market potential by successfully positioning its product against its rivals NVIDIA and Intel. Apple introduced tablet form factors in the PC industry to fill the gap between phone and PC users. Figure 3-5 shows the PC market segmentation. Product managers can assess the semiconductor PC market segmentation and market trends along with internal SWOT assessment to identify the potential product market segment opportunities and growing markets to serve.

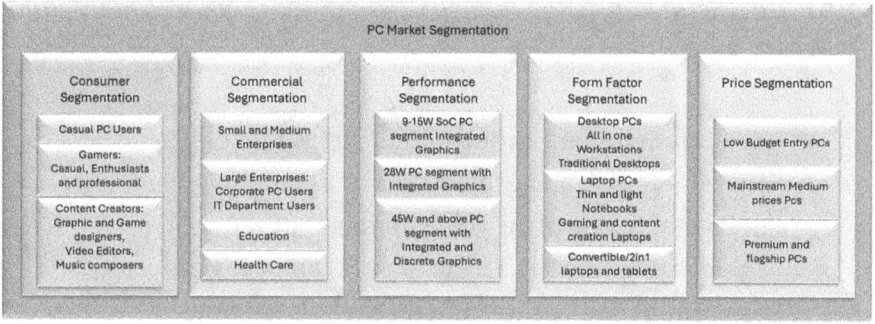

Figure 3-5. PC market segmentation

External Industry and Competitive Analysis

The last critical input into the strategic framework can be divided into three types: the industry's external forces, competitors, and competitive environment assessment, as shown in the Figure 3-6. These three are crucial factors in shaping the competitive product strategy by thoroughly assess the state of affairs in the semiconductor industry and competitive rivalry.

CHAPTER 3   COMPETITIVE SEMICONDUCTOR PRODUCT STRATEGY

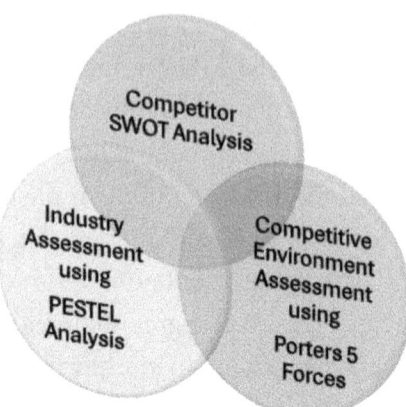

Figure 3-6. *Semiconductor industry, competitive environment, and competitor assessment tools*

- The external semiconductor industry is micro-environmental, and geographical influence factors define the scope of the semiconductor product strategy (e.g., the CHIPS Act of 2022) and geographical restrictions (e.g., using PESTEL analysis to know external forces).

- The current semiconductor competitor analysis reveals the potential opportunities by analyzing the competitor's product offerings and weaknesses relative to market needs.

- Semiconductor competitive environment assessments help assess the intensity of the competition and threats from suppliers, buyers, and indirect competitors within the semiconductor industry to get a market landscape of the competition of the semiconductor industry.

CHAPTER 3   COMPETITIVE SEMICONDUCTOR PRODUCT STRATEGY

PESTEL Analysis

External industrial influencers in the semiconductor industry providing insights into the industry's macro-environmental factors, the external environment in which semiconductor companies operate. For example, if a country implements strict TDP regulations for PC products which directly influences the product sales in that country if the products TDP doesn't fall within that country's set limit. A PESTEL analysis is a strategic tool to evaluate the macro-environmental factors that can impact an industry. Product managers can utilize the PESTEL framework to assess the semiconductor industry's political, economic, social, technological, environmental, and legal influence and input into competitive product strategy development. Figure 3-7 shows potential PESTEL influencers in the semiconductor PC industry for product managers to assess before developing a competitive product strategy to target domestic and global markets.

Semiconductor PC Industry PESTEL Analysis	
Political Influencers	Government Policies and Trade Relations, Subsidies and support programs like THE CHIPS ACT 2022, Geopolitical risks due to conflicts and regulatory restrictions
Economic Influencers	Global Economic Growth, Supply chain Costs, Currency Exchange Rates and Consumer Demand Cycles
Social Influencers	Technology Adoption, Workforce Skillset, Consumer Preferences and Behavior
Technology Influencers	Innovation and R&D investments, Moore's Law/Transistor technology, Emerging Technologies like AI, AR, VR, Near Memory compute etc.
Environmental Influencers	Sustainable and carbon Neutral Product Manufacturing, Semiconductor Material and Resource Scarcity, Energy Consumption and Climate Change risks
Legal Influencers	Regulatory and Standard compliance, Intellectual Property Laws to protect innovations in the industry

Figure 3-7. Semiconductor industry PESTEL analysis

CHAPTER 3   COMPETITIVE SEMICONDUCTOR PRODUCT STRATEGY

After the external industry analysis, the next input is the competitive environment analysis, which can be implemented using Porter's Five Forces.

Porter's Five Forces[1]

Porter's Five Forces framework is a strategic tool that can be used to analyze the competitive environment of any semiconductor industry. In the PC semiconductor industry, these forces help to assess the various factors that impact the PC industry's structure, competition, and profitability within the consumer and commercial PC segments. For example, the open PC ecosystem is dominated by the Microsoft Windows operating system although there are PCs available using ChromeOS and LinuxOS. The semiconductor PC industry is highly competitive, with strong barriers to entry, high supplier and buyer power, a low threat of substitutes, and intense rivalry among existing competitors, as shown in Figure 3-8. From Porter's Five Forces, it can be understood that product managers need significant investment in R&D, likely negotiate better manufacturing prices or identify other manufacturers to lessen the supplier opportunity costs, effectively manage supply chains, and continuously innovate to gain competitive advantage. Therefore, these factors must be critical to developing the overall competitive strategy for the long-term success of the products.

---

[1] Michael E. Porter, who introduced it in his 1979 Harvard Business Review article, "How Competitive Forces Shape Strategy."

CHAPTER 3   COMPETITIVE SEMICONDUCTOR PRODUCT STRATEGY

Porters 5 Forces in Semiconductor PC Industry	
Intensity of competition	Intense competition among Microsoft Windows OS and Apple MacOS, Silicon design companies AMD, Intel, Qualcomm, Apple and Nvidia, OEMs system manufacturers DELL, HP, Lenovo, Microsoft, Apple and others.
Thread of substitutes	The threat of substitutes in the semiconductor PC industry is low due to the lack of viable alternatives that can replicate the performance and cost-effectiveness of current semiconductors
Thread of New Entrants	High barriers of entry due to the operating system dependency, significant capital investment required in research and development (R&D), manufacturing facilities (fabs), and technology. Economies of scale from semiconductor design and manufacturers, OEMs cannot be met by the new entrants but already established semiconductor companies can enter to compete in PC industry. New entrants face significant challenges in navigating the complex landscape of intellectual property rights and regulations, further increasing the barriers to entry.
Bargaining power of suppliers	The PC semiconductor industry relies on a few specialized suppliers for raw materials, advanced equipment, and technology. For instance, companies like ASML dominate the supply of lithography machines essential for semiconductor manufacturing, TSMC in advanced process node manufacturing have higher bargaining power.
Bargaining power of buyers	Large number of PC manufacturers like Dell, HP, Lenovo and others purchase in large volumes, giving them considerable bargaining power to negotiate prices and terms. The PC market is highly competitive, and manufacturers are sensitive to component costs to maintain competitive pricing. This sensitivity can pressure semiconductor companies to offer more competitive pricing.

Figure 3-8. *Porter's Five Forces in the semiconductor PC industry*

Competitor SWOT Analysis

A competitor SWOT analysis is a strategic tool used to evaluate a competitor's strengths, weaknesses, opportunities, and threats. It helps product managers learn the competitive landscape and identify areas where they can capitalize on competitors' weaknesses or defend against their strengths. Semiconductor product managers must derive a SWOT analysis for each of the direct and indirect competitors as shown in the Figure 3-9 to assess their competitive strategies, such as AMD, Intel, NVIDIA, Apple, and Qualcomm for semiconductor design, TSMC and Intel foundry for semiconductor manufacturing, Dell, HP, Lenovo, Apple, Microsoft, and others for OEMs, and Microsoft, Google, Apple, and others for operating systems. This analysis should fuse into the competitive strategic framework to develop a robust and competitive product strategy with sustained competitive advantage.

75

CHAPTER 3   COMPETITIVE SEMICONDUCTOR PRODUCT STRATEGY

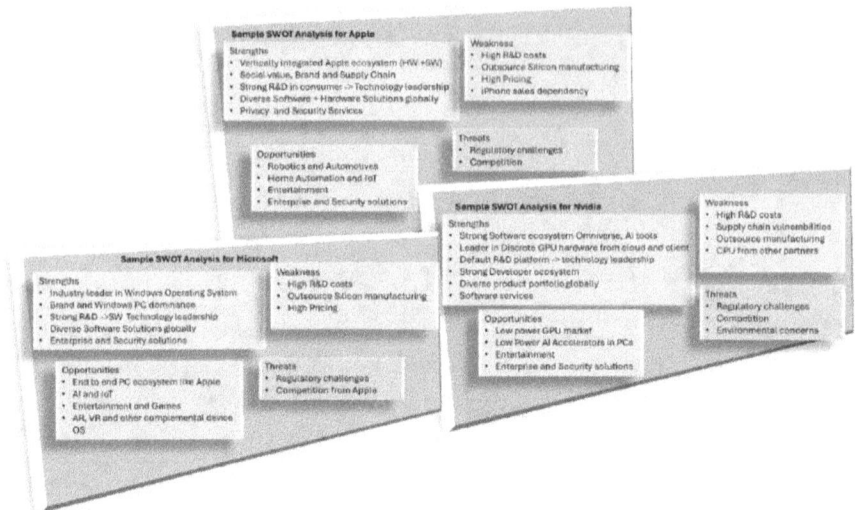

Figure 3-9. Examples of a SWOT analysis

All the input requirements and analysis gathered per the competitive strategy development framework ensure product managers have a holistic competitive landscape view in the semiconductor PC industry. The next step is to develop a competitive product strategy based on the inputs to the competitive strategic framework. Let's discuss the strategy development in the semiconductor PC industry.

Semiconductor Products Strategy Development

Product managers developing competitive product strategy must systematically develop a robust product strategy for short-term and long-term semiconductor product success. By following the competitive strategy development framework, product managers have the input to begin drafting product strategy. Information and insights on current competitor SWOT analysis, Porter's Five Forces, PESTEL analysis, market analysis, and a value chain and SWOT analysis provide a complete landscape view of the market, industry, competition, and their own company's core competencies required to develop a robust semiconductor

CHAPTER 3 COMPETITIVE SEMICONDUCTOR PRODUCT STRATEGY

product strategy. The product managers can develop product strategy in a systematic method using the mentioned competitive semiconductor strategy development framework, as shown in the Figure 3-10. Using this framework helps product managers clearly define why, where, and how the product is positioned to create customer value for short-term and long-term success. Additionally, this systematic framework helps product managers revise the product strategy as needed based on the changes to the strategic analysis inputs.

Figure 3-10. Semiconductor products strategy development

CHAPTER 3   COMPETITIVE SEMICONDUCTOR PRODUCT STRATEGY

Strategic Product Decisions

Product managers can take a three-step approach to developing the semiconductor product strategy. The first step is to make product-related decisions such as strategic product positioning, sustainability, and renewal plans and objectives. Let's discuss the three product decisions.

Strategic Product Positioning

Strategic product positioning is to define the semiconductor product's value proposition with a competitive advantage in the market. It is important for product managers to define product positioning to have a competitive advantage to stand out in the market. For example, Intel SoC-based PCs have the Windows ecosystem's vast applications as a competitive advantage compared to the Qualcomm SoC-based PC in the market. Although both SoCs are positioned to compete directly against each other, Intel has a platform competitive advantage compared to Qualcomm. The competitive advantage-based product positioning strategies ensure the product's success in the market. However, product managers must continuously revise the strategy development to ensure the competitive advantage remains intact or develop new methodologies to gain competitive advantage if competitors approach challenging competitive advantage.

In strategic product positioning, product managers can choose to position the semiconductors with differentiation in product features, deliver the same product features at a lower cost, or both tailored to customer segments. As the semiconductor industry is the basis of technological advancements, the products are usually positioned with feature differentiation rather than cost leadership. Therefore, product managers should drive continuous patented innovations and features to maintain the differentiation in the short term and long-term product positioning. For example, Apple intelligence provides its users with unique differentiation to its users compared to other competitors in AI use cases.

CHAPTER 3   COMPETITIVE SEMICONDUCTOR PRODUCT STRATEGY

The PC industry has multiple products with strategic product positioning with competitive advantage. As discussed in Chapter 1, the PC ecosystem of OEMs, semiconductor SoC design and manufacturers, ISVs like Microsoft, Apple, and so on. Products these companies offer provide a differentiated competitive advantage in the relevant PC customer segments.

Tables 3-3, 3-4, and 3-5 list some of the product positioning with differentiated competitive advantages from the various PC industry companies. Semiconductor product managers developing product strategy must have a thorough knowledge of market dynamics, a focus on innovation, and the ability to differentiate the products in a highly competitive landscape. By leveraging a company's core competencies, addressing market needs, anticipating future trends, investing in R&D, and strategically positioning the products, product managers can build a sustainable competitive advantage and drive growth in the PC market. Adaptability and a keen eye for emerging trends are crucial in maintaining relevance and success.

Table 3-3. *Product Positioning of OEMs in the PC Industry*

OEM	Product Positioning
DELL Technologies	Customization, strong supply chain, global direct sales model, strong business services and solutions, reliability, and innovation
Lenovo Group of Technologies	Value for money, global reach, diverse product portfolio, reliability, and innovative design
HP Hewlett-Packard Company	Comprehensive product range and life cycle approach, quality and durability, sustainability, and advanced security features
Apple Inc.	Apple ecosystem, strong supply chain, privacy, brand, connected platform and devices, innovation, quality, and reliability

Source: hp.com, Lenovo.com, Dell.com, and Apple.com as of July 2024

Table 3-4. Product Positioning of SoC in the PC Industry

SoC	Product Positioning
Intel Corp.	Product leadership, open platforms, semiconductor design and manufacturing at scale, broad ecosystem compatibility, innovation, research, brand
AMD Corp.	High-performance and adaptive computing leader, open ecosystem, research, innovation, and quality
NVIDIA Corp.	Leader in AI and deep learning, unmatched GPU performance and cutting-edge graphics technologies, broad industry applications using NVIDIA's technology across gaming, professional visualization, data centers, automotive

Source: Intel.com, AMD.com, Nvidia.com as of July 2024

Table 3-5. Product Positioning of ISVs in the PC Industry

ISV	Product Positioning
Microsoft Windows	Broad hardware and software compatibility, secure and user friendly, commercial and consumer OS with extensive customization, dominant gaming platform with DirectX support, and backward compatibility for legacy systems
Apple macOS	Seamless integration with the Apple ecosystem, unmatched user experience and design, optimized hardware-software integration, strong security and privacy features, and robust support for creative and professional tools

Source: Microsoft.com and Apple.com as of July 2024

CHAPTER 3   COMPETITIVE SEMICONDUCTOR PRODUCT STRATEGY

A competitive strategy development framework helps product managers make relevant product decisions on product positioning and differentiated value propositions by feeding the relevant inputs. Once the product positioning is decided, the next step in the strategy development is defining the strategic sustainability and product renewal plans.

Strategic Sustainability and Product Renewal Plans

This aspect of the strategy development framework ensures product managers define the measures to sustain product differentiation until the next product generation is out and the cadence of the product itself makes most of the sales in the marketplace. The idea is to focus on building and maintaining a long-term competitive advantage that is difficult for competitors to replicate. For example, Apple developed an end-to-end ecosystem and various product offerings, creating a walled garden for long-term sustainable competitive advantage.

Semiconductor product managers must estimate the number of SoCs needed to be manufactured based on the partner design wins, market analysis and TAM to capture maximum product sales and the timeline for product renewal. This estimate must be converted into the manufacturing capacity the semiconductor fabrication facilities need to facilitate a smooth product supply and cost required to develop the SoCs. Generally, the profit margin is higher in the technology industry, but there could be supplier opportunities in semiconductor manufacturing, which may impact the profit margin. Therefore, product managers must carefully analyze the cost requirements to ensure the SoC maintains healthy profit margins.

Additionally, product managers must ensure the design wins from OEMs like DELL, Lenovo, Microsoft, and others distribute the SoC capacity to ensure the market gets the inventory globally. For example, NVIDIA launched its GeForce RTX series GPU every year, as shown in Table 3-6 from 2018 to 2022. Intel launched its respective PC SoCs every year (see Table 3-7). On the other hand, Apple followed a yearly cadence from

CHAPTER 3   COMPETITIVE SEMICONDUCTOR PRODUCT STRATEGY

2022 and took a two-year cadence from 2020 to 2022 (see Table 3-8). Therefore, the cadence can be decided based on the value chain, market, and other factors contributing to or affecting the semiconductor product renewal plans.

Finally, product managers should decide when to EOL the semiconductor products to move to the next generation after the current generation semiconductor products are launched. After the launch, product managers should also ensure the implementation of customer feedback and learning methodology to assess customers' behavior and growing needs. This feedback and learnings need to be feedback to the inputs of strategy analysis to make the product development strategy a cyclic process to plan and implement the leanings in the next product renewal to stay competitive.[2]

Table 3-6. *NVIDIA GeForce RTX GPU Launch Timelines from 2018 to 2022*

Year	Products Released
2018	NVIDIA GeForce RTX 20 series GPUs based on Turing Architecture
2020	NVIDIA GeForce RTX 30 series GPUs based on Ampere Architecture
2022	NVIDIA GeForce RTX 40 series GPUs based on Ada Lovelace Architecture

Table 3-7. *Intel PC SoC Launch Timelines from 2021 to 2023*[2]

Year	Products Released
2021	12th Generation Intel Core processor based on Alder Lake Architecture
2022	13th Generation Intel Core processor based on Raptor Lake Architecture
2023	14th Generation Intel Core processor based on Meteor Lake Architecture

[2] As of July 2024, Wikipedia

CHAPTER 3   COMPETITIVE SEMICONDUCTOR PRODUCT STRATEGY

Table 3-8. *Apple PC SoC Launch Timelines from 2020 to 2024*[2]

Year	Products Released
2020	Apple M1 custom silicon SoC, Apple's first ARM-based processor for Macs
2022	Apple M2 custom silicon
2023	Apple M3 custom silicon
2024	Apple M4 custom silicon

Strategic Roadmap Objectives

The final set of product decisions that need to be taken is quantizing the product's positioning, competitive advantage, and sustainable and renewal plans as clear, measurable objectives to acquire with a timeline associated with it. Product managers' decisions in strategic product positioning and sustainable renewal plans feed in as clear measurable objectives in the long-term product roadmap. These objectives are the targets for product managers to monitor during the execution cycle to achieve planned design, manufacturing, cost, SoC performance, and business objectives. By setting clear, measurable goals that align with the chosen competitive strategy, such as market share growth, profitability targets, customer satisfaction, or innovation milestones, the objectives help gain more insights into the market and business for continued growth. To start defining objectives, product managers should maintain a long-term product roadmap, preferably five years or longer, with clear objectives like performance, TDP, cost, area, launch, and EOL, as shown in Figure 3-11. The semiconductor SoC roadmap development and execution are discussed in upcoming chapters.

The strategic roadmap objectives help product managers define products with tangible metrics to quantify competitive advantage to help achieve design wins in the open PC ecosystem or launch SoC based devices with unique value propositions. The objectives should be compared to top

CHAPTER 3 COMPETITIVE SEMICONDUCTOR PRODUCT STRATEGY

competitors to ensure the strategic product decisions create and capture its value in the market and are perceived as such by the customers with a strong go-to-market strategy. For example, Apple releases Macs based on their SoCs with performance improvements relative to their prior generation. Besides just semiconductor performance, each launch adds application features enabled directly through a semiconductor performance increase, creating a unique value proposition for their PC industry users.

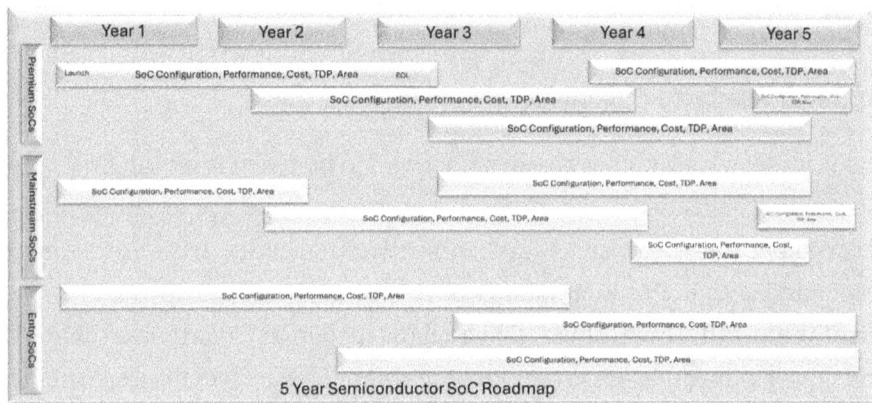

Figure 3-11. An example of a five-year roadmap

The competitive strategy development framework based on strategic product decisions ensures that product managers define a robust product strategy for success. The product positioning, strategic sustainability and renewal plans, and strategic roadmap objectives for products create a unique value proposition and maintain a sustainable competitive advantage for long-term product success.

When organizing and setting clear objectives and targets for product roadmaps, product managers must also define a path for achieving the competitive KPI targets while requiring product managers to have a clear insight on roadmap KPIs to track and different ways to achieve them. You learn more about implementing semiconductor product roadmaps after better understanding the product strategy execution elements.

Strategic Innovations and Investments

The next step in the competitive strategy development framework helps product managers avoid situations such as BlackBerry. Its unique value proposition of secure communications was eventually implemented by its competitors in the mobiles. In a highly competitive environment like PC, mobile, and other semiconductor industry segments, the competition is so severe that the innovative or unique value proposition a company holds will be challenged by other companies with their R&D and innovations. Therefore, it is important for product managers to develop a product strategy to consider the industry's fast-changing competitive dynamics. The competitive strategic development framework ensures that product managers include strategic innovations and investment strategies to increase the competitive edge continuously to avoid feature stagnancy. Product managers must explore opportunities for disruptive innovation that could redefine the market or create new markets and position the company as a leader in emerging trends. Product managers must analyze the emerging technologies and startups in the industry to acquire or partner with to continuously enhance the semiconductor product value. Attending technology events and conferences, sponsoring new and innovative business ideas and technology competitions, and supporting academic research are some methods to help product managers analyze the possibilities.

For example, AMD acquired Xilinx to increase the FPGA, embedded and AI capabilities to amplify its competitive edge in the semiconductor industry. Moreover, upon acquisition of Xilinx, AMD developed SoCs integrating Xilinx IPs to execute new capabilities in their products further increasing competitive advantage in the market.

CHAPTER 3   COMPETITIVE SEMICONDUCTOR PRODUCT STRATEGY

Strategic Risk Identification and Mitigation

The competitive strategy development framework ensures product managers consider the worst scenarios and prepare ahead for any unwanted situations during or after the launch of the products. By strategic risk identification and mitigation plans, product managers can identify potential risks that could undermine the developed competitive strategy, such as market disruptions, competitor actions, or regulatory changes. Following the competitive strategy development framework, product managers should develop contingency plans and risk mitigation strategies to address potential threats and ensure business continuity. Product managers should develop and prepare for multiple scenarios when the dependencies have a certain degree of uncertainty to ensure a robust risk identification and mitigation. For example, economic downturn, technological disruption, brand management, and skillset dependency to ensure the strategy remains resilient and adaptable.

Sony's AIBO (AI RoBot) was an early Sony attempt to create a household robot to help with chores. But at its launch, the AIBO's buggy technology was not sophisticated enough to handle even simple tasks reliably. Rather than selling a household robot with unreliable performance, Sony decided to position the AIBO as a robotic pet for entertainment. With this "low-expectations" positioning, consumers were delighted when their pet completed even the simplest tasks, and the customers particularly enjoyed "training" it to correct its mistakes.[3]

Conclusion

The competitive strategy framework provides a comprehensive systematic approach for product managers to implement a robust semiconductor product strategy. By including required strategic analysis inputs from

---

[3] A Havard-published case study available to purchase

CHAPTER 3 COMPETITIVE SEMICONDUCTOR PRODUCT STRATEGY

competitive, industry, a product manager can develop a recurring semiconductor product strategy with clear objectives. These objectives are quantifiable and measurable in terms of product value, potential market share growth and competitive advantage while ensuring strategic innovations and investments for long-term competitive sustainability and risk mitigation. By following this framework, product managers can better navigate complex, competitive semiconductor industry environments, achieve strategic goals, and maintain a strong market position over the long term.

Semiconductor Products Strategy Execution

The competitive product strategy developed using the competitive strategic development framework needs to be executed using the semiconductor product life cycle, which is part of the framework. The life cycle executes SoC and system architectural design and definition to determine the performance KPIs for SoC and system followed by physical products using semiconductor manufacturing technology. During these phases, the product managers need to execute performance management of the semiconductor design and physical SoC. While these phases are in progress, the product manager must also execute the stakeholder management to ensure the SoC is developed into an end-user PC device with a competitive advantage. Each of these execution stages is a broader concept, and product managers must pay close attention as multiple key concepts and dependencies are carefully addressed to ensure product success. The semiconductor products strategy execution five aspects shown in Figure 3-12 are covered in upcoming chapters to fully discuss how to help product managers implement the execution effectively.

CHAPTER 3 COMPETITIVE SEMICONDUCTOR PRODUCT STRATEGY

Figure 3-12. *Semiconductor products strategy execution*

Summary

The competitive semiconductor product strategy encourages product managers to formulate a plan for sustainable competitive advantage in the market. A competitive semiconductor product strategy development framework helps product managers with a systematic approach to developing a robust competitive product strategy by accounting for market trends with potential emerging technologies while assessing competitor strategies using a customer-centric approach with the help of effective tools, along with providing external factors like political and economic headwinds influencing the product management. After developing a product strategy, the execution depends on some key product decisions by the product managers, such as a decision on strategic product positioning. As part of product strategy execution, product managers pave a path for strategic innovations and investments for long-term sustainability by identifying and mitigating risks. With a comprehensive strategy development, the next step for product managers is to execute the product strategy. As a first step the product managers should be technically competent in semiconductor SoC architecture to define the roadmap KPIs targets. The SoC architecture is discussed in an upcoming chapter.

CHAPTER 4

SoC Architecture and Power Management

If you think good design is expensive, you should look at the cost of bad design.

—Dr. Ralf Speth

This chapter discusses the technical concepts, such as the typical architecture of the latest SoCs with CPUs, GPUs, NPUs, and other peripheral IP (intellectual property) components of a semiconductor product, and concepts of efficient power management. The chapter provides a simple and easy way to understand the complex technical concepts of semiconductor product architecture and power management essential for delivering competitive, higher performance, and power-efficient semiconductor products. The SoC architecture of the modern PC is explained using real-world examples.

There are various electronic form factor products manufactured using a variety of SoCs for the users to choose from like smartphones, tablets, desktops, and laptops. These different form factors are meticulously designed and manufactured with specialized SoC configurations to meet the computing needs of various semiconductor product user segments. Therefore, SoC is a critical component of electronic devices as its features are implemented based on the SoC capabilities. Therefore, the success of electronic computing devices such as PCs and smartphones heavily depends on implementing SoC architecture.

System on a chip, also known as *system-on-chip* or SoC, is an integrated circuit that integrates major components of an electronic computing device into a monolithic semiconductor die or disaggregated multi-chip module (MCM) design within the same package. The modern client SoC typically includes a central processing unit (CPU), a graphics processing unit (GPU), a neural processing unit (NPU) for AI, memory, media, and other peripheral interfaces, as shown in the Figure 4-1 designed into a monolithic die or disaggregated package.

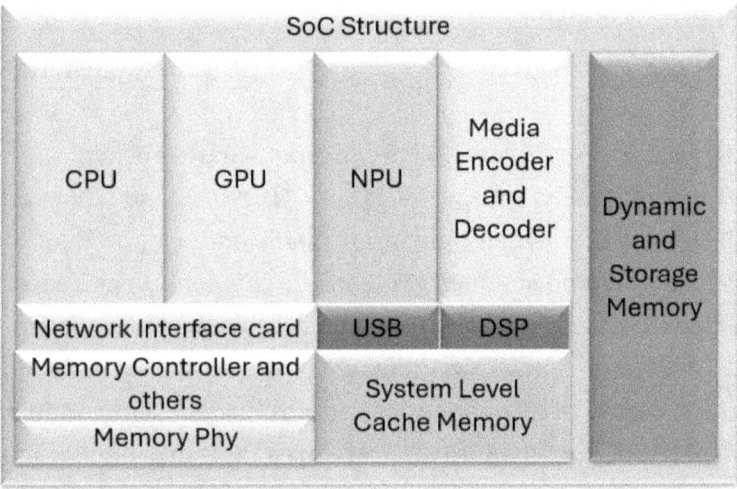

Figure 4-1. *SoC architecture*

A monolithic SoC integrates all the components manufactured using single semiconductor manufacturing process technology into a single die. This die structure is laid out with the most efficient floor plan of the SoC components placement to obtain the optimal die size and product cost. On the other hand, a disaggregated multi-die design

CHAPTER 4   SOC ARCHITECTURE AND POWER MANAGEMENT

integrates the components into multiple individual dies using one or more semiconductor processing technologies packaged into a single package like the Intel Meteor Lake[1] processors.

To design a competitive PC SoC, all the individual components like CPU, GPU and NPU need to be designed and developed with efficient architecture along with advancements in other IPs like memory, storage, and I/O interfaces. If an application uses CPU, GPU, Memory, and network card in an SoC, the application can only be performant when all these components execute their tasks well in all the application scenarios. One small miss in any of these components affects the application's performance. For example, if a PC user is watching a game's live stream and the Wi-Fi network card in SoC is not functioning properly. The user cannot watch the game even though other parts of the SoC are working perfectly well. Therefore, it is important for all the components of an SoC to work in collaboration with each other to deliver a smooth PC user experience. Table 4-1 shows some examples of SoCs available in the market as of mid 2024.

Table 4-1. *Example of SoCs Available in the Market as of 2024*

Examples of x86 SoCs from Intel	Examples of x86 SoCs from AMD	Examples of ARM ISA SoCs from Apple	Examples of ARM IP SoCs from Samsung
Raptor Lake Series	Zen 4 Ryzen 6000 series	M2/M2 Pro/M2 Max	Exynos 2200
Meteor Lake Series	Zen 5 Ryzen 7000 series	M3/M3 Pro/M3 Max	Exynos 2400

---

[1] https://en.wikipedia.org/wiki/Meteor_Lake

These SoCs are placed in original equipment manufacturing (OEM) PC devices like Dell Latitude, Microsoft Surface Pro, MSI Stealth, Lenovo ThinkPad, and HP EliteBook. OEMs partner with semiconductor product managers for SoCs to manufacture PCs and assemble other peripherals needed for PC manufacturing, like motherboards, screens, and operating systems. Some semiconductor design companies like Intel and AMD deliver SoCs to OEMs for PC manufacturing. Other full-stack design companies, such as Apple, design and manufacture their own PCs, like the MacBook Pro and Samsung Galaxy. Some companies, such as Samsung, design and manufacture electronic devices with their own SoCs manufactured in their fabrication facilities and partnering with other SoC vendors to maintain competitive advantage, as shown in the Figure 4-2.

Figure 4-2. *Different PC form factors*

The SoC designs that go into the PCs have multiple SKUs and product lines differentiated in CPU, GPU, memory, and other system design choices to fit the needs of customer segments like gaming, content creation, and commercial. Product managers should implement a flexible and scalable SoC IP component architecture to be scaled into multiple product lines. Implementing unified IP design methodology

CHAPTER 4　SOC ARCHITECTURE AND POWER MANAGEMENT

across product lines and scaling into various integrated SoCs increases the economic value of the product by reducing design costs and helping to cover more market segments. Integrating the SoCs with these highly scalable IPs should be designed with the right mix of individual IPs for competitive performance and power characteristics.

Semiconductor companies make differentiated SoC configurations by choosing several CPU and GPU cores and other components to meet customer needs. For example, Intel and AMD have good, better, and best product SKUs i3/Ryzen 3, i5/Ryzen5, i7/Ryzen 7, and i9/Ryzen 9 to differentiate the SoC to meet the needs of the target segments in price and performance. At the same time, Apple designs multiple SoCs like M3, M3 Pro, M3 Max to target different PC segments. The differentiation in SoCs is a crucial advantage as not all segments need everything PC can offer, like content creation. PC users need high graphics performance SoC with decent battery life, while commercial PC users who travel a lot need longer battery life with decent computer performance. Product managers need to make several SoC design and manufacturing choices to meet the needs of these different segments of PC users. There is no defined approach to meet these choices. But the key is to design a competitive SoC architecture critical to meeting these needs and ultimately delivering a competitive PC product in different segments.

CPU Architecture

CPU is a common term for a central processing unit, a primary SoC component capable of executing various PC workloads. A CPU consists of cores built using a control unit, arithmetic and logic units (ALU), memory unit, and input and output ports, as shown in Figure 4-3. CPU executes programs in the form of instructions with the help of basic arithmetic, logic, control, and input/output (I/O) operations. For the programs and applications to provide a competitive advantage in performance, the

CHAPTER 4   SOC ARCHITECTURE AND POWER MANAGEMENT

building blocks of the CPU need to be deeply understood to deliver a competitive CPU design. Therefore, knowing the CPU architecture and KPIs is imperative to set the right targets.

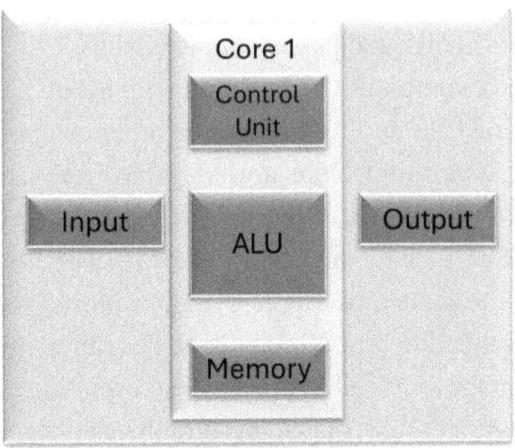

Figure 4-3. *Typical CPU core components*

CPU architecture refers to a CPU's design and application functional methodology to process various instructions, data management, and interactions with other hardware components within and beyond the SoC. It defines the organization of the CPU's internal components like support for various instruction types, microarchitecture, hyperthreading, memory hierarchy and their interconnections. Product managers must collaborate with architects and engineers to design a CPU architecture utilizing relevant patented innovations to deliver a competitive CPU with differentiated market positioning in the PC user segments for long-term success.

Instruction Set Architecture (ISA)

Instruction set architecture (ISA) is the connecting layer between CPU hardware and software applications. Benchmarks/applications are software code written to run on CPU hardware in a software programming language. ISA converts the software programming language into machine code instructions that CPU hardware can execute. Assessing different types of ISAs and their characteristics is crucial for product managers to continuously improve customer use cases by leveraging the capabilities of semiconductor technology with the help of engineering architects.

There are two types of popular ISAs[2] in the PC industry: *reduced instruction set computer* (RISC) and *complex instruction set computer* (CISC). With these two types of ISAs, there are three popular CPU architectures in the PC industry: x86, ARM, and RISCV as shown in the Figure 4-4. Let's discuss them.

- **x86**: The x86 architecture is primarily based on CISC design extended from the 8086 class of microprocessors designed by Intel and is named x86[3]. The x86 CPU cores have variable instruction lengths capable of executing pipelined, superscalar, and out-of-order execution with simultaneous multi-threading with two threads per core. A thread is a logical core capable of performing a single-core workload using virtual instruction sequences. In an x86 CPU, each core can have two threads per physical core. Intel and AMD primarily follow the x86 CPU core architecture.

---

[2] https://dl.acm.org/doi/pdf/10.1145/106972.107003
[3] https://en.wikipedia.org/wiki/X86

CHAPTER 4   SOC ARCHITECTURE AND POWER MANAGEMENT

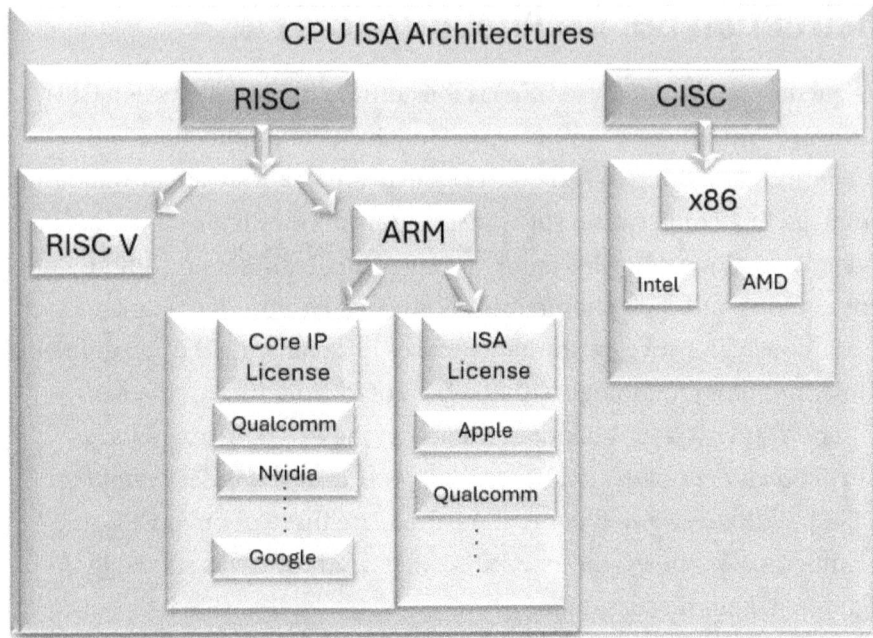

Figure 4-4. CPU ISA architectures

- **Advanced RISC Machines (ARM)**: The ARM architecture[4] is primarily based on RISC design.[5] The ARM CPU has a fixed instruction length capable of executing pipelined, superscalar, and out-of-order execution. Typically, in PCs from Apple and Qualcomm, ARM cores don't support simultaneous multi-threading with two threads per core, but some ARM cores support multi-threading. The ARM CPU architecture is proprietary to ARM Limited, and it licenses its IP to companies like Apple, Qualcomm, and Google for designing their own CPUs in their SoCs.

---

[4] https://dl.acm.org/doi/pdf/10.1145/143559.143570
[5] https://en.wikipedia.org/wiki/ARM_architecture_family

CHAPTER 4   SOC ARCHITECTURE AND POWER MANAGEMENT

Due to the differences in variable and fixed instruction length, the ARM and x86 architectures take different approaches to executing a single task of multiple instruction types.

- The x86 CPU aims to complete an instruction in multiple CPU clock cycles with fewer lines of code per CPU task, making each instruction complex.
- The ARM CPU focuses on executing an instruction in one CPU clock cycle with more lines of code per CPU task with simple instructions but taking more CPU cycles to complete the task.

Both approaches are valid, and there are products in the market with both architectures. These CPUs are differentiated mainly by how their architecture implements the applications. Since the computer is a complex machine and the technology industry is moving to rapid advances year over year. Application execution has become more complex, and a machine that can decipher and execute complex tasks with greater speed provides the best customer experience at a reasonable price.

From the definition, ARM-based CPUs are specialized for simple tasks, whereas x86-based CPUs are specialized for complex tasks. The technology industry is getting complex occasionally and demands continuous support for executing complex instructions with fewer computer cycles to keep up with the pace of the industry. Until recently, the industry has seen x86-based CPUs as leaders[6] in the market. However, Apple started challenging x86 CPUs with their M series ARM CPU implemented using a hardware-software design approach starting in 2020. However, many ARM-based CPUs were out in the market, which revealed ARM-based CPUs not ideal for the PC segment. Apple likely, in contrast, used hardware and software co-design approaches to mitigate the bottlenecks other ARM CPUs were

---

[6]https://ieeexplore.ieee.org/abstract/document/6522302

facing in the industry to deliver optimal application performance. Apple designed an ARM-based CPU with microarchitectural choices to deliver competitive performance to an x86-based CPU. Table 4-2 provides an example of x86 and ARM CPU performance (for reference only).

Another possible reason for ARM CPUs not becoming popular in Windows PCs is that the Microsoft Windows OS has focused on x86 SoCs for a long time due to performance leadership. Recently, we have seen Windows on ARM operating systems getting focused updates with native and prism-emulated applications. Transitioning from x86, Apple paved its ARM SoCs success utilizing already popular macOS with HW-SW Co-design to implement hardware and macOS design tailored to the application needs.

Table 4-2. *CPU Performance Comparison (from Geekbench.com July 2024)*

Benchmark Version 6.3	**SoC-based on ARM ISA**	**SoC-based on x86 ISA**
Geekbench CPU performance score	3063	2459

The same instruction types supported by an ISA can be implemented on different hardware types with an impact on the performance. Therefore, product managers designing a CPU need to understand the behavior of the ISA in different or the same instruction types in various workloads including competitor's products. For example, AMD and Intel can run a program using the same x86 ISA. But the program's performance is different on both hardware due to microarchitecture differences in CPU, although ISA is the same. Some of the instructions supported by x86 ISA are VNNI, AVX512, and AVX256. AVX512 has performance benefits compared to AVX256 on applications due to twice as many vector sizes. It is up to architects and product managers to support few or all these instructions depending upon the end goal of the CPU design.

Apple designs CPUs with ARM ISA released by ARM in a regular cadence. Product managers can choose to support versions of choice like ARMV8 or ARMV9, depending on the need and license agreements. For example, the Apple M4 CPU supports ARMV9, whereas Qualcomm's Snapdragon X Elite CPU is based on ARMV8. There are major performance updates on ARMV9 like updates to scalable matrix extensions (SME) compared to ARMV8.

Therefore, the choice and compatibility of the ISA make a huge difference in the overall execution of a CPU program, especially when working across x86 and ARM architectures[7]. Once the ISA is chosen and microarchitecture is decided for the CPU cores, scalable configuration decisions like performance and performance per watt need to be decided based on the target consumer segments by managing frequency and voltage scaling.

The third category, RISC V CPUs, is derived from a reduced instruction set architecture like ARM but follows the open specification of instruction, giving designers full control of instruction type implementation without any license, unlike ARM. RISCV is in the initial stages of market penetration and implementation. Due to its flexibility, it is highly regarded in the industry, and many industry leaders are already part of the community to collaborate on this open platform. Product managers can explore RISCV design options if they can bridge the gap in the ecosystem dependencies like operating systems and native applications support. Although x86 and ARM are mostly utilized in the industry today, product managers should keep track of the RISC V evolution for the future to be competitive in the AI era, which is a dynamically changing environment. RISC V gives the flexibility to implement any type of instruction to meet the dynamics of the industry and can be a potential choice for CPU designers in the future.

---

[7] https://minds.wisconsin.edu/handle/1793/64923

CHAPTER 4   SOC ARCHITECTURE AND POWER MANAGEMENT

Microarchitecture

While ISA connects the software to hardware, CPU microarchitecture defines the hardware design that executes those instructions. It involves the design and organization of the internal components of the CPU to execute ISAs, as shown in the Figure 4-5. It determines how efficiently the CPU executes instructions, manages data, and interacts with other hardware components. Advances in microarchitecture, such as pipelining, out-of-order execution, and branch prediction, superscalar architecture have significantly improved CPU performance and efficiency over the years. CPU microarchitecture is essential for optimizing hardware and software to achieve the best possible performance.

For the CPU to execute any programs consisting of multiple instructions, A pipeline mechanism is designed to fetch the instructions and decode them so it can be executed on the ALU units by accessing the required data stored in the memory and writing the executed result back to the memory. This might seem like a simple task, but the number of instructions in the CPU pipeline for a modern PC application is in the order of 2^{64}. Therefore, the pipeline is integrated with other techniques like out-of-order execution to execute the instructions in any sequence to avoid delays and increase efficiency. There is a branch predictor for predicting the navigations within the instructions without having to wait for its full execution to deliver faster execution of the instructions, feeding into the overall performance of the programs. Modern CPUs have wider pipelines with many decoders for improved instruction efficiency and performance for the evolving PC workloads.

CHAPTER 4 SOC ARCHITECTURE AND POWER MANAGEMENT

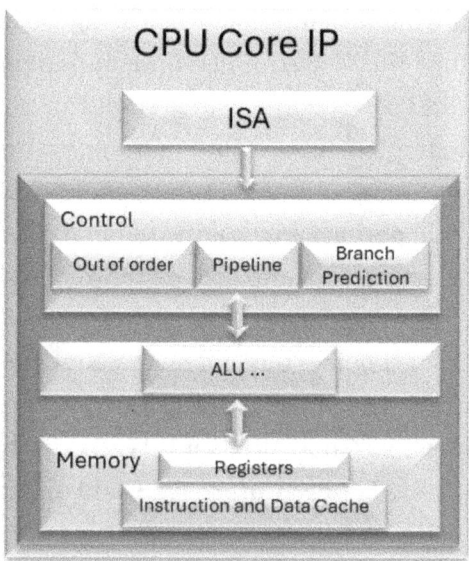

Figure 4-5. Typical CPU core IP architecture

Product managers aiming for competitive CPU core IP design can pick any ISA and design a competitive CPU with efficient microarchitecture; the bottleneck is not necessarily the choice of x86 or ARM ISA but depends on the implementation of the CPU microarchitecture using either x86 or ARM ISA. Consider ISA as the ingredients in the recipe, and cook is the microarchitecture. The better the cook, the better the chances that the meal turns out to be good. Therefore, product managers should design CPUs with efficient microarchitecture for the supported ISA. There are many ways this can be achieved. Product managers should brainstorm ideas with architects and engineering teams, seek customer feedback, and model different scenarios with older product data to improve the performance of the CPU IP in upcoming chapters.

CHAPTER 4 SOC ARCHITECTURE AND POWER MANAGEMENT

Modern CPUs are made of multiple cores using scalable CPU core IPs, as shown in the Figure 4-6. Modern CPUs have multiple types of cores implemented as hybrid cores. Performance cores run at peak frequencies and are employed to implement computing-hungry tasks as they consume much power running at higher and peak frequencies. Efficiency cores engineered for optimal performance, as the name suggests, are designed to perform tasks efficiently, consuming lower Power, as shown in the Figure 4-7. Some CPUs today have a third core type, called a *medium core*. The core count and type choices depend on the target product segment the SoC is positioned. Apple M3 series SoCs have four performance and four efficiency cores, while Google Tensor G3 CPU has three types of cores using 1x ARM Cortex X1, 4x ARM Cortex A715, and 4x ARM cortex A510.

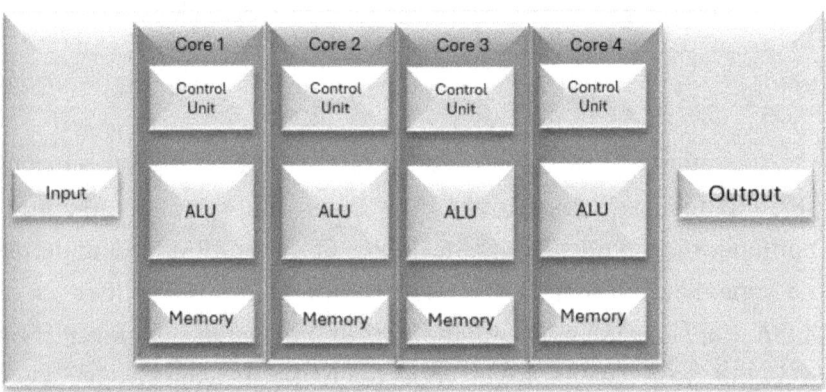

Figure 4-6. *Typical CPU multi-core design components*

CHAPTER 4   SOC ARCHITECTURE AND POWER MANAGEMENT

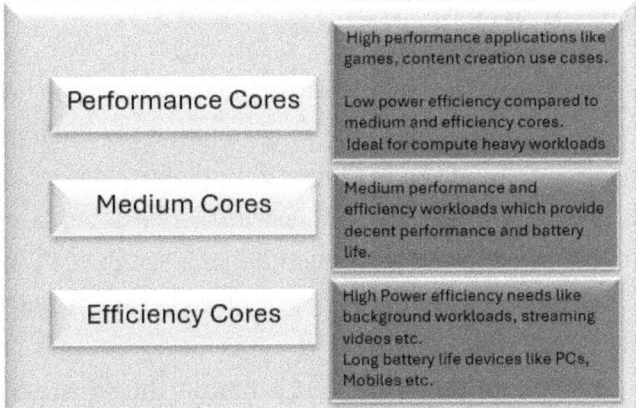

Figure 4-7. Examples of different types of CPU cores

Why do we need performance or medium cores? Can a CPU only have all efficiency cores or all performance cores? A PC performs a variety of tasks where few require higher performance, like blender simulations, and few efficient performances like playback videos. Hence, a good mix of performance and efficiency cores would be ideal for a PC CPU.

Product Manager defining CPU for a segment should target competitive performance on all CPU cores or pick a combination that best suits the requirements of applications in PC user segments.

A typical CPU use case can be single-core utilizing only one CPU core or multi-core utilizing two or more CPU cores. For a single-core, the CPU usually picks the higher-performing core, which is often a performance core. Competitive single-core performance is attained by delivering the maximum number of instructions a single-core can execute in a clock cycle. Competitive multi-core is derived from combining two or more cores delivering maximum instructions in a clock cycle. Single-core and multi-core performance is dependent on CPU design. Therefore, to design a competitive CPU, the product manager's decisions are based on the number of CPU cores, types of cores, ISA, and microarchitecture of the CPU, along with the continuous innovations in the CPU design.

CHAPTER 4   SOC ARCHITECTURE AND POWER MANAGEMENT

Memory Hierarchy

If ISA can be considered the "ingredients," microarchitecture is the "cook," and memory hierarchy is the "kitchen and tools and equipment." A cook's efficiency depends on the organization of the kitchen and the cooking equipment. Similarly, the CPU performance depends on cache hierarchy, DRAM capacity, and bandwidth that helps the CPU access the required data at a minimum latency. Each CPU usually has three tiers of cache: L1 as the first-level cache, L2 as the second-level cache, and L3 as system system-level cache. L1 is usually the private cache available for each core. Depending on the design, L2 is shared by a core complex or set of cores. L3 is shared by all the IPs in the SoC, including the CPU, as shown in the Figure 4-8.

CPU cores execute input instructions to provide output data, and the input and output data are acquired and stored in the caches. For the CPU to execute a program faster, the caches must supply and store the input and output in line with CPU speed. Any discrepancy is an added latency and increases the cycles the CPU takes to execute an instruction, impacting the CPU execution time and performance.

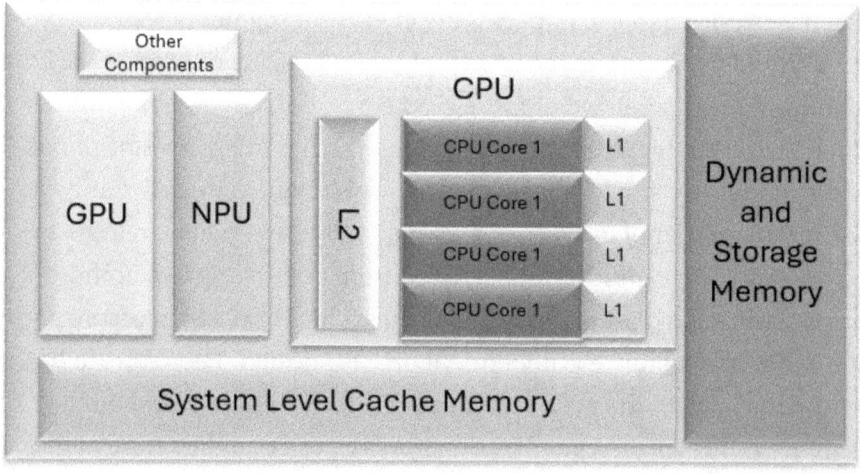

Figure 4-8. Typical SoC cache hierarchy

Similarly, the DRAM capacity and bandwidth affect the performance of the CPU.

L1, L2, L3, and DRAM are memory that stores executable programs. DRAM holds the bulk of the data compared to L3, L2, and L1 and supplies the data and instructions needed for the executable program. So, if a CPU needs information while executing an instruction, it first searches in the L1 cache. If the data is unavailable, called an *L1 miss*, the search moves to the L2 cache, a slightly bigger cache than L1. If L2 is also a miss, the request goes to the bigger L3 cache and eventually to DRAM if data is unavailable in all three caches. The full cycle of DRAM in search of data is called *memory latency*. The lower the memory latency, the faster the CPU executes the instructions. So, the more the L3 and DRAM bandwidth, the faster the data gets transferred to the CPU, increasing the performance of CPU applications. However, a fine balance can be achieved between L3 and DRAM memory targets as one can slightly compensate for the other to some extent if implemented deliberately. Product managers should focus on memory latency and hierarchy as they are critical drivers of CPU performance.

Usually, x86-based CPUs for a long time had two channels of 128-bit DRAM until Apple entered the ARM CPUs and designed 128-bit, 256-bit, 512-bit, and 1024-bit CPUs for Macs. While Apple used DRAM bandwidth to provide more flexibility to their CPU, AMD has implemented VCache, a 3D cache that acts like a shared L3 cache for the CPU with 128-bit DRAM configuration. All these methodologies are a way to provide better CPU performance influenced by the cost of packaging, scalability and others are discussed in upcoming chapters.

CPU KPIs

To begin the product competitive landscape, we would need to have performance quantifiers to establish the capabilities of the CPU for better market positioning and performance assessment.

The performance of the CPU can be quantized for single-core and multi-core applications. Single-core is the performance of one core working on a single task-based workload like web browsing in a single web window. Multi-core is the performance of more than one core working to finish the task like using video editing software to edit a scene. The single-core and multi-core CPU performance of Apple SoC shown in Table 4-3 looks very competitive to other x86 CPUs in the market.

Table 4-3. Geekbench CPU Results (for reference only)

Version 6.3[8]	Apple SoC	x86 SoC from Intel	x86 SoC from AMD
Geekbench single-core score	3063	2459	2202
Geekbench multi-core score	11692	13360	11421

One major step is to grasp the measuring methodology of single-core and multi-core CPU performance metrics to accomplish this. The basic factors affecting the performance of CPUs are instruction type support, single-core performance, number of cores, available cache memory, DRAM and bandwidth, and the thermal limit. For a single-core CPU task, the number of cores can be ignored.

Generic CPU performance (single-core or multi-core) = 1/the time the CPU takes to finish a program (CPU program time).

---

[8] Source: https://browser.geekbench.com/ml/v0/inference

CHAPTER 4 SOC ARCHITECTURE AND POWER MANAGEMENT

A program is a set of instructions that can be measured in instructions/program. Instructions are executed in CPU cycles and can be quantized in time as the number of cycles the CPU takes to execute one instruction, generally known as CPI (cycles per instructions).

> CPU program execution time or CPU performance equation
>
> = Instructions/program * cycles per instruction * CPU clock cycle
>
> = Total instructions in a program * CPI * CPU clock cycle

A CPU that takes shortest time to execute a program compared to the available CPUs in the market is perceived as competitive. Product managers aim to get the lowest time for task execution on the CPU compared to the competitors. Product managers should spend enough time on thoroughly analyzing the available competitors' CPU execution time on a few mostly used CPU programs of the target segment vs. theirs. In an ideal case, the fastest CPU time can be attained by few instructions per program, fewer cycles per instruction, and a faster CPU clock cycle. However, these three vectors depend on multiple factors like the type of program, compiler, ISA, CPU organization, cache methodology, DRAM memory and bandwidth, and the operating system running the application.

Programs can be benchmarks or applications meant to provide a full performance metric of the CPU like CineBench, Geekbench, or actual user use cases like web browsing or application-related workloads like gaming, blender, Premiere Pro, and Final Cut Pro. These measure the real-time performance of a CPU for a target segment under different scenarios. During the CPU positioning, product managers must develop a list of a few top segment use cases/benchmarks and win on all or most of the performance KPIs (Key Performance Indicators). For example, CPUs in gaming segments should deliver competitive performance (frames

CHAPTER 4 SOC ARCHITECTURE AND POWER MANAGEMENT

per second) on popular AAA games[9] compared to the other CPUs in the market. The winning or losing performance over the previous generation or competition should be understood thoroughly. The dependency can be anywhere from microarchitecture to the application level to approach a fix if possible. Sometimes if there are multiple choices of compilers to run a program, differences in the compiler execution of that program can be sensitive to the CPU performance.

CPU performance positioning is often based on configurations like thermal design power (TDP), which indicates the average power a CPU is expected to dissipate under a typical performance load. Lower TDP values are preferred for energy efficiency and thermal management, especially in laptops and mobile devices. Power is discussed further in the coming chapters.

Besides TDP and power, the CPU positioning is differentiated by the number of cores, frequency of the cores, and DRAM bandwidth. Intel and AMD positioning on CPU is based on the U, H, and HX segments, where U has a lower number of cores, frequency and TDP than H and HX, as shown in the Table 4-4. It is important to factor in the right competitor's product while designing a CPU. For example, a 15W TDP CPU comparison should include only 1355U, 5400U, and M3 from the preceding list. A 5900HX would be an invalid comparison while accessing the performance of a 15W CPU as HX doesn't compare to U segment CPU performance, TDP, or the price point. TDP and frequency depend on the process technology, Cdyn, and power management of the SoC, which is discussed later.

---

[9] AAA Games: is an informal classification used in the video game industry to describe games with large budgets and high profiles.

CHAPTER 4   SOC ARCHITECTURE AND POWER MANAGEMENT

Table 4-4. *Various CPU Configurations (Source: Intel.com, AMD. com, Apple.com/Geekbench.com)*

	No. of CPU cores	Frequency	TDP
Intel Core™ i5 1355U	10	5/3.7Ghz	15W
Intel Core™ i7 13800H	14	5.2/4Ghz	45W
Intel Core™ i7 13700HX	16	5/3.7Ghz	55W
AMD Ryzen™ 3 5400U	4	4 Ghz	15W
AMD Ryzen™ 5 5600H	6	4.2 Ghz	45W
AMD Ryzen™ 9 5900HX	8	4.6 Ghz	45+W
Apple M3	8	4.05/2.45Ghz	15W
Apple M3 Pro	12	4.05/2.45Ghz	30W
Apple M3 Max	16	4.05/2.45Ghz	30W

Therefore, to design a competitive CPU, the decisions and KPIs for product managers are CPU clock speed, IPC, Number of CPU cores and threads, types of cores, ST and MT performance, memory latency, cache hierarchy and size, DRAM bandwidth and size, TDP, power consumption and efficiency during idle and various performance stages and CPU real-world applications and benchmarks that best represents the user of the target segment. Product managers should compile this list with targets for the products and ensure these KPIs targets are met across all semiconductor life cycles, as shown in the Figure 4-9.

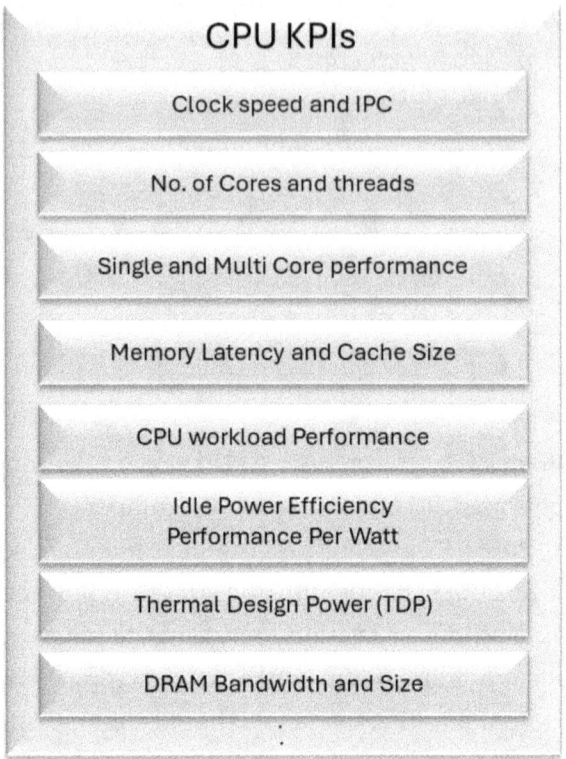

Figure 4-9. *CPU KPIs*

CPU AI

Besides general-purpose computing, CPUs can also execute AI workloads. CPU is considered a general-purpose compute engine, and matrix multiplications, which are the instructions that execute neural networks, were also supported by the CPU for the longest time. The support for these matrix multiplication instructions is either included in the CPU core or added as a separate AMX IP in the SoC. AMX (advanced matrix extensions) helps to optimize and accelerate deep learning training and inferencing workloads based on matrix calculations. A CPU executing normal workloads compared to AI workloads with AMX is an entirely different implementation because AMX uses a systolic framework that accelerates AI instructions. The performance on inference-based tasks with AMX supported CPU is far more performant than a generic CPU executing AI workloads. Although a generic CPU can run matrix instructions, AMX IP is added to accelerate the AI instructions to enable faster AI workload performance on the CPU.

As shown in Figure 4-10, AMX heavily accelerates the performance of a machine learning workload, given it meets other requirements like memory bandwidth and cache. To lead in the CPU AI performance, product managers must effectively choose the number of CPU cores + AMX + cache + bandwidth required to get the desired performance[10].

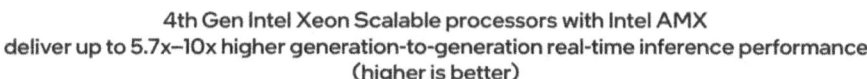

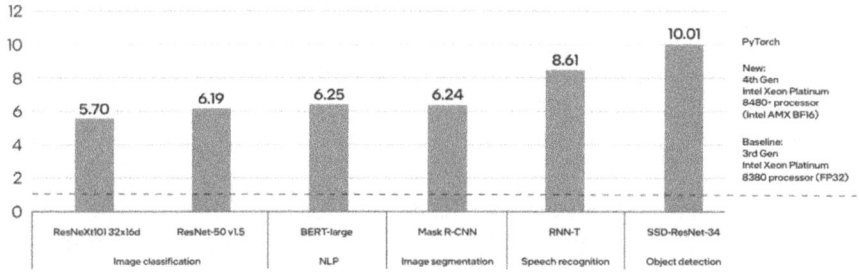

Figure 2. 4th Gen Intel Xeon Scalable processors with Intel AMX accelerate PyTorch real-time inference performance[5]

Figure 4-10. *AMX performance on Intel CPUs*

The evolution of the CPU started with microcontrollers and microprocessors designed to implement arithmetic operations of integers. As the research and innovation evolved, microcontrollers and microprocessors transformed from executing a few simple arithmetic operations to trillions of operations per second. So, the CPU became a

---

[10] https://www.intel.com/content/www/us/en/products/docs/accelerator-engines/what-is-intel-amx.html

generic microprocessor designed to execute generic instructions, and an efficient CPU design supports instructions required to run on any type of PC program. The instructions are usually in integer (int) or floating-point data types. The data commonly supported by PC CPUs are int8, int4, FP16, FP32, and FP8. The data type support depends on the academic research and innovation in the technology which enables new or efficient capabilities in executing workloads. Multiple workloads solving important customer problems became the heart of technological innovation. One such use case is display screens that are used to watch prerecorded pictures and videos. Display screen implementation is running the multiple instructions with a larger dataset, revealing the CPU's strengths and weaknesses. CPU can efficiently execute single instruction, multiple data workloads but other workloads like display content on screens implemented using single instruction and multiple threads were slow. As CPUs showed inefficiency in executing these heavily parallel workloads, an accelerated parallel instruction processing unit was designed to help CPUs deliver efficient performance on the parallel workloads. Hence, the GPU became a popular PC component to deliver accelerated parallel instructions in collaboration with the CPU. A point to note here is GPU is designed to supplement the CPU, not as a complement, as we still need the CPU to initiate the task and let the GPU execute rendering workloads. Let's discuss the GPU architecture.

GPU Architecture

A GPU is a graphics processing unit designed to execute accelerated graphics rendering and other parallel workloads; this is also known as a *GPU accelerator*.[11] Unlike CPUs, designed for any general-purpose execution,

---

[11] https://picture.iczhiku.com/resource/paper/WyiWoZOZoDZWgvxN.pdf

CHAPTER 4   SOC ARCHITECTURE AND POWER MANAGEMENT

GPUs are designed to accelerate specific sets of parallel instructions like rendering required to support the CPU to finish a program. Companies like NVIDIA, AMD, Intel, Apple, and Qualcomm have few major GPU designs. The design of GPU is not tied to x86 or ARM architecture, it is a logic to implement parallel instructions. GPUs are made of smaller and more specialized cores for accelerating parallel workloads like gaming, graphic visuals, and content like video/audio/photo editing on a PC or Phone. CPU and GPU work collectively to deliver a great application experience to the PC user by collaborating to accelerate performance.

Consider a gamer playing a game. To progress into the game, the gamer must make moves, and the entire screen must keep up with the gamer and reflect the gamer's moves as fast as possible so the gamer has a seamless gaming experience. While the CPU manages the control execution, the GPU executes the visual updates on many or all parts of the screen. To keep up with the fast-paced game play to show the effects on the screen, GPU divides the screen into smaller sections and executes sections of screen updates in parallel for better detail capture. A good GPU design meticulously breaks the screen into smaller sections to capture finer details and execute in parallel. They can be rated based on their ability to meticulously divide the screen and execute parallel tasks.

Like CPU, GPU is also made of cores, also called *execution units*, *compute units*, or *streaming multiprocessors*. These cores comprise multiple ALUs grouped into Single instruction Multiple threads (SIMT). The multiple ALUs in one execute parallel operations with a single instruction. Hence, the instructions fetch and decode are relevant per SIMT block and not per ALU, unlike CPU. Modern GPUs have different types of cores targeted for specific workloads, like tensor cores, shader cores, and ray tracing cores. Each core type is specialized in specific instruction execution, serving distinct purposes in parallel computational tasks. Shader cores are versatile and handle general-purpose tasks, tensor cores excel in accelerating mathematical operations for deep learning, and ray tracing cores enhance the realism of lighting and reflections in graphics through real-time ray tracing. Each type of core contributes to the overall capabilities of a GPU in different ways, making it suitable for a range of applications like gaming, 3D effects and rendering, physics and model simulations, and AI workloads.

Shader cores execute the rendering pipeline, including vertex, pixel, and geometry shaders with higher texture details. These shader cores are crucial for general-purpose computing tasks, rendering graphics, and implementing various shading techniques in game development and graphics processing.

Tensor cores are specialized hardware units designed to accelerate multi-dimensional matrix multiplication operations extensively used in deep learning and machine learning workloads. Tensor cores significantly enhance the performance of AI and neural network workloads, providing a substantial speedup in tasks such as training and inference in deep learning models. Tensor cores are also called XMX (Xe Matrix Extension) cores by Intel.[12]

Ray tracing cores are dedicated components designed to accelerate real-time ray tracing, which is a rendering technique that simulates the behavior of light to produce highly realistic lighting, reflections, and shadows in computer graphics programs. Ray tracing cores are instrumental in improving the visual fidelity of graphics in gaming, computer-aided design (CAD), and other applications that require highly realistic lighting and reflections.

---

[12] https://www.intel.com/content/www/us/en/support/articles/000091112/graphics.html

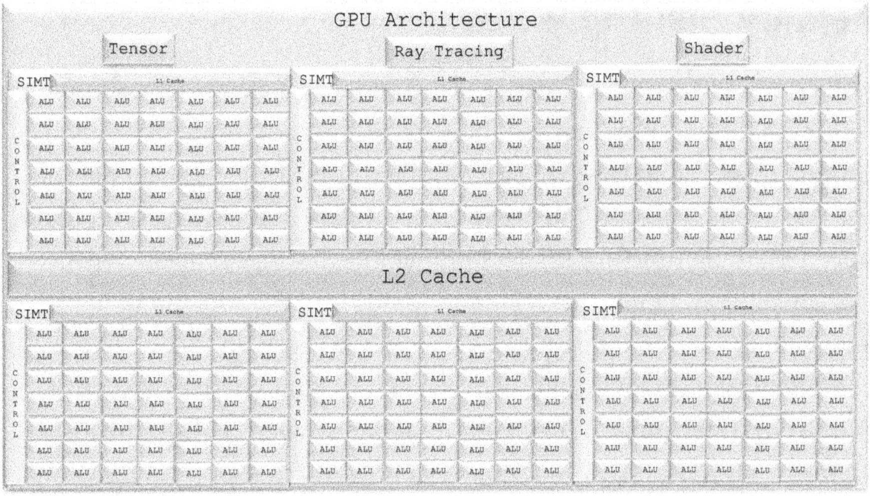

CHAPTER 4   SOC ARCHITECTURE AND POWER MANAGEMENT

Figure 4-11. GPU architecture

Unlike CPUs, where there are only three popular architectures, GPUs can be designed in many ways to accomplish the needs. Product managers should quantify the performance with a few KPIs to evaluate the GPU compared to competitors and their prior generations. As different types of GPU cores are made of ALUs, A well-known KPI to evaluate the performance of the GPU is its ALU's ability to execute operations in unit time, called FLOPS (floating-point operations per second). The value proposition of the GPU is its higher throughput and better accuracy, given its ability to render a screen by dividing it into small frames with higher accuracy in parallel. The default data type in GPU is usually floating point because it is more accurate than integer data types due to its richer representation with decimal points.

The performance of a GPU can be measured in floating-point operations per sec, often called Giga, GFLOPS, or Tera, TFLOPS. Another way to quantify the GPU performance is by running an application-like game to capture the fps (frames per second). The GPU delivering higher fps is said to be better performant.

CHAPTER 4   SOC ARCHITECTURE AND POWER MANAGEMENT

Memory Hierarchy

Besides power, GPU performance is dependent on other SoC components. A GPU is a throughput-based engine. Its performance depends on the memory latency and DRAM bandwidth to support GPU's faster parallel data processing speeds. The discrete GPUs use a dedicated fast memory called GDDR memory for higher bandwidths to support the faster-moving data capabilities. On the other hand, Apple has differentiated their higher configuration integrated GPUs like M3 Max with 512-bit DRAM memory delivering up to 500 GB/sec memory bandwidth to meet the GPU needs. Intel and AMD, in their integrated lower TDP graphics SKUs, use the usual 128-bit DRAM memory bandwidth to support the segment. There are continuous cache upgrades to mitigate the 128-bit bottleneck on their SKUs. So, there is more than one way to meet the data transfer speed requirements in GPUs, product managers should evaluate the best choice for their products based on the long-term vision with design flexibilities. I found Apple's integrated GPU with larger unified memory a better long-term solution in handheld PCs as a major value proposition of the PCs is the performance per watt and heterogeneous compute where the SoC components work as a team to deliver a seamless application performance. Software and operating systems have the flexibility to run workloads efficiently and can promptly respond to industry dynamics.

A GPU is an accelerator engine to support the CPU in parallel instruction. Product managers need to make sure besides memory speed, the CPU is not hindering the GPU workload execution. This can happen when the GPU is waiting for the CPU to hand off the executable instruction, which adds to the delay in the user experience of an application. Product managers should ensure that the choice of frequency on CPU, GPU, and memory is such that no one is waiting on each other, and most or all the target segment application KPIs are part of the evaluation test plan to completely exclude these corner cases.

CHAPTER 4　SOC ARCHITECTURE AND POWER MANAGEMENT

The choice of integrated or discrete graphics has pros and cons, but OEM PC manufacturing with SKU differentiation gives most PC users a good grasp of picking the right SKU for their needs. With the revolutionary success of social media platforms, many influencers have channels to help users pick the right PC for their needs.

Integrated graphics in the SoCs are mainly available in lower 60 watts PCs except for Apple M3 Max-based MacBook Pros with over 130 watts (source: Apple.com). The integrated GPU SoC has easy access to the data from the CPU and other IP components in the SoC to resolve any data dependencies. Discrete GPU is often connected by PCIe link to the SoC. Because of this implementation, the data processed by the CPU and GPU have duplicate copies in two separate locations, unlike the integrated design. Apple integrates GPUs in the SoC to leverage the unified memory shared between all the SoC IPs to avoid storing multiple data copies. This method has its own advantages but comes with a larger monolithic die area which has yield limitations when manufactured using advanced semiconductor technologies.

Although limited to the PCIe link to the SoC, NVIDIA's discrete GPU design implemented hardware and software design approaches to mitigate latency losses with PCIe data transfer. It would be interesting to see how MediaTek and NVIDIA bring ARM SoC to the market in 2025. The market has different types of implementations and no ground rules for picking these choices. Hardware and Software collaboration can drive any design implementation to be efficient. NVIDIA is the leader in discrete GPUs, while Apple also has competitive performance with integrated GPU design. Product managers must evaluate the choices that best fit their strengths and implement them for the best efficiency.

CHAPTER 4   SOC ARCHITECTURE AND POWER MANAGEMENT

GPU KPIs

Product managers should have clear KPIs to quantify GPU performance to deliver a competitive GPU IP, assessing various aspects of a GPU's capabilities and efficiency for the target segments. The following are some KPIs and methods used to quantify GPU performance.

- Number of GPU cores and core frequency as shown in Table 4-5.
- Memory latency, cache sizes, and memory bandwidth
- TDP of the GPU
- GPU shader pixel fill rates, texture-to-pixel mapping rates, and rendering pipeline efficiency
- Frames per second measured on GPU generic and game benchmarks with advanced features like ray tracing and super-resolution supported to enhance the user experience of the gamer
- Theoretical general compute performance measures the GPU core's ability to perform general-purpose calculations, often expressed in FLOPS as measured by FP8/FP16/FP32/FP64 precision points. FLOPS can be calculated as frequency * number of ALU's operations per cycle * no. of cores
- Real-world workload performance

Table 4-5. FLOPS

Apple GPU SoC	M3	M3 Pro	M3 Max
Number of GPU cores	10	18	40
Peak frequency	1.4	1.4	1.4
Theoretical FP16 Operations/Cycle	256	256	256
FLOPS Peak	**3.584**	**6.4512**	**14.336**

Source: Apple.com

Tensor operations performance quantization measures the GPU's ability to accelerate machine learning operations. These can be measured using benchmarking tools like Procyon AI or tokens per second running large language models (LLMs) and others that specifically assess tensor core performance.

There are several other synthetic benchmarks available to assess the performance of GPUs which are based on specific applications or use cases, such as gaming, content creation, scientific simulations, or machine learning. Product managers can use popular benchmarks like Geekbench GPU, CineBench GPU, and 3D Wildlife or run real-world scenarios to assess performance. Similar to CPU, a target segment-based list of benchmarks and applications comes in handy for product managers to design, update, and maintain competitive performance. Moreover, GPU performance is multifaceted as GPU is used in a variety of user segments, and different applications may prioritize different aspects of the KPIs. Therefore, Benchmarking tools, manufacturer specifications, and real-world testing are essential for accurately quantifying GPU performance across various workloads.

CHAPTER 4   SOC ARCHITECTURE AND POWER MANAGEMENT

Table 4-6. *TFLOPS of GPU on PC SoCs*

	Intel GPU Core Ultra7 155H	NVIDIA GPU RTX4060	Apple GPU M3
TFLOPS	~4.5	15	3.6

Source: Intel.com, Nvidia.com and Apple.com

Like CPU configuration offerings based on core count for user segment differentiation, GPUs are also differentiated based on the throughput requirements for the target user segments. Some SoCs have the GPU IP integrated into the SoC, while others have a discrete GPU depending on the segment's GPU performance needs. Table 4-7 shows some of the products offered by Apple, Intel, and AMD with various GPU configurations.

Table 4-7. *Products Offered by Apple, Intel, and AMD with Various GPU Configurations*

Apple Integrated GPU	Intel GPU Offerings	AMD GPU Offerings
M3 with 10-core GPU	Intel Core Ultra 185H with 8-core GPU	AMD Ryzen 5 Pro 8540U with 4-core GPU
M3 Pro with 18-core GPU	Intel Core Ultra 165U with 4-core GPU	AMD Ryzen 5 Pro 8640HS with 8-core GPU
M3 Max with 40-core GPU	Intel Core Ultra processors +NVIDIA discrete GPU	AMD Ryzen 9 Pro 8945HS with 12-core GPU

The GPU differentiation on Apple is based on GPU theoretical FLOPS ranging from 3-15 and higher TDP. Apple positions the M3, M3 Pro, and M3 Max devices for the users to choose the right SKU based on their needs. The focus of the positioning is based on the throughput needs of the users,

CHAPTER 4   SOC ARCHITECTURE AND POWER MANAGEMENT

like high-end content creators need powerful GPU. On Intel and AMD, the lower TDP segments (e.g., U P or H) have integrated graphics, while higher TDP HX usually has a discrete GPU IP from NVIDIA. Intel and AMD have discrete GPUs but NVIDIA dominates the discrete market with its competitive performance and programmability. Although NVIDIA has leadership in GPU IP, in the PC world, it relies on Intel or AMD CPUs and OEMs to integrate their discrete GPU in the higher TDP PCs. At Computex 2024, NVIDIA announced its partnership with MediaTek to bring an ARM-based SoC with NVIDIA GPU to the market. It would be interesting to know if the partnership is building the same discrete GPU or designing an integrated GPU with collaboration to enter the integrated GPU segment. Integrated GPUs are designed for low power, whereas discrete GPUs often are more power-hungry. GPU power management is the KPI for product managers as the high throughput demands more power draw and should aim to design an optimal power usage for the given throughput delivery of the GPU. GPU performance per watt is discussed later, along with CPU power.

GPU Programmability

Unlike CPU, which relies on ISA to interface hardware and software, GPU capabilities are mostly dependent upon the programmability of the GPU, as the hardware architecture is based on executing parallel instructions. Consider GPU as an empty canvas and programmability can be compared to the tools available to the artist implementing the art. The quality of the art is dependent on the tools available to the artist. Similarly, GPU efficiency depends on the programmability and frameworks available to the application developers. CPU and GPU take different approaches because there is no specific design methodology for the GPU, unlike CPU, and it relies extensively on programmability to efficiently execute parallelized operations. The programmability of GPUs focuses on dividing SIMT with huge parallel operations like graphs or screen vertex so parallel

CHAPTER 4 SOC ARCHITECTURE AND POWER MANAGEMENT

operations are executed to achieve higher performance while managing efficient bandwidth and cache utility. Product managers' key KPI for GPU design should be the programming capabilities and tools available to the developers to develop applications that run efficiently on their GPUs.

Many proprietary or open source programmable frameworks are available on different GPUs in the market, like NVIDIA has CUDA and TensorRT and metal for Apple GPU and so on. Let's discuss GPU programmability.

The GPU programmability frameworks cater to different hardware ecosystems and provide tools for developers to leverage the capabilities of specific GPU architectures for various computing workloads like gaming, deep learning, and inference. The choice often depends on the target hardware and the preferences and requirements of the developer or independent software vendors (ISVs). OpenCL, ROCM (Radeon Open Compute), CUDA, TensorRT, Triton inference server, DirectX, Metal, and OpenVino (open visual inference and neural network optimization) are a few popular software frameworks and toolkits developed by different companies for generic GPU programming, deep learning, and AI acceleration. Each has its focus, compatibility, and strengths.

CUDA (compute unified design architecture) is a parallel computing platform and programming model developed by NVIDIA. It is designed for general-purpose GPU computing and is widely used for GPU-accelerated applications, including deep learning. Support is exclusive to NVIDIA GPUs, and the framework is proprietary. CUDA has a mature ecosystem with many libraries, frameworks, and applications developed for GPU acceleration. NVIDIA created a massive CUDA developer community over the years. It is considered a go-to platform for innovation and research with a matured hardware and software ecosystem that paved its path to being the market leader in artificial intelligence.

ROCm (Radeon Open Compute) is designed for AMD GPUs and is an open source framework for GPUs so that the development community can contribute to its improvement.

CHAPTER 4   SOC ARCHITECTURE AND POWER MANAGEMENT

Metal is a low-level graphics and compute API developed by Apple to help developers in GPU programming and is mostly used in graphics rendering, general-purpose computing (GPGPU), and machine learning tasks. Metal is a proprietary framework available to Apple GPUs only.

Microsoft DirectX is a graphics computing API developed to help Windows GPU applications, especially games. DirectX supports all the Windows-supporting GPUs and is not tied to a single type of GPU. NVIDIA, Intel, AMD, and Qualcomm GPU support DirectX on their GPUs, and is a popular programming API on integrated GPU Windows PCs.

Multiple open source and proprietary GPU programming frameworks are available in the industry today. Vulkan and OpenGL are a few other open source frameworks available. Product managers should provide support for open source and aim to accelerate proprietary framework usage like CUDA so the performance is optimized on their GPU hardware. And ensure the developer ecosystem gets used to programming on their hardware, increasing engagement and problem-solving capabilities of the hardware and software. NVIDIA achieved leadership because of its vast penetration into the developer ecosystem with hardware and software. This led to short turnaround times for fixes and continuous innovation on their GPU IP.

The CPU is the faster-running compute engine in PC SoC, followed by other components. GPU is designed to accelerate parallel operations but the number of applications using parallel operations has grown, like shaders, tensors, and ray tracking, Figure 4-12 shows various GPU KPIs. There are specific cores for each type of operation, and given the throughput and memory usage, the power consumption of GPU has become a problem, especially on integrated PC SoCs. GPUs can accelerate tensor operations faster. However, AI applications like always on display, screen wake up using voice, and background AI applications demand an accelerated tensor core engine with substantially lower power consumption. This gave way to having another AI acceleration compute unit called am NPU in PC SoCs. NPU is a neural processing unit that accelerates machine learning operations at low power. Let's learn more about NPU.

125

CHAPTER 4   SOC ARCHITECTURE AND POWER MANAGEMENT

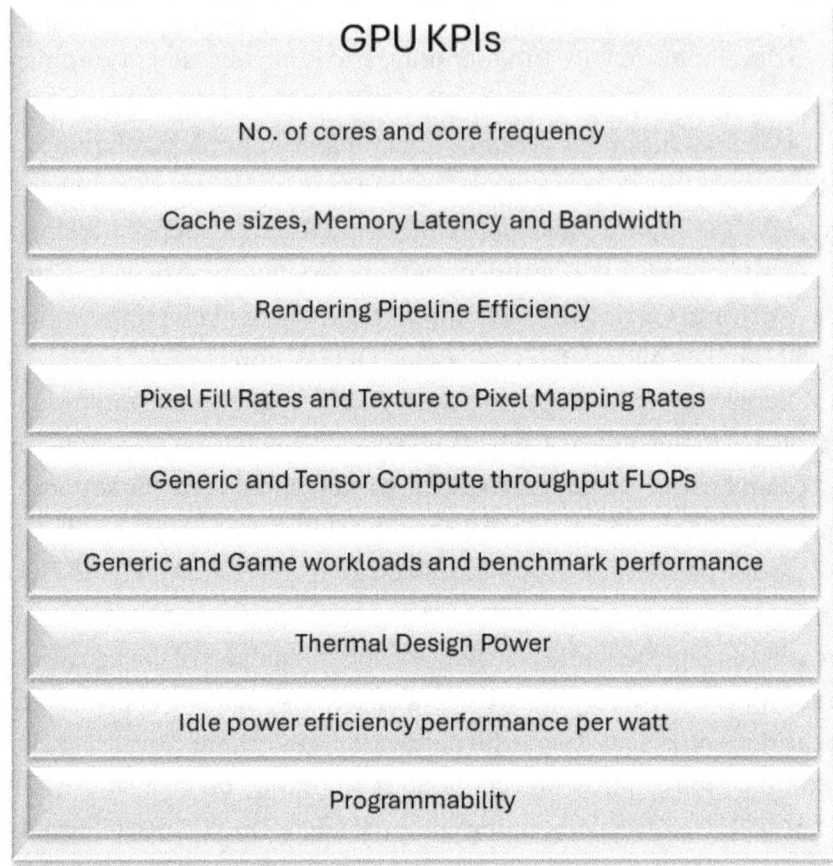

Figure 4-12. GPU KPIs

NPU Architecture

NPUs excel in AI and deep learning tasks, offering energy efficiency. GPUs—originally designed for graphics rendering—have evolved into powerful general-purpose and AI processors capable of handling diverse parallelizable workloads, including machine learning. The choice between NPU and GPU depends on an application's specific requirements and use cases.

CHAPTER 4 SOC ARCHITECTURE AND POWER MANAGEMENT

As the ecosystem became more driven by artificial intelligence, the need for accelerated AI performance at lower power started to trend in the industry. This led to the addition of the third major block called an NPU, specialized to deliver accelerated AI performance at lower power compared to CPU and GPU. CPU and GPU can execute similar AI workloads but are inefficient in power. NPU is aimed to deliver AI performance without much impact on the battery life of the PC. With low power consumption, NPUs are dedicated high-performance compute blocks designed to accelerate performance on neural networks and transformer model-based AI applications. PC SoCs started to implement NPU with Qualcomm Snapdragon PC SoCs and Apple M series PC SoCs, both are industry leaders in designing mobile SoCs with longer battery support. Qualcomm and Apple have already implemented low power AI using NPU on their phone SoCs and brought the same idea to PCs for longer battery life and accelerated AI performance.

One way to measure the performance of NPU is TOPS (trillion operations per second). In AI neural or transformer networks, TOPS is reported for a basic AI operation called a *multiply and accumulate operation* (MAC). All the AI programs can be executed with MAC instructions, which are a type of SIMT operation. The key differentiation is GPU accelerates all types of SIMT parallel instructions whereas NPU accelerates only MACs instructions at low power ideal for AI inference and training workloads. Each NPU can be designed with multiple core configurations similar to CPU and GPU and each core can have a certain number of MACs set to run at a frequency.

The architecture of NPUs is similar to GPU as both are targeted to execute SIMT parallel operations. The value proposition of NPU is more on lower power execution of MACs, which can be achieved by optimizing NPU architecture to support only one specific SIMT operation unlike GPU with general-purpose SIMT operations, as shown in the Figure 4-13. The key is designing a low power MAC engine meeting the performance needs to clearly differentiate GPU and NPU. To improve throughput and reduce power consumption, NPUs often perform computations using lower-precision data types like Int8 (8-bit integer precision) or Int4

(4-bit precision). This allows for faster processing while maintaining acceptable accuracy for neural network tasks.

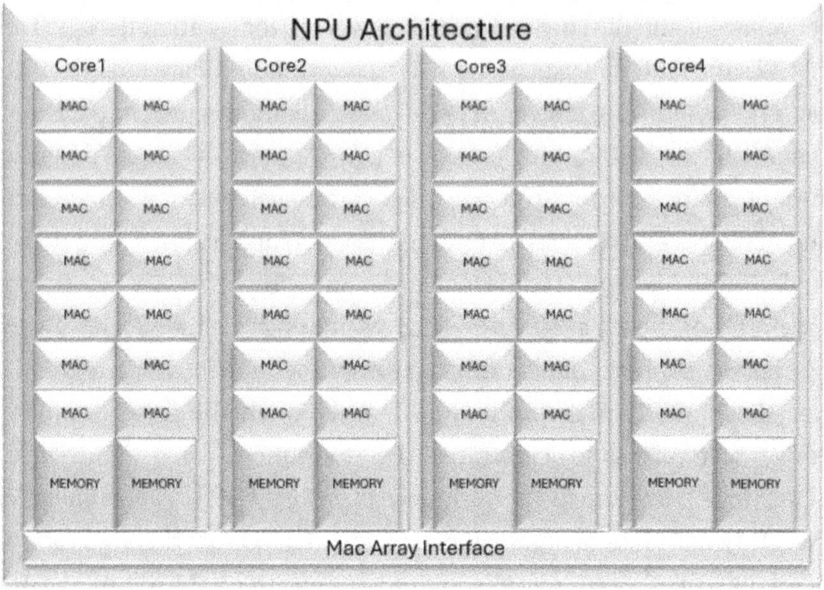

Figure 4-13. Typical NPU architecture

The large precision data types like FP16 have lower throughput than low precision data types like int8, but moving from higher precision data to low precision data types like FP16 to int8 impacts the accuracy because the floating points carry decimal points, which help for accurate AI response generation. Product managers can look for innovative methods to implement the right data type and ensure minimal accuracy losses. For example, AMD with RDNA3-based NPU architecture introduced BlockFP16 data type hardware implementation, which aims to have int8 throughput and FP16 accuracy so the users of RDNA3 benefit from Int8 performance and accuracy of FP16, Source: AMD.com. There is extensive research in this field, like 1-bit LLM. Product managers should be on top of these innovations to incorporate the implementation into their architecture to increase the value proposition of their SoCs.

CHAPTER 4 SOC ARCHITECTURE AND POWER MANAGEMENT

NPUs typically have on-chip memory hierarchies optimized for the specific memory access patterns to accelerate AI network computations. As NPU architecture prioritizes energy efficiency, these engines are well-suited for deployment in edge devices, mobile devices, and other power-constrained environments besides PCs. To achieve scalability, NPUs are designed with configurations similar to CPU and GPU to serve various segment devices with different computational requirements. This scalability makes NPUs suitable for diverse applications, from small embedded devices to larger data center deployments.

NPU performance is measured in TOPS similar to CPU. Peak TOPS (pTOPS) is a theoretical way of calculating the maximum performance of an AI engine using MAC operations, the number of cores, and the frequency of operation on an AI engine.

pTOPS = MAC Ops/clock/core * no. of cores/tiles of AI engine * frequency

Another KPI of NPU is the power consumption when running AI workloads. Performance per watt can be captured while running an AI workload like stable diffusion or LLMs running on NPU and compared with older generations and competitors' NPU IPs to evaluate the power and performance of this application on NPU. AI benchmarks like Procyon AI, Procyon Stable Diffusion, MLCommons, and Procyon LLM are emerging to measure AI performance on NPU.

Table 4-8. Examples of Peak TOPS

	Intel Core Ultra Lunar Lake NPU	**AMD Ryzen 9 370 HX NPU**	**Apple M4 NPU**
Integer 8 Peak TOPS	48 Peak TOPS	50 Peak TOPS	38 Peak TOPS

The programming model for NPUs depends on the manufacturer and the specific NPU architecture. Some NPUs may have proprietary programming models, while others may support open standard frameworks like TensorFlow or PyTorch. As Programming NPU follows the same steps as GPU, they can be integrated with popular open source AI and deep learning frameworks available on GPU, allowing developers to leverage its capabilities. Integration with these frameworks simplifies the development and deployment of AI applications on devices with NPUs because the PC industry has just started to adopt NPU KPIs are shown in the Figure 4-14.

Starting with CPUs, the PC technology industry evolved to innovate GPUs and NPUs to bring efficiency and performance to the workloads. Innovation has the power to transform existing ways of implementation for a better user experience. Therefore, product managers must be flexible to embrace positive change, keep up with research, implement innovative ways, and bring augmented features into their products.

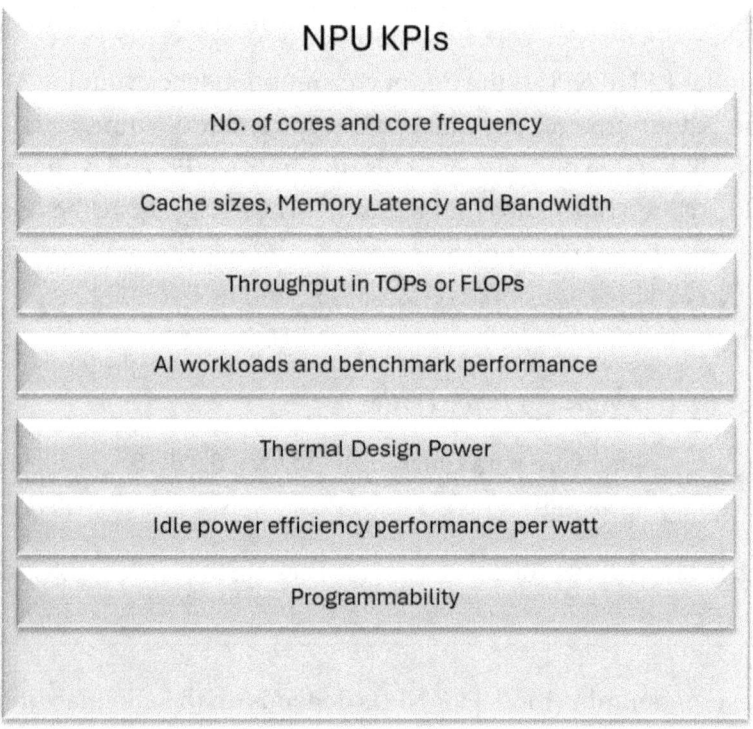

Figure 4-14. *NPU KPIs*

CHAPTER 4   SOC ARCHITECTURE AND POWER MANAGEMENT

Media

A Media Block is one of the components in the PC SoC, a specialized hardware designed to handle multimedia processing tasks, such as video encoding/decoding, image processing, audio processing, and display rendering. The PCs are the center of the developer ecosystem and with the increase in multimedia-based applications in consumer electronics, capabilities in media hardware in PCs can significantly increase the competitive advantage. A Media Block provides the necessary hardware acceleration for efficient and high-quality video, audio, and graphics processing. By offloading these tasks from the main CPU, the Media Block enhances performance, reduces power consumption, and delivers a superior user experience.

SoC Integration

System-on-chip (SoC) integration involves combining various components and subsystems like CPU, GPU, and NPU into a single chip to achieve a high-performance and power-efficient system of a chip with a compact layout design. The configurations of each IP that goes into SoC integration can be chosen based on the user segments, Figure 4-15 and Table 4-9 provides details on Apple SoCs.. The differentiation can be in the number of CPU, GPU, and NPU cores and the DRAM bandwidth and cache sizes to help deliver the required performance on the chosen SoC configurations. For example, Apple M3 series SoCs have different CPU, GPU, cache sizes, and DRAM bandwidth configurations integrated into three SoCs scaled using the same CPU, GPU core IPs, and other components. The IP floorplan in the SoC is chosen meticulously to have better interconnection between the IPs to ensure optimum performance of the SoC. The product managers should have clear KPI targets, as shown in the Figure 4-16 at the individual IPs and SoC level to ensure the integration of various components IPs delivers seamless SoC performance and power efficiency. [13]

---

[13] Source: https://www.apple.com/newsroom/2023/10/apple-unveils-m3-m3-pro-and-m3-max-the-most-advanced-chips-for-a-personal-computer/

CHAPTER 4   SOC ARCHITECTURE AND POWER MANAGEMENT

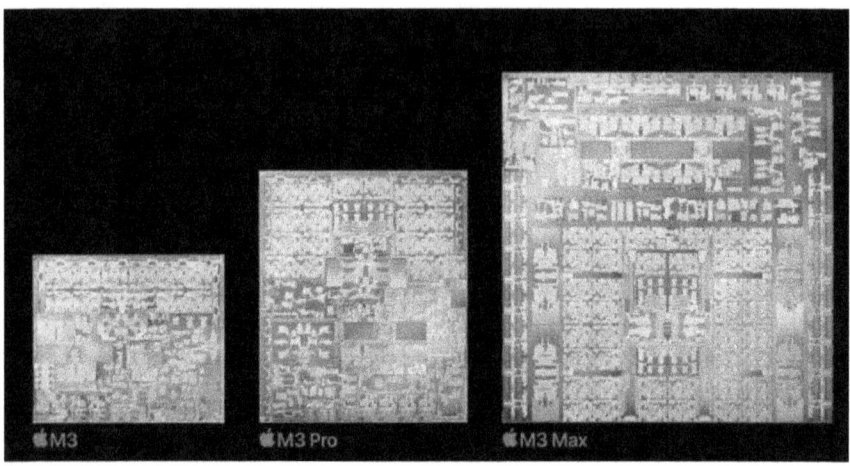

Figure 4-15. *M3 Series SoCs (source: Apple.com)*

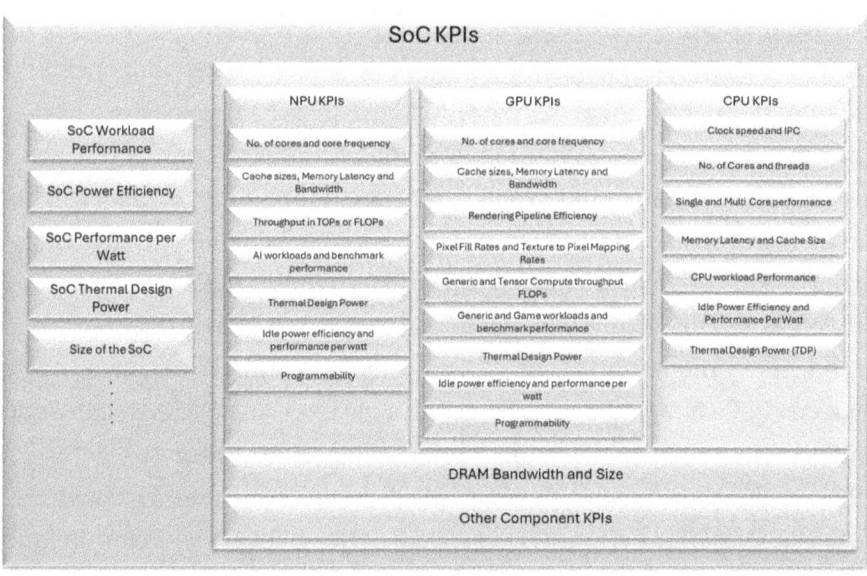

Figure 4-16. *PC SoC KPIs*

Table 4-9. Apple M3 Series SoC Configurations

	M3	M3 Pro	M3 Max
CPU	4 performance cores 4 efficiency cores	6 performance cores 6 efficiency cores	12 performance cores 4 efficiency cores
GPU	10 cores	10 cores	40 cores
DRAM bandwidth	102.4 GB/s	153.6 GB/s	307.2 GB/s and 409.6 GB/s

Source: Apple.com

SoC integration represents a pivotal advancement in semiconductor technology, offering significant performance, power efficiency, size reduction, and cost efficiency benefits. The integration combines multiple functional components, such as CPUs, GPUs, memory, DSPs, ISPs, codecs, and connectivity modules, into a single chip or package for the most efficient performance.

Product managers should meticulously plan SoC integration with component and SoC-level KPIs responsible for driving the development of high-performance, efficient, and compact PC devices. As technology evolves, SoCs play an increasingly critical role in shaping the future of PC electronic devices. Product managers should consider design and architectural advancements to innovate and excel in the competitive consumer and industrial electronics landscape. Now that you have learned about SoC architecture, let's look at another key pillar in SoC design: power management.

Power Management

> *It's a vicious cycle. While systems become denser, their energy efficiency has decreased. Devices are getting smaller and smaller, but they are getting hotter.*
>
> —Bob Gill

Semiconductor SoCs have efficiency and control as their main metrics. Efficiency in how a job gets done and control on who can do the job better, like generic latency-driven workloads are taken care of by CPU, generic parallelized operations by GPU, and dedicated MAC SIMD operations by NPU. The semiconductor compute ecosystem has evolved to specialize the SoC components to implement workload-driven design and architecture for better control and efficiency.

For the CPU, GPU, or any other component in the SoC to do an efficient job with a well-designed architecture, the SoC should be capable of using the lowest power possible to get applications running at higher performance. So, the product can hold the battery power for a longer time of the day or use less power in general and still execute applications at a higher performance. This is possible by an efficient power management architecture across the SoCs.

Let's consider an example, consider a machine capable of writing is tasked to write an email, to do so, the machine should be given some power to accomplish the task. The machine consumes the power, and the email is written. The power used by the machine is dissipated in the form of heat as per the laws of thermodynamics (energy can only be converted from one form to another but cannot be created or destroyed). Similarly, for a PC or smartphone to finish a task, SoCs are supplied with power as a function of voltage and current, so the SoC can perform the task by executing its instructions, as shown in the Figure 4-17. A power-efficient SoC utilizes the least amount of power to finish the task faster to deliver higher performance per watt. This generates less heat as the power to finish the task is lower. Therefore, power management in semiconductor SoCs is to get more work done by consuming little power as possible and maintaining low temperatures on the devices. Hence, a product manager's role is designing the SoCs for competitive performance and having competitive performance per wattage (power) used.

CHAPTER 4　SOC ARCHITECTURE AND POWER MANAGEMENT

Product managers can follow a systematic process to maintain power efficiency at all stages of semiconductor product management to deliver the target product with higher performance per watt. But what is power? How do SoC components get it? Electrical power is generated by current and voltage: P=IV, as shown in the Table 4-10. So, the electrical power is passed to SoC by input voltage and current. The voltage is again a function of current and resistance. Therefore there is always a resistance in any circuit supplying voltage (and current) that impacts the circuit's behavior, besides many other factors.

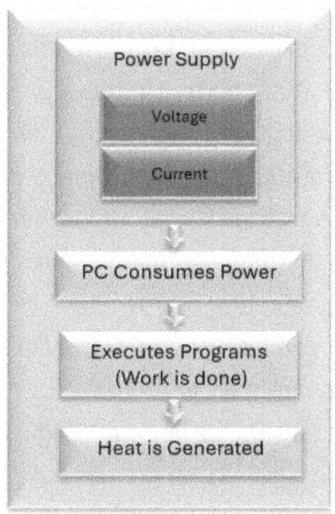

Figure 4-17. *PC power management*

CHAPTER 4 SOC ARCHITECTURE AND POWER MANAGEMENT

Table 4-10. Electrical Power Formulas and Abbreviations

P = I * V[14]	(P is power, I is current, and V is voltage) measured in watts
V = I * R	Voltage is measured in volts, where I is current and R is resistance (Current is measured in Amps or Amperes and resistance in ohms)
P = I * I * R	Power loss measured in watts, where I is current R is resistance
E = P * T	E is energy, P is power, and T is time, E is measured in Joules
V α K f*f	V is the voltage at the time t, K is constant, and f is frequency

To develop leading performance PC products, the CPU and other SoC components need to run at higher frequencies to achieve performance targets. The higher frequencies demand higher voltage as $V = Vo \sin 2\pi ft$ as voltage is directly proportional to frequency, and P = I * V. Voltage is directly proportional to power. Therefore, higher frequency demands higher voltage, and higher voltage consumes more power dissipating more heat(temperature), affecting performance per watt. As shown in Figure 4-17, power management is a function of voltage, current, and temperature. Efficient power management controls voltage currents and keeps the losses at a minimum without reaching the temperature limits. Usually, TDPs are fixed to a design, so the heat dissipated is controlled by throttling if the limits of power are pushed.

In the modern semiconductor industry, efficient power management is the key to delivering competitive performance per watt and the main driver of SoC design complexity. All the IP components in the PC SoC and the entire platform should implement power power-efficient design so the PC provides a good customer experience for longer battery hours. Therefore, the critical KPI for a PC to be tracked by the product manager is

---

[14] https://courses.lumenlearning.com/suny-physics/chapter/20-4-electric-power-and-energy/

CHAPTER 4   SOC ARCHITECTURE AND POWER MANAGEMENT

performance per watt in all the applications the PC serves to its segment customers. The aim is to be the product leader with better performance per watt over all the products available in the market, maintaining leading application performance. Achieving competitive performance per watt is a very complex task due to the voltage and current losses associated when trying to supply power regulating voltage and current.

This complex task can be accomplished using a systematic approach and making the right choices applicable to the design requirements, starting from SoC and platform planning, execution, manufacturing, and OEM assembly of a PC to meet the required performance and power targets. The key is to meticulously implement this choice across all stages of product development without missing to avoid huge power penalties. The complexity only increases as delivering a full product to the customers involves collaborating with one or many partners like OEMs and process technology manufacturers. Therefore, the role of a product manager in designing a SoC is very challenging. But the challenge is worth implementing as product managers across the electrical industry regardless of focus area like data center, enterprise, PC, embedded strive for better performance per watt as one of the KPIs. Hence, this area is always a disruption and allows product managers to deliver augmented PC products.

Let's start the power management architecture from the planning phase: The SoCs are designed and manufactured on semiconductors made of billions of transistors. The basic building block of the SoC is a transistor, so the first stage in SoC power management is realizing the power limitations of transistors. The transistor technology is designed by semiconductor manufacturers such as Intel, TSMC, and Samsung and delivers advanced process technologies at a cadence with improved transistor capabilities in power, performance, and area (PPA) by innovating in extreme ultraviolet (EUV) lithography, which is crucial for creating smaller and more efficient transistors to enable higher performance, power, and area.

CHAPTER 4　SOC ARCHITECTURE AND POWER MANAGEMENT

Transistor Threshold Voltage

The starting point is to know the type of transistor offered by the process manufacturing companies. The semiconductor manufacturing industry preferred MOSFET transistors (metal oxide semiconductor field effect transistors), as shown in the Figure 4-18, which are voltage-controlled and have high switching speeds compared to other current-controlled transistors. The biggest advantage of MOSFET is that it is much easier to control voltage over current.

Semiconductor manufacturing companies innovate on the FET transistors for better voltage controls, higher switching speeds, and a lower transistor area. MOSFET transistors have evolved a lot since the beginning of semiconductor manufacturing to provide better control and augmented features to accelerate innovation in the semiconductor industry

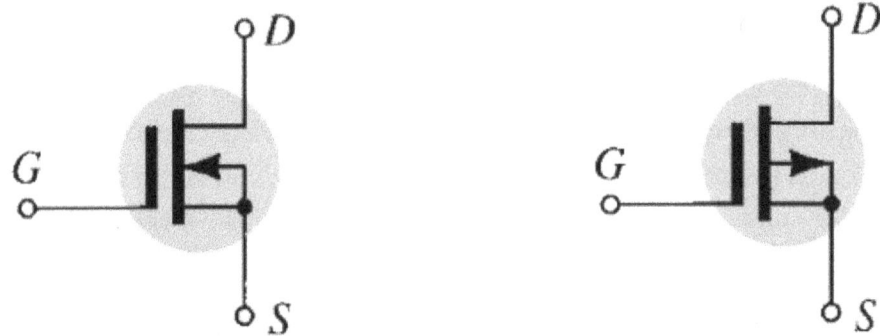

Figure 4-18. *Basic MOSFET transistors with gate, drain, and source*

The standard transistors used in PC SoCs are voltage controlled, and these transistors require a minimum voltage to turn it on, known as *threshold voltage* (Vth). Ideally, we would need the threshold voltage to be as low as possible with higher switching speeds, but this is in the control of process technology manufacturers delivering advanced nodes. So, the first step to know is the Vth flexibility of the transistor technology in which the SoC is manufactured. Starting at 7nm TSMC started providing multi-Vt options to its customers based on the product design needs.

CHAPTER 4   SOC ARCHITECTURE AND POWER MANAGEMENT

The implications need to be understood thoroughly to choose from the available Vth option so an educated decision can be made on minimum voltage requirements. If the transistor's gate-to-source voltage (VGS) is close to Vth, the current leakages are higher than transistors with VGS slightly above the Vth. This is because transistors fundamentally operate based on the moment of charged electrons between source and drain regulated by the gate. A few electrons always move against the flow, leading to leakage currents and voltage losses due to subthreshold voltage. Subthreshold voltage occurs when a transistor's VGS is below the gate threshold voltage of a MOSFET. A small amount of current (IDS) flows between the drain and the source. The aim is to lower this voltage and current leakages as low as possible so the power (P = IV) is not lost significantly without performing any work.

Therefore, the first set of choices a product manager must make is the decision on the Vth of the transistors to avoid significant power loss at the product level. Looking at Figure 4-19, isn't Vth4 the best choice? Yes, but only for a power-efficient design, it is the best choice. The aim of the product manager is choosing the best performance as well, not just power. The performance at lower threshold voltage ranges like Vth0 to Vth2 is higher as the frequency of operation can be pushed higher compared to Vth3 and Vth4. As a result, a good design methodology is working with manufacturing companies and defining a set of Vths to manage performance and power per the product needs. There is no defined metric at a product level to track the Vth choices, so having a KPI might not be ideal, but worth modeling these scenarios for better product offerings in the long term.

CHAPTER 4   SOC ARCHITECTURE AND POWER MANAGEMENT

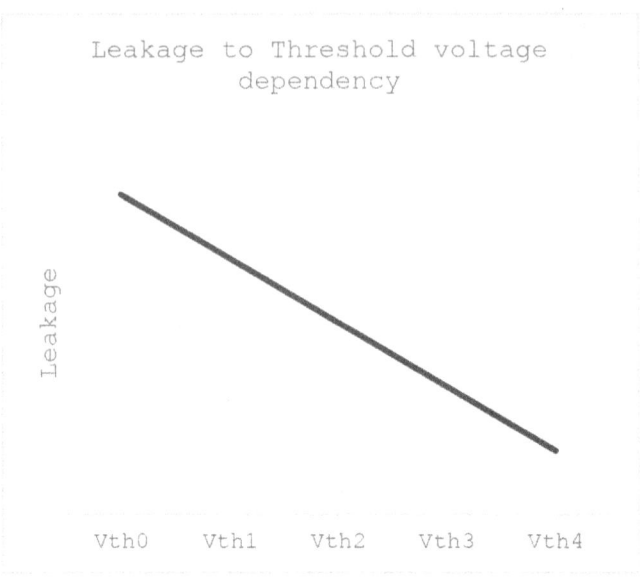

Figure 4-19. *Voltage to leakage dependencies*

The choice of Vth is very useful when product managers follow one IP design and release multiple products like Apple, AMD, NVIDIA, and Intel. These companies design one IP like CPU, GPU and other IPs and deploy them across multiple product lines with different TDPs, frequency of operation, and core configurations. Table 4-11, Table 4-12, and Table 4-13 provide examples of IPs designed once and released into many products with different thermal designs, frequencies, and core configurations.

Table 4-11. *IPs and Products from AMD (source: AMD.com)*

Company	AMD	Products based on the IPs
IP 1	Zen 4 CPU	AMD Ryzen™ 8000 series desktops available in 35W and 65W
IP 2	RDNA 3 GPU	AMD Ryzen™ 8000 series laptops available in 28W and 45W

CHAPTER 4 SOC ARCHITECTURE AND POWER MANAGEMENT

Table 4-12. *IPs and Products from Apple (source: Apple.com)*

Company	Apple	Products based on the IPs
IP 1	M2 CPU IP with P core and E core	M2 MacBook Pro M2 Pro MacBook Pro M2 Max MacBook Pro
IP 2	M2 NPU IP	M2 MacBook Pro M2 Pro MacBook Pro M2 Max MacBook Pro

Table 4-13. *IPs and Products from Intel (source: Intel.com)*

Company	Intel 14th Generation Processors	Products Based on the IPs
IP 1	Raptor Cove P core	Intel 14th generation laptops and desktops
IP 2	Gracemont E core	Intel 14th generation laptops and desktops

Choosing to pick a Vth helps design better power and performance efficiency in products using the same IP in the product lines like CPU. Product managers can pick the lower Vth for higher performance, trade off some power loss on the desktop products as they operate at higher TDPs, and pick a slightly higher Vth for mobile products for lower TDP limit. Hence, the mobile products have lower leakages, saving power. Therefore, there can be a lot of advantages if the product managers have a preferred Vth for the same IPs deployed in different products, giving more flexibility in taking educated risks in power management and performance right from the initial planning phase.

CHAPTER 4   SOC ARCHITECTURE AND POWER MANAGEMENT

Operating Voltage and Frequency

At this stage of product design with fixed transistor technology, the product manager should be able to have the design's frequency and threshold voltage limits. The next step is to design a power management unit to drive power through the SoC by controlling the voltage so the SoC components run at a frequency. Transistors are voltage-controlled as it is more flexible than controlling current in semiconductor electronics circuits. Therefore, voltage is the main controller for power and current in semiconductor products. Power and current can be controlled by voltage. How is the frequency of logic and clocks controlled by voltage?

The Vf curve drawn for a SoC manufactured on an advanced process technology is shown in Figure 4-20. The voltage is directly proportional to the square of the frequency. Therefore, a smaller frequency doesn't require much higher voltage. But as the frequency limits are pushed to target higher performance, that is when the voltage requirements increase exponentially, resulting in higher power consumption and affecting the temperature of the SoCs. Therefore, a few preferred spots of voltage to frequencies are chosen for a design from its VF curve based on the process technology flexibility. The spots can range from base frequency to turbo frequency for the CPU IP and the optimal desired frequency of operation for GPU, NPU, and other IPs.

CHAPTER 4 SOC ARCHITECTURE AND POWER MANAGEMENT

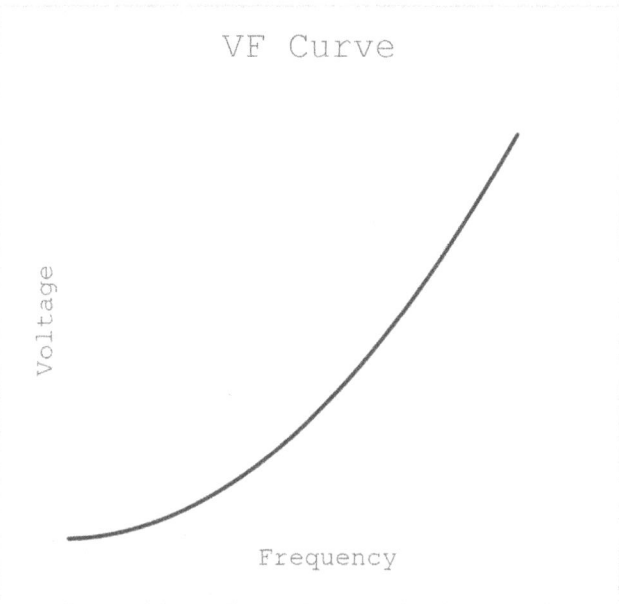

Figure 4-20. *Example of VF curve*

At this stage, we have our transistor threshold voltage and voltage-frequency ranges for tuning the IPs for desired performance and power options. The next step is to set the power limits for the VF selections so the same SoC or IP can be differentiated in one or many form factors with required performance tuning.

Thermal Design Power (TDP)

When voltage-to-frequency characteristics are studied on a design, product managers can also request performance characteristics of the design for the VF curve on a set of workloads that represents different user segments like content creators, gamers, and casual PC users. Then, based on the voltage and frequency characteristics and performance of user applications, different TDP levels can be set to differentiate the products based on the performance needs of the user segment.

CHAPTER 4 SOC ARCHITECTURE AND POWER MANAGEMENT

For example, Table 4-14 shows Apple M2 SoC-based products with different TDP designs.

Table 4-14. *Apple M2 SoC-based Products with Different TDP Designs*

Apple M2 SoC-based Devices	Description
MacBook Air	Fan-less M2 laptop design with a 13-inch and 15-inch screen
MacBook Pro 13-inch	Fanned M2 laptop design with a 13-inch screen
iPad Pro	Fan-less M2 tablet design with an 11-inch and 12.9-inch screen
Mac Mini	Fanned M2 desktop design
Vision Pro	Fan-less M2 wearable design
iPad Air	Fan-less M2 tablet design

Although Apple used the same M2 SoC to make different types of devices, the TDP of the SoCs is set to different levels for each of these devices; for example, iPad Air can be around 10 watts, and MacBook Pro can be set to 61 Watts based on the performance needs and temperature sensitivity of the device when used (Source: Apple.com). Nobody wants a laptop or tablet to heat too much, so the user experience gets impacted. Therefore, product managers must consider factors like temperature, performance, and voltage-to-frequency characteristics and set the design TDP so that the overall product delivers power efficiency and performance across the chosen product segments. Any work done by the processor processes heat to regulate the heat-produced fan designs or cooling solutions are implemented for faster heat dissipation, so the device doesn't overheat and throttle.

CHAPTER 4 SOC ARCHITECTURE AND POWER MANAGEMENT

SoC design TDP limits, form factor decisions are entirely made by Apple because its is the designer and OEM; whereas companies like Intel, AMD, Qualcomm, and NVIDIA design SoCs with predefined TDPs for OEMs to choose from to manufacture different form factors based on performance needs.

To prevent overheating, the SoCs need a controller to control heating behavior as the IPs are designed to execute instructions and are mostly unaware of the amount of heat dissipated. A dedicated power management controller is designed to monitor the SoC's maximum power, current, and temperature to avoid thermal throttling; the controller significantly reduces the operating frequency, impacting performance, known as the *thermal throttling phenomenon*.

Product managers aim to design an effective power management unit capable of efficiently managing and controlling the SoC's power and performance. It is directly proportional to the device's battery life and can be improved by avoiding scenarios like thermal throttling.

At this stage, we have threshold voltage, VF characteristics, design TDPs, and a power management unit to control the power, temperature, and performance (voltage and frequency). The next step is to control the supply of power the SoCs need to deliver the desired performance aligned with TDP. Let's examine the SoC power supply.

IP Power Management

Each IP is designed with logic and clocks capable of implementing several instructions. As discussed earlier, CPUs are general-purpose compute engines, GPUs are specialized for general-purpose SIMT operation, and NPU is specialized in AI operations. As they are designed for running various applications, practically not all the logic is utilized by the user running all types of workloads at a given time. The reality is only one or few instructions are executed on the SoCs at a given time. So, when power is supplied to SoCs, logic implementing the workload consumes active dynamic power. Other logic and clocks consume the power to stay on without doing any work. This power is called *leakage power*. As a result, not all the power supplied to the IPs results in work done.

Total IP Power = Dynamic Power + Leakage Power

Dynamic power is workload-dependent as the workloads can implement different logic based on the instructions implemented in the application. Therefore, dynamic power needs to be measured for all applications that a user can implement in the target segment. The dynamic power can be controlled by setting a limit to the maximum dynamic power of the IP to avoid exceeding dynamic power in any corner cases.

The next step in power management is to implement a way to control leakage power. This is implemented by stopping the clocks (clock gating) or completely cutting off the power (power gating) to the logic not in use. Clock gating has leakage power as there is some leakage from the logic, whereas power gating has zero leakage power but comes at a price is latency to power it back on. For modern PCs, there is a need for lower turnaround time. Therefore, the controllers need to implement a balance of clock gating and power gating depending on the need.

Another popular use case for PC users is keeping the PC idle. In this stage, the PC is waiting to accept any task from the user. Therefore, the logic consumes some power, and a few clocks of the IPs to snoop for the user's input are called *idle dynamic power*. There is also some leakage power in an idle stage, so the total idle power = Idle dynamic power + leakage power.

Idle power is a critical KPI in power management, as the power consumed in an idle state decides the battery life of the PCs. A SoC's idle power should be as low as possible for competitive performance per watt.

So far, you know that the power management in an SoC is implemented by choosing the right voltage threshold, voltage, and frequency combinations for optimal performance per watt of an IP. At the IP level, control leakage power by implementing clock or power gating and control idle power.

CHAPTER 4   SOC ARCHITECTURE AND POWER MANAGEMENT

SoC Power Supply and Delivery Management

When we want to supply power to the PC, phone or any other used daily, we connect the battery to the available power supply to charge. The SoC power supply is derived from the battery supply, but it must undergo multiple changes before it reaches the SoC. The regular power supply is ~120V AC, and the SoC needs much more than the ~12V DC to operate. The PC motherboard has AC to DC converters to supply the SoC in DC voltage. Within SoC, each IP voltage requirement is different as they operate at different frequencies; some may need higher voltage, and others need low voltage. For example, the Apple M2 performance core operates at 4.05 GHz, the efficiency core operates at 2.7 GHz, and the GPU operates at 1.3 GHz.

DC-to-DC converters supply these varied voltage requirements, the complexity arises due to the resistance in the electrical circuits. The power losses need to be managed for effective DC-to-DC conversion. Multiple types of DC-to-DC converters are available to control power loss, such as LDO (low drop out) converters and buck converters, as shown in the Table 4-15. Depending on the requirements, these converters are implemented in the motherboard to deliver the required power to the SoC. These converters can also be added to the SoC to control voltage within the SoC.

Table 4-15. LDO vs. Buck DC-to-DC Converters

LDO (low drop out) DC-DC converter	Buck DC-DC Converter
Low Efficiency	High efficiency
Idle for low dropout rates as they have high power loss	Low power losses as charge are stored as inductance L and capacitance C to supply in switch converters
Example: input is 3.5V, and output is 3.2V	Example: capacitance
Requires Less transistors	Requires more transistors, increasing die area
Cheaper and easy to implement	Cost is higher and is slightly complex to implement

The required power is supplied to the SoC through power rails using a DC-to-DC converter, and decisions like the number of power rails can significantly affect the power, temperature, and performance. Not all the IPs in an SoC are active at a given point in time. For example, consider a PC user working on a Word document on its screen. To complete the work, CPU IP + GPU IP+ DRAM IP and Storage IP are needed; other SoC IPs like NPU and media encoder-decoders are not required to finish the task. If SoC has a single power rail to supply power to all the IPs, the IPs not in use consume some power that otherwise could have been saved. Hence, having a granular power supply to the IPs gives more control over power management to reduce power losses.

The power supply rails can be divided per IP in an SoC or per block of an SoC. However, more granularity increases the cost of the SoC. The product managers must make decisions with certain tradeoffs in power losses or cost depending on the flexibility. Generally, in a monolithic die, the CPU and GPU have a dedicated power rail, while all the other IPs are powered by uncore rail (other than CPU and GPU IPs). However, having a dedicated power rail per IP component has granular power supply and control advantages. For example,

CHAPTER 4 SOC ARCHITECTURE AND POWER MANAGEMENT

Qualcomm implemented a dedicated power rail for NPU in their Snapdragon X Elite SoCs.[15] There are no actual rules to having a certain number of rails. Product managers can decide the number of power rails for better power management, which comes at a cost and communicate to OEMs so they can implement required power delivery to the rails.

At this stage, we have TDP limits set, power supply rails are decided, and the power supply is available to the IPs. The next step is IP power management.

Implementing Power Management from IP to Device

We know that turning the power off or gating the clock is implemented at the hardware IP level, and there could be several IPs in an SoC which adds a lot of complexity in power management from IP to device level. To simplify the power management from small IP components to SoCs and the entire device, power management states are defined to give hardware and software more flexibility. These state choices provide more control of power based on the device features and execution to deliver better performance per watt. There are many power states to block or reduce power to IP-specific blocks in an SoC, and both the operating system and hardware have access to these states for flexible switching from one state to another. The states have become a standard with defined implications to power, like C states and P states[16]. to give granular power management controls to hardware and operating systems to implement at runtime.

---

[15] https://www.qualcomm.com/content/dam/qcomm-martech/dm-assets/documents/Unlocking-on-device-generative-AI-with-an-NPU-and-heterogeneous-computing.pdf

[16] https://edc.intel.com/content/www/us/en/design/ipla/software-development-platforms/client/platforms/alder-lake-desktop/12th-generation-intel-core-processors-datasheet-volume-1-of-2/009/power-management/

CHAPTER 4 SOC ARCHITECTURE AND POWER MANAGEMENT

These states can be implemented at IP level, SoC level, package level, system level, and device level to deliver efficient power management across the PC device, as shown in Table 4-16.

Table 4-16. Example of Power Management States

Power Management States	Description
C States	C states help control active and idle power in the SoC IPs. They come in C0-Cn states.
	C0 is active, and C1-Cn helps reduce or turn off selected functions to control idle power in IPs.
	These states help SW and HW control idle power leakages in parts of the IPs not used at a given time.
P States	Performance states help SW and HW to control the voltage and frequency of the IP to have better control on the power base to tune workload performance with the P0 to Pn range.
	Examples of P state examples are best performance and balance power modes.
S States	System power states supported by Windows help SW and HW to have control power to the system with S0 to Sn.
	State S0 is the working state. States S1, S2, S3, and S4 are sleeping states that reduce power consumption but can return to a working state without a restart. State S5 is the shutdown or off.
D States	Device states help control power to the PCs.
G States	Global power states apply to the system and are usually visible to the user.

Source: learn.Microsoft.com

CHAPTER 4   SOC ARCHITECTURE AND POWER MANAGEMENT

Therefore, efficient SoC power management involves product managers making decisions in every phase of the SoC implementation, from planning, design, and manufacturing to the software program execution, as shown in Table 4-17. Power profiling tools can be a great asset to access power management at each phase. This assessment reveals any discrepancies in the power expected to the actual consumption. To deliver competitive performance per watt, the same profiling can be done on the available competitor products or model projections for the expected performance per watt of the future competitors. Product managers must aim to deliver targeted performance per watt compared to their older generation SoC and outperform the competitors with the best-known competitive assessment.

Table 4-17. Power Management Phases

Power Management Phases	Usage
Vth Transistor leakages	Helps decide the peak frequency to power leakage limits
VF Curve	Helps decide optimal operating voltages and frequency for a given design
TDP limits	Limits power to the SoC design to avoid throttling
Power supply rails	Granular power supply helps better power management
Clock gating and power off	Helps granular control of the power supplied to the IPs
Leakage power, idle power, and dynamic power	Gives insight as to where the power can be optimized
Control voltage and frequency of operation	Enables different performance modes required for better power management based on the performance needs

(*continued*)

Table 4-17. (*continued*)

Power Management Phases	Usage
Power management states	Well-defined power states with controls on HW and SW provide flexible power management
Thermal throttling	A fail-safe method to prevent overheating by reducing power supply significantly impacts performance
TDP and cooling solutions	Required for limiting dynamic power PL1 and PL2 of CPU for giving more power to GPU to control SoC power and dissipating temperature
Power delivery	PMICs/VRs using minimal loss power converters

These phases need not be implemented in the given order; they can be implemented in any way that works best for the product manager's development strategy. However, the goal is to have better control over SoC power and deliver competitive performance per watt.

Performance per Watt

The performance per watt is determined by measuring the power consumed by a workload to deliver the measured performance. The workloads can be actual customer applications or benchmarks relevant to the customer segments. The other power KPI measures the battery life of the PC running individual workloads like web browsing, video streaming or running a set of workloads. The measurements can be at the IP level, like CPU, GPU, or NPU, or at the system, like the battery life running the workloads.

CHAPTER 4   SOC ARCHITECTURE AND POWER MANAGEMENT

There are several ways to capture power utilized by an IP or SoC level or system battery level. The finer and more accurate way to measure power is by instrumenting the device inductors (output of the converters) connecting the power rails of the IPs SoCs. This time-consuming and complex method has the advantage of granular power data analysis. The battery level measurements are done by measuring the device's battery capacity before and after running the workloads, and the delta is the measure of power utilized by the workload.

Usually, design companies have tools to measure power and performance analysis, like EMON from Intel and power metrics from Apple, which are designed specifically to report data for their hardware architecture. Platform-independent software profiling tools like HWiNFO run on almost all Windows systems hardware and report performance and power characteristics. These tools are run along with the workloads to measure the performance and power of the workload. The tool might consume some power and compute power, but generally, proprietary tools are developed with a sensitivity analysis to help distinguish the tool's power. Third-party tools like HWiNFO are good proxies for power and performance characteristics but are not as accurate as proprietary profiling tools.

Measuring a set of workloads is important to define the performance per watt of SoC or CPU for a user segment. As discussed earlier, not all applications might enable all the logic in the IP. Hence, a mix of instructions-based applications must be measured to analyze the IP's performance per watt. For example, for a content creator, an average of popular usages like video editing, video playback, applying effects, video conversions, and power and performance can be measured for analysis. The industry has benchmarks like SPECrate, Puget Bench, and Geekbench designed to access the SoC's performance running different instruction use cases. These can run along with power profilers for performance-per-watt analysis.

CHAPTER 4   SOC ARCHITECTURE AND POWER MANAGEMENT

Companies like Apple, Intel, AMD, and others compare performance per watt as a value proposition during product launches. The comparison can be made against the previous generation IPs or SoCs and available competitors' IPs or SoCs, so the new product being launched performs better than their previous IP and available competitors. For example, Figures 4-21 and 4-22 are comparisons made by Apple during the M2 launch. Apple compared the power and performance to Intel SoC. Similarly, AMD, Qualcomm, Intel, and others use this power KPI to advocate their SoC's competitive positioning in the market.

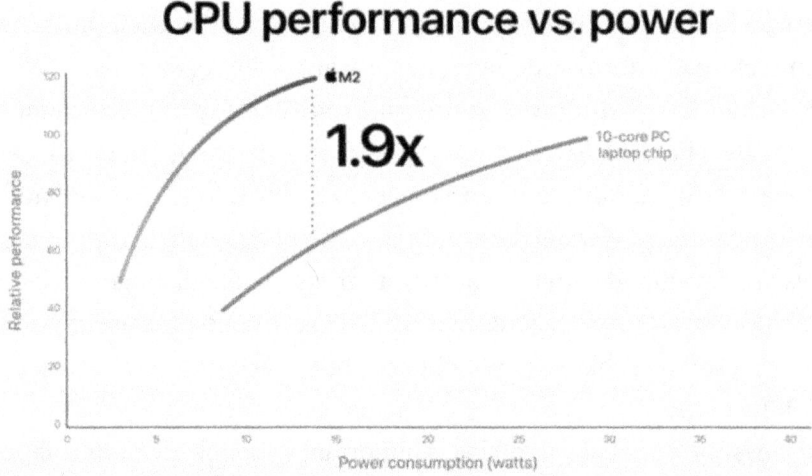

Figure 4-21. Example of performance per watt comparison (source: Apple.com)

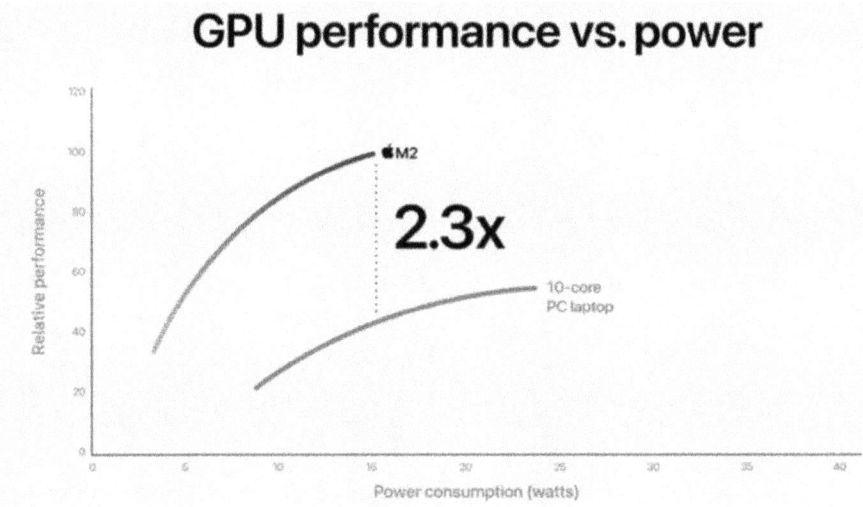

Figure 4-22. Example of performance per watt comparison (source: Apple.com)

Summary

Efficient and competitive SoC architecture involves designing multiple IPs for higher performance and capabilities at low power consumption compared to the competitors. A low power management architecture is implemented from system to transistor level in collaboration with operating system vendors, OEMs, and advanced process technology manufacturers for systems to keep the power low.

CHAPTER 5

Semiconductor Manufacturing

If the auto industry advanced as rapidly as the semiconductor industry, a Rolls Royce would get half a million miles per gallon, and it would be cheaper to throw it away than to park it.

—Gordon Moore

This chapter discusses the impact of transistor process technology in manufacturing high-performance semiconductor products. Competitive landscape, pricing, and performance metrics in the manufacturing industry. It also discusses the impact of political factors like the CHIPS Act on semiconductor product management and the role product managers can play in mitigating risk and identifying opportunities.

Semiconductor manufacturing is a rapidly changing and complex process involving specialized skills and methodology. The key aspect in semiconductor manufacturing is owning the latest process technology and how well that technology is scaled for mass-produced semiconductors. As the cost of manufacturing determines the profit margins of semiconductor manufacturers, semiconductor product designers, and electronic device sellers, it is crucial that semiconductor manufacturers not only produce cutting-edge process technology but also make it highly scalable and efficient to fully reap the benefits.

Let's discuss the steps involved with the semiconductor manufacturing process, beginning with the purification of silicon to create single crystal silicon called *ingots*, which are sliced into thin wafers like salami. These wafers undergo a series of photolithography steps, also known as *semiconductor lithography*, a vital process in manufacturing semiconductor devices like microprocessors and solid-state memories. It involves applying a photoresist to the silicon substrate and exposing it to a pattern of ultraviolet light through a photomask to form patterns of circuits followed by diffusion to dope specific areas with impurities, altering their electrical properties to meet desired needs.

After circuit patterns are formed, layers of various materials, such as silicon dioxide or metal interconnects, are deposited, and unwanted material is removed using techniques like etching. Multiple layers are built up using chemical/physical vapor deposition (CVD/PVD), with precise alignment and patterning at each step, to form the complete integrated circuit.

Finally, the wafers are tested, diced into individual chips, packaged, and tested again to ensure functionality and reliability. This highly controlled process requires efficient equipment and sterile environments to prevent contamination and achieve the high precision needed for semiconductor devices. Even after taking critical steps with higher scrutiny and efficiency, yield rate determines its manufacturing costs. The semiconductor yield rate is a percentage of the total number of good dies produced on one wafer (one single salami). The number of good dies produced from a wafer is usually less during the initial manufacturing of the cutting-edge process technology. However, the yield improves significantly as the process gets more mature and highly scalable.

Yield rate percentage = total no. of good dies produced / total dies that can be produced on a wafer

Usually, semiconductor manufacturers negotiate pricing with fabless product design companies based on yield rate or price per good die. For example, consider a cutting-edge process like 3nm transistor process technology; the early yield rate could be between 40% and 60% roughly, meaning each wafer manufactures only 40%–60% usable dies with the rest as defects and considered a sunk cost. So, the cost per die becomes higher when the yield rate percentage is low, which usually happens in the early stage of the latest process technologies. As the technology matures yield rate can reach 97%–98%, lowering the per-die cost. So, the dies manufactured using the latest process technologies cost more.

Transistor Technology

Why do companies need the latest process technology although the process is expensive and gives less yield?

As discussed, the two main KPIs for major SoC components are clock frequency and power efficiency. In the latest process technologies, the size of the transistor continuously decreases, which is measured in nanometers, such as 7nm or 5nm. The transistor gate sizes get smaller with a reduction in transistor area, which enables the latest process transistors to switch faster, reducing the signal propagation time through the transistor. This faster switching capability allows transistors to run at higher clock frequencies. This is achieved using advanced silicon materials that reduce the leakages and provide more gate control, enabling improved transistor performance at higher operational frequencies. Besides improving individual transistors, Improved materials using multi-level metallization designs reduce resistive and capacitive delays, enabling faster signal transmission and higher frequencies throughout the wafer from which SoCs are manufactured.

CHAPTER 5   SEMICONDUCTOR MANUFACTURING

The advanced process technologies ensure higher frequencies are achieved at low power consumption. Innovating advanced silicon material techniques to lower the leakages allows for lower operating voltages without significant power loss. The lower operational voltages and leakages improve power efficiency, which is the other KPI in SoC components. Modern CPUs use dynamic voltage scaling to adjust the voltage in real time based on performance needs. The underlying silicon technology determines the efficiency and range of the voltage and frequency scaling, as shown in the Figure 5-1. Therefore, advanced semiconductor process technologies are key contributors to frequency and power efficiency, directly impacting the performance and performance per watt in electronic devices.

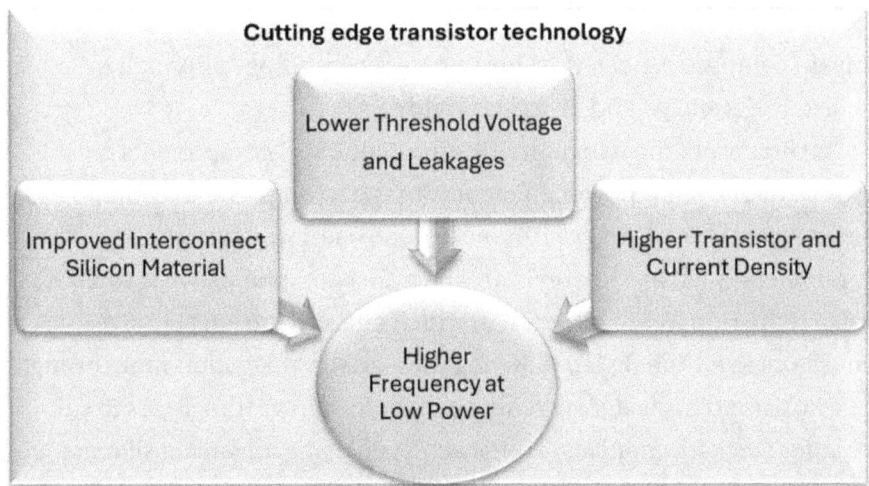

Figure 5-1. *Advanced transistor technology components*

Usually, semiconductor product companies rely on process technology improvements to get performance upgrades on their products every generation. If more than one semiconductor product vendor uses the same cutting-edge process, its performance and power benefits are available to anyone who uses the latest process. Product managers should not just rely on process technology benefits but look for new features to attain competitive advantage with innovations and continuous SoC and IP architectural improvements on their product roadmaps.

Manufacturing

Fabless semiconductor product managers can leverage their company's strengths from SWOT analysis to negotiate a better cost and capacity with semiconductor manufacturers. Manufacturing a higher volume of the same IP can be less hassle for semiconductor manufacturers and help get volume discounts and more capacity. When a company leverages these negotiations, sometimes the overall cost of dies becomes lower than competitors giving a better performance per dollar advantage.

Product managers can aim to reuse the IP across their product lines for volume discounts like Apple. Apple usually takes up most of the capacity from Taiwan Semiconductor Manufacturing Company (TSMC), and given Apple has one 1 IP for CPU, GPU, NPU, and media across product lines, it can likely give Apple volume-based negotiations. Let's discuss more about the manufacturing leaders in today's market, political and other factors that influence semiconductor manufacturing and checklists for semiconductor product managers to ensure the success of their products.

When fabless companies finish design to enter production, the handouts to manufacturing companies are in the form of tape-out and masks containing the blueprint of the chip.

CHAPTER 5   SEMICONDUCTOR MANUFACTURING

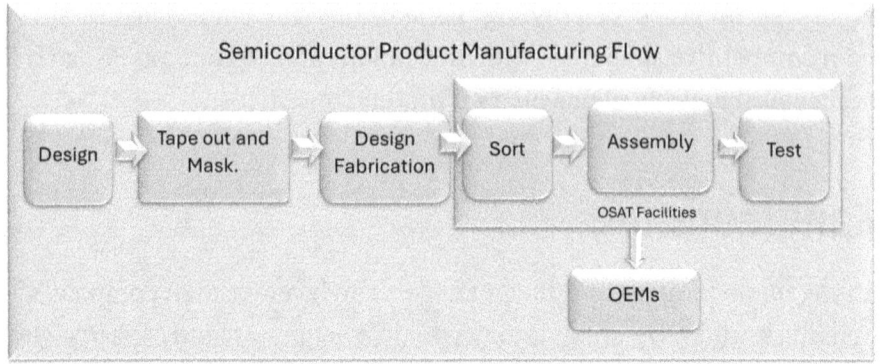

Figure 5-2. *The flow of the full semiconductor product manufacturing*

Once the blueprint is sent to the manufacturing company, the design is fabricated, and individual dies are sorted to filter out nonfunctional dies. The good dies are assembled and tested for power and performance characteristics by OSAT (outsourced semiconductor assembly and test) vendors and eventually sent to OEMs for electronic product manufacturing, such as PCs and smartphones.

The first step in manufacturing a wafer fabrication can be done as a monolithic or disaggregated die. Smaller monolithic dies are lower in cost than larger monolithic dies, as the yield rate reduces as the size of the die increases. Disaggregated SoCs are a group of smaller dies connected through die-die interconnects, which are more cost-effective than large monolithic dies. Monolithic and disaggregated (often called multi-die) designs have advantages and disadvantages. Product managers must make critical decisions to decide what suits them best based on capabilities and price to position the product in the market. This can only be possible if product managers know the market, especially competitive supplemental offerings.

CHAPTER 5 SEMICONDUCTOR MANUFACTURING

Before going into the details of monolithic and disaggregated types, let's look at why there are two choices and their purpose. Process technology innovation is long influenced by Moore's law, which states that the number of transistors that can be placed in a unit area doubles every two years. This ensures two times more transistor density per unit area every two years so similar size chips theoretically can have twice as many capabilities to the increasing performance needs of the industry. However, there has been slow progress in Moore's law over the last few years, as shown in Table 5-1. Some industry leaders started to believe Moore's law was dead, while some still believe in it.

Table 5-1. TSMC, Intel, and Samsung Process Node Delivery Over a Decade

	TSMC Manufacturing Technology	Intel Manufacturing Technology	Samsung Manufacturing Technology
2010	40nm	32nm	45nm
2011	28nm		
2012		22nm	32nm
2013			
2014	20nm	14nm	28nm
2015	16nm		14nm
2016			10nm
2017	10nm		
2018	7nm		8nm
2019		10nm	7nm
2020	5nm		5nm
2021			
2022	4nm	Intel 7	4nm
2023	3nm	Intel 4	3nm
2024		Intel 3	3nm
2025	2nm	Intel 20A	

163

CHAPTER 5   SEMICONDUCTOR MANUFACTURING

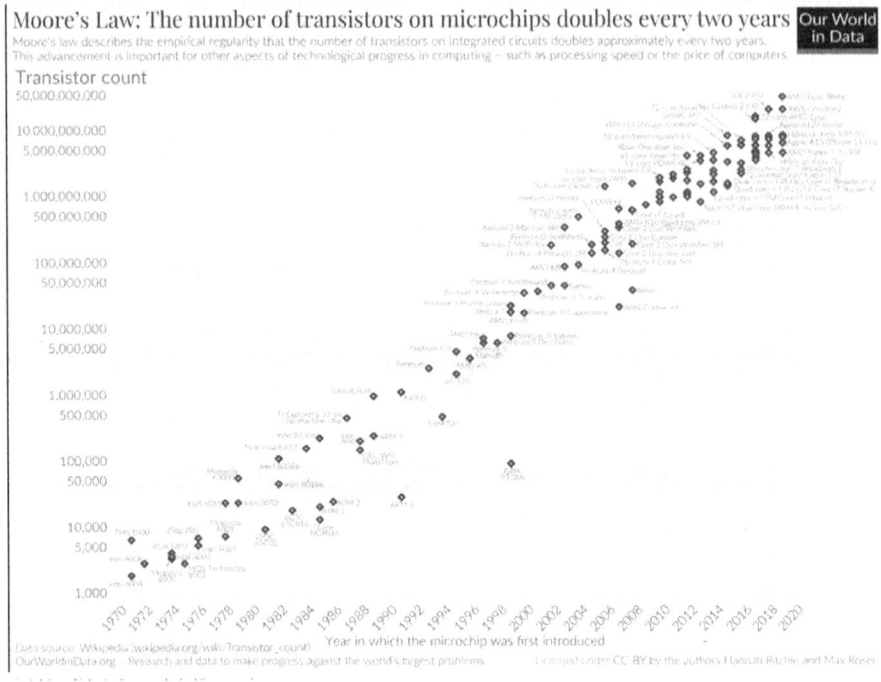

Figure 5-3. *Picture representing Moore's law*

In a perfect Moore's law world, having a monolithic design would be a great choice, given transistor count doubles on the die every two years to increase the die's capabilities. But as the process technology progress is slow compared to the needs of the industry in the last few years, the disaggregated (multi-die or multi-chip module (MCM)) method emerged to offset some of its effects. Besides Moore's law, the cost of multi-die chips is lower than large monolithic dies as there is a higher yield rate percentage on small dies than single large die.

CHAPTER 5   SEMICONDUCTOR MANUFACTURING

Let's look at an example. Case A has a single monolithic die of 500 mm². Case B has a multi-die with two dies of 250 mm², each connected die to die. Assume that there is a 12-inch wafer size and defect density is 0.1.

Case A gives 63 good monolithic dies, whereas case B gives 83 good disaggregated multi-die chips (173/2=83). Conventionally, muti-die chip cost is lower due to higher yield rates as the price is determined by the no. of good dies produced per wafer.

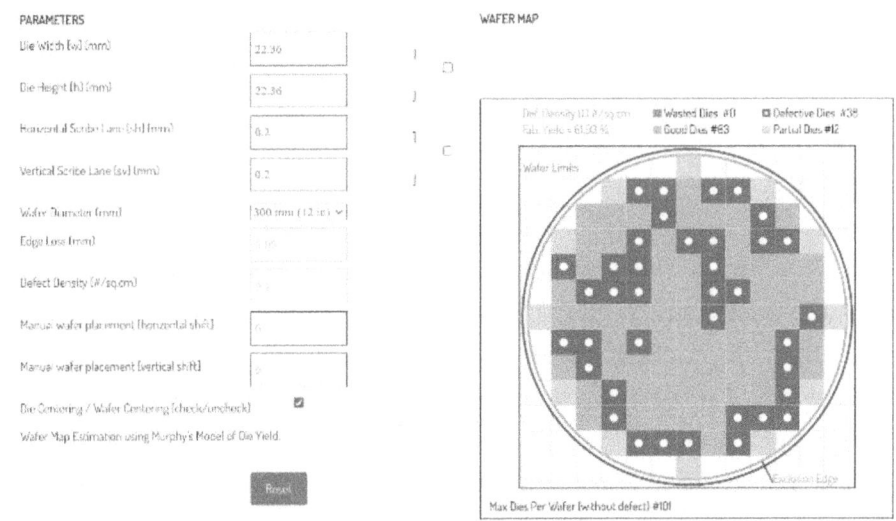

Figure 5-4. *Case A[1]*

---

[1] Data generation. Source: mooreelite.com

CHAPTER 5   SEMICONDUCTOR MANUFACTURING

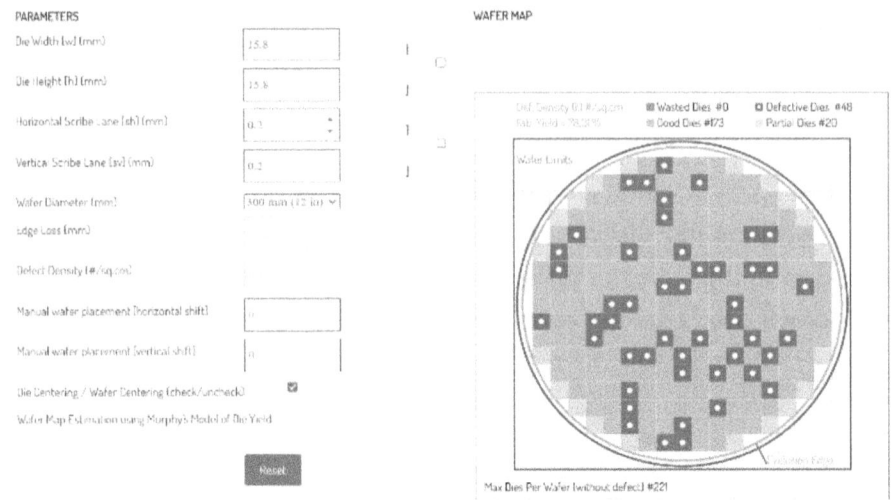

Figure 5-5. *Case B*

It is not very simple to conclude that larger monolithic dies always cost more than multi-die chips. From the full manufacturing flow of semiconductor products shown in Figure 5-2, two more steps after fabrication and sorting affect the overall pricing of the monolithic and disaggregated design.

A monolithic die has a single phase of assembly and testing per die after fabrication and sorting. In contrast, in multi-die, there is assembly and testing per die, which needs to be implemented for all the dies. So, the product managers must determine the net price of the SoC design only after pulling all these pieces together before making critical decisions.

Monolithic and Desegregated Dies

In a PC SoC, the critical IPs, including CPU, GPU, NPU, and others, are fabricated in the same process technology sorted, assembled, and tested, whereas multi-die design involves heterogeneous and homogeneous design. In heterogeneous design, each of the many dies connected die

CHAPTER 5 SEMICONDUCTOR MANUFACTURING

to die can be manufactured in different process technology, while in homogeneous design all the dies are manufactured in the same process technology. The one that provides better ROI after all the stages is the cost-effective solution. Let's consider the examples shown in Figures 5-6, 5-7, and 5-8 and Table 5-2.

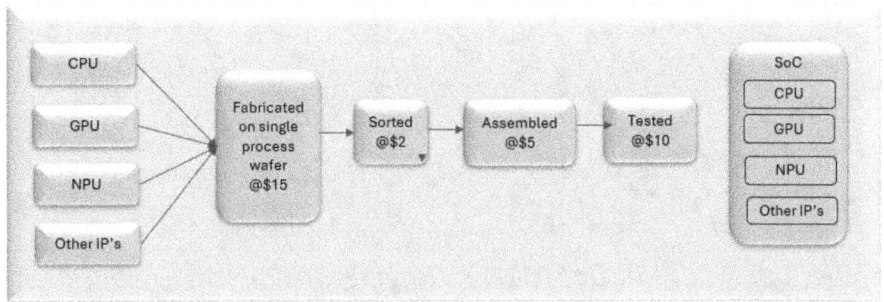

Figure 5-6. *Monolithic die design*

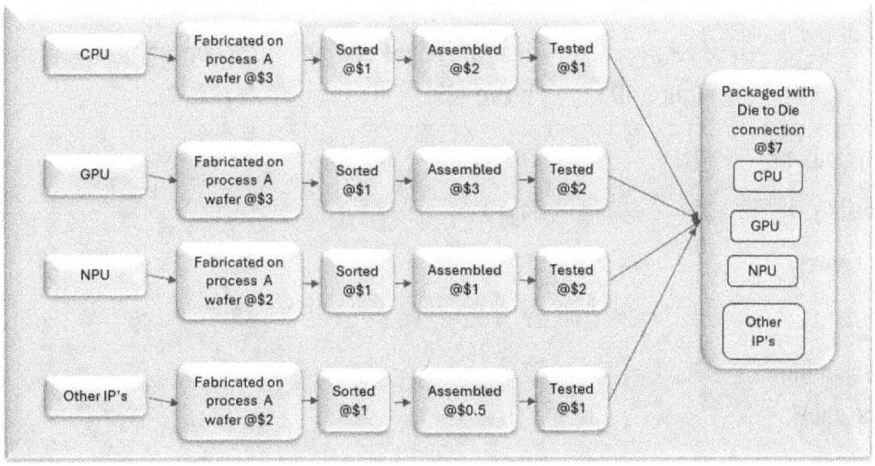

Figure 5-7. *Multi-die or MCM or disaggregated homogeneous design*

CHAPTER 5   SEMICONDUCTOR MANUFACTURING

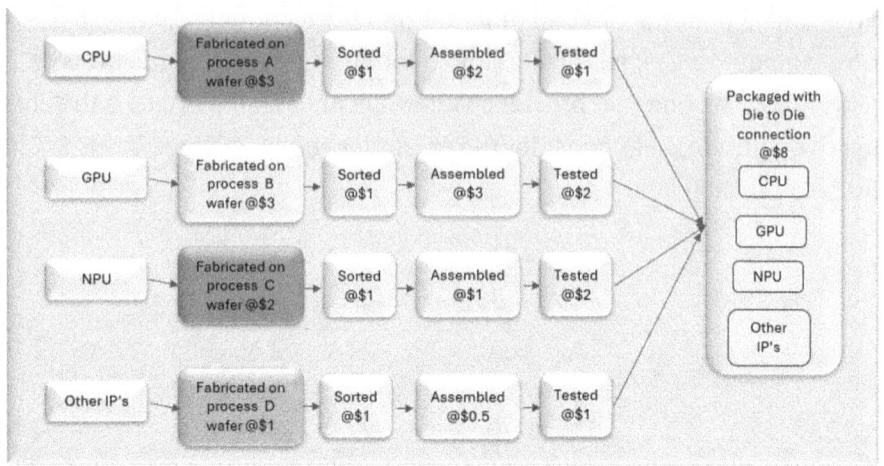

Figure 5-8. Multi-die or MCM or disaggregated heterogeneous design

Table 5-2. Types of SoC Designs

	Monolithic design Figure 4D	Homogeneous disaggregated design Figure 4E	Heterogeneous disaggregated design Figure 4E
Fabrication	$15	$10	$9
Sorting	$2	$4	$4
Assembly	$5	$6.5	$6.5
Testing	$10	$7	$5
Packaging (die-die)	—	$7	$8
Total Cost	$32	$34.5	$31.5
Margin	Baseline	-8%	+1.5%

CHAPTER 5   SEMICONDUCTOR MANUFACTURING

It is not necessary that monolithic is always the cost-aggressive solution. Combining packaging costs and the complex multi-die manufacturing process can also result in a margin hit. Product managers need to evaluate the pricing of their product vs. the relevant competition at a given timeline to determine the manufacturing design strategy. The monolithic die has better latency, power, performance, and unified memory shared across all IPs. In contrast, the disaggregated design has higher latency and power, affecting the performance of the packaged SoC. This cost modeling is crucial to bring the product at the right price into the market. Product managers should simulate these pricing models with multiple scenarios to pick the best cases. What stands apart is to include competitors' product pricing models and best-known intelligence of the pricing and costs. Certain logical assumptions can be made as it is highly unlikely to figure out all the numbers for competitors due to its sensitivity. Product managers can make better-learned decisions on design style when the die pricing model includes self and competitive products.

Another important consideration product managers can look into is utilizing partial dies to position binning SKUs to get revenue out of these dies. Good dies are fully functional dies with 0% die defect, whereas partial dies have a certain defect percentage. Product managers can do scenario modeling to have product lines with partial dies, many fabless semiconductor product companies already follow this method to bring partial dies to the market. A few best-known scenarios use probability analysis followed by defect analysis. Figure 5-9 shows AMD's product SKUs on the single AMD Ryzen Pro 8000 series. The top product SKUs with 8 CPU cores and 12 GPU cores a good die with differences in power segments thermal design power, while SKUs with six cores of CPU and 8/4 cores of GPU are perhaps binned after sorting based on the defect percentage of partial dies.

CHAPTER 5   SEMICONDUCTOR MANUFACTURING

AMD Ryzen PRO 8000 Series									
Name	Graphics Model	# of CPU Cores	# of Threads	Max. Boost Clock	Base Clock	Graphics Core Count	AMD Ryzen AI	Default TDP
AMD Ryzen 9 PRO 8945HS	AMD Radeon 780M	8	16	Up to 5.2 GHz	4 GHz	12	Available	45W
AMD Ryzen 7 PRO 8840U	AMD Radeon 780M	8	16	Up to 5.1 GHz	3.3 GHz	12	Available	28W
AMD Ryzen 7 PRO 8845HS	AMD Radeon 780M	8	16	Up to 5.1 GHz	3.8 GHz	12	Available	45W
AMD Ryzen 7 PRO 8840HS	AMD Radeon 780M	8	16	Up to 5.1 GHz	3.3 GHz	12	Available	28W
AMD Ryzen 5 PRO 8640U	AMD Radeon 760M	6	12	Up to 4.9 GHz	3.5 GHz	8	Available	28W
AMD Ryzen 5 PRO 8645HS	AMD Radeon 760M	6	12	Up to 5 GHz	4.3 GHz	8	Available	45W
AMD Ryzen 5 PRO 8640HS	AMD Radeon 760M	6	12	Up to 4.9 GHz	3.5 GHz	8	Available	28W
AMD Ryzen 5 PRO 8540U	AMD Radeon 740M	6	12	Up to 4.9 GHz	3.2 GHz	4	Not Available	28W

Figure 5-9. *AMD Ryzen Pro 8000 series product offerings (source: AMD.com July 2024)*

As an example of a modeling scenario for product managers, consider a typical case of die manufacturing with good, partial, and bad dies. Of the total partial dies, the percentage of a defect in 25% of dies is identified as 10%, 40% in 60% of partial dies, and 60% in the remaining 15%. Based on the defect percentage on partial dies after thorough sorting and segmentation, the partial dies are positioned with fewer CPU or GPU cores based on the defect percentage on the die. This method of product offering from partial dies has become very popular to get the most out of the limitations in the advanced process technology yield.

CHAPTER 5 SEMICONDUCTOR MANUFACTURING

Fabless semiconductor product companies make these bin offerings to get the last dollar out of the partial good dies by positioning at different segments and use cases. To conclude, semiconductor product managers must make critical decisions from design to manufacturing and, eventually, product bin positioning in the market. These decisions are complex and require extensive modeling scenarios to pick the case that suits the needs. Adding competitive data to the list besides their product helps make things transparent. It helps product managers to take educated decisions with risks estimated ahead of time to timely plan risk mitigation plans.

OSAT

OSAT (outsourced semiconductor assembly and test) plays a critical role in the semiconductor technology industry by providing essential services that complement the work of semiconductor manufacturers. OSAT facilities handle the physical encapsulation of semiconductor chips into packages to help OEMs easily integrate the semiconductor chips into the PC or smartphone motherboards using various packaging technologies. They may also integrate multiple chips into a single package if the design methodology is disaggregated or MCM. Product managers must choose a packaging method suitable for integrating the semiconductor chips onto the motherboard by close collaboration with OEMs responsible for assembling the final product. Some of the popular packaging methods are ball grid array (BGA), land grid array (LGA), and pin grid array (PGA).

BGA packages have an array of solder balls on the bottom surface of the package shown in Figure 5-10. These balls serve as the electrical connections to the motherboard and allow for high pin density in relatively small areas with short connection paths. The short paths help to reduce signal interference and improve performance. The BGA package connected to the motherboard provides effective heat dissipation due to its large surface area. The BGA package must be soldered to the motherboard and cannot be easily replaceable.

PGA packages have pins arranged in a grid pattern on the bottom, as shown in Figure 5-10. These pins are inserted into holes on the OEM motherboard to connect, providing a strong mechanical attachment. These pins help easy removal of packages simplifying replacement and repair if needed. The straightforward design of PGA packages makes them easy for OEMs to handle; however, the risk of broken pins is higher, making PGA a less reliable method.

LGA packages feature flat, conductive pads called *lands* on the bottom of the package instead of pins, as shown in Figure 5-10. The OEM motherboard has corresponding contact pads that align with these lands. Similar to BGA, LGA allows for a large number of connections in a compact footprint. The LGA contacts do not bend like pins in a PGA package, which helps improve reliability. Due to direct contact with the motherboard, LGA packages improve heat dissipation and are widely used in high-performance SoCs.

Figure 5-10. Examples of LGA PGA and BGA packaging methods

Every packaging method, including package on package (PoP) and SiP (system on package), has benefits and tradeoffs. Product managers must collaborate with OSAT facilities and OEMs to choose a packaging method that suits the OEM requirements based on the specific needs of the motherboard and other considerations such as size, performance, cost, and reliability.[2]

---

[2] Source: https://www.pcbaaa.com/bga-something-you-need-to-know/

CHAPTER 5   SEMICONDUCTOR MANUFACTURING

In addition to packaging, OSAT facilities test semiconductor wafers before they are diced into individual chips to ensure functionality and performance. After assembly, OSAT facilities conduct various tests, such as electrical, thermal, and mechanical, to verify that the packaged chips meet required regulatory specifications and are free from defects. They also conduct detailed inspections throughout the assembly and testing processes to ensure high-quality standards. As part of the testing process, OSAT facilities perform failure analysis to diagnose and address issues related to defects or performance problems to ensure KPI targets are met using the DFT and DFD methodology, which is discussed in a later chapter. In summary, OSAT facilities are vital partners for product managers to ensure the required performance and quality control of the semiconductor chip packages. Product managers can partner with OSAT facilities for packaging, testing, and supply chain services like assisting OEM inventory management.

Semiconductor Manufacturing Leaders

TSMC, Samsung, GlobalFoundries, and Intel are four of the most prominent players in the semiconductor manufacturing industry. TSMC and global foundries specialize in manufacturing semiconductor products, unlike Samsung and Intel, which designs and manufactures semiconductor products.

TSMC has recently emerged as a leader in developing advanced process nodes. They have expertise in new manufacturing technologies like 7nm, 5nm, and 3nm processes at scale. TSMC has heavily invested in extreme ultraviolet (EUV) lithography which is crucial for creating smaller and more efficient transistors to enable higher performance and performance per watt. TSMC's capacity for new process nodes has huge demand, and its client base includes major technology companies like

CHAPTER 5 SEMICONDUCTOR MANUFACTURING

Apple, AMD, and Nvidia, as shown in the Table 5-3. Additionally, due to TSMC's process leadership, Intel sometimes utilized TSMC technology for example Intel Core Ultra series 2 for high-performance, cutting-edge chip manufacturing. However, major fabless companies can manufacture their products using the latest technology. Product managers designing products should also ensure differentiation from other microarchitectural features along with the latest process technology benefits.

Table 5-3. Products on TSMC Process Technology

TSMC Process	NVIDIA Products	Apple Products	AMD Products
7nm		A12 Bionic	
5nm		M1 and M2 series, A14 Bionic	Ryzen 7000 series
4nm	RTX 40 series, Blackwell series	A16 Bionic, M3 series	Ryzen 8000 series
3nm		M4, A17 Pro	

Source: Apple.com, Nvidia.com, AMD.com

Intel designs and manufactures its semiconductor products and controls the entire production process from R&D to fabrication. Intel has historically been a leader in semiconductor innovation, focusing on microprocessor development and advanced packaging technologies. Intel's IDM 2.0 strategy involves expanding its foundry services to produce chips for other companies, aiming to become a significant player in the global foundry market. To achieve this, Intel has made substantial investments in expanding its manufacturing capabilities in the United States, aligning with the goals of The CHIPS Act.

Samsung has a diverse semiconductor portfolio that produces memory chips and logic chips. They are a significant player in both and are competitive in advanced node technologies, such as 7nm, 5nm, and

3nm processes. Samsung combines its semiconductor capabilities with its strengths in other electronic products, from smartphones to household appliances, creating a robust ecosystem.

GlobalFoundries focuses on specialized processes and does not focus on the leading-edge nodes like TSMC and Samsung. They specialize in mature and specialty process technologies. This includes radio frequency, IoT (Internet of Things), and automotive chips. GlobalFoundries offers flexible, customized, tailored solutions for specific industry needs like home security embedded wearables, making them a vital player for customized and niche semiconductor applications. With fabrication facilities around the world, GlobalFoundries provides a diversified manufacturing base, which is critical for supply chain stability.

Semiconductor Manufacturing Pricing

You have seen cost modeling analysis from fabless design product managers, which is complex, another aspect of pricing from manufacturers. Then, pricing methodology in semiconductor manufacturing, particularly from industry leaders like TSMC and Intel, involves several complex factors besides yield-related factors mentioned earlier. These factors include production costs, technological capabilities, market demand, and strategic considerations based on the manufacturers' strengths in scale and R&D. Let's discuss the pricing of the two top leaders in manufacturing.

TSMC

TSMC typically calculates the total cost of manufacturing a wafer, which includes raw materials, labor, overhead, and equipment depreciation. A profit margin is added to the production cost to determine the final price. The margin can vary based on the complexity of the process node and the customer's order volume and is known as *cost plus pricing*. Product managers can add margin to the wafer price and implement their modeling.

CHAPTER 5   SEMICONDUCTOR MANUFACTURING

> Wafer price from TSMC: Total wafer cost + Margin

Cutting-edge process node wafers like 7nm, 5nm, and 3nm are priced higher due to the increased complexity and lower yields in the early stages of production. These nodes require more expensive equipment and R&D investment. Older nodes like 28nm and 45nm are priced lower as the technology is well-established, and yields are higher. The equipment and processes are fully depreciated, reducing overall costs. In the heterogeneous multi-die design, product managers can evaluate options for some die manufacturing in older nodes to reduce the price if possible. This pricing method is generally known as *process node differentiation*, as TSMC leads in producing advanced nodes, and customers pay higher wafer prices for TSMC.

Large orders from major clients like Apple, AMD, and NVIDIA can receive significant discounts. Higher volumes lead to economies of scale, reducing the per-unit cost for TSMC. Customers committing to long-term agreements might also receive price incentives.

Intel

Intel designs and manufactures its chips, allowing for a different pricing approach than foundries. The overall product strategy often influences pricing rather than just manufacturing costs. Intel can bundle its semiconductor products with other technologies and services, adding value beyond semiconductor manufacturing. Packaging and other services can be done in one place, which has advantages and, at times, can reduce the price per die as implementation can be done at scale for these services and integration at the same place. Intel refers to this as IDM (integrated device manufacturing). Intel is gearing up for IDM 2.0,[3] a revised product manufacturing strategy that can bring another set of goodness to their one-point semiconductor design and manufacturing solution.

---

[3] Source: https://www.intc.com/filings-reports/all-sec-filings/content/0000050863-24-000010/0000050863-24-000010.pdf

CHAPTER 5   SEMICONDUCTOR MANUFACTURING

On the wafer pricing plus pricing, Intel considers the production costs, including raw materials, labor, R&D, and equipment depreciation, similar to TSMC. Advanced process nodes have lower initial yields, which can increase the per-unit cost. As yields improve, costs decrease, potentially lowering prices over time. Premium pricing is applied to high-performance and cutting-edge products, such as those used in data centers, AI, and high-performance computing.

Wafer price from Intel: Total wafer cost + Margin

Large enterprise customers can negotiate custom pricing based on volume commitments and long-term supply agreements because prices for original equipment manufacturers (OEMs) can vary based on the strategic importance of the partnership and the scale of the orders.

Overall, the pricing methodologies of TSMC and Intel are multifaceted, involving a mix of cost-based, value-based, and market-based approaches. Both companies consider production costs, technological capabilities, market demand, and competitive dynamics. While TSMC, as a foundry, focuses on manufacturing and volume discounts, Intel's IDM model allows it to bundle products and services, offering differentiated pricing strategies across its product lines. There are a few other general factors that influence any industry pricing, like the availability of raw materials, geopolitical factors, and supply chain disruptions that have the potential to influence pricing. Global economic conditions, like inflation, currency exchange rates, and trade policies, can also affect the overall pricing strategy.

Semiconductor product managers can leverage the factors that suit them the best. Depending on the strengths, companies can get volume discounts and/or leverage long-term contracts to negotiate pricing. Apple, due to its volume strength can get volume discounts and contract-based advantage from TSMC. AMD and NVIDIA, on the other hand, often differentiate from Intel by manufacturing their semiconductor from TSMC's cutting-edge technology. To keep track of these dynamics of each semiconductor product company, a competitive landscape of

CHAPTER 5   SEMICONDUCTOR MANUFACTURING

semiconductor manufacturing comes in handy to product managers. Sometimes, the performance is solely derived from the frequency uplift gained from manufacturing semiconductor products on a cutting-edge process technology. In the product roadmap, it would be worthwhile to add performance per watt, performance of the node and the reasoning can be provided as process technology where applicable. This offers a better understanding of strengths and weaknesses and allows product managers to take measures accordingly.

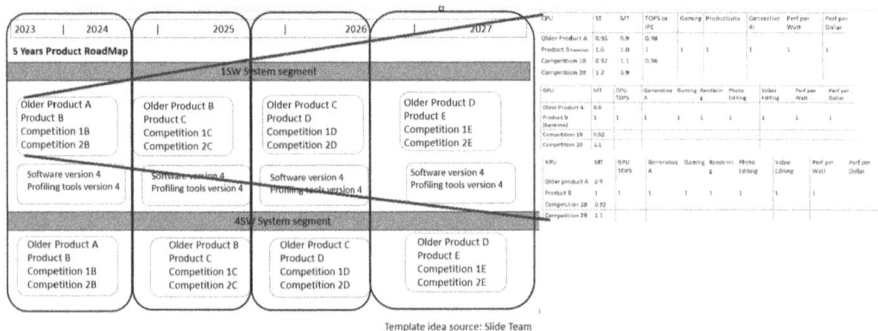

Figure 5-11. Example of a product roadmap

The other factor is IP scalability—if a single IP is utilized for multiple product segments, the design time and resources are reduced significantly, lowering the semiconductor product's design cost. Given the same IP is manufactured for all the product segments, additional customizations and testing efforts needed by semiconductor manufacturers per IP can be reduced, which can affect pricing and, in turn, can help semiconductor product companies to place binned parts efficiently in various segments as the sorting gets efficient.

Most companies like Apple, NVIDIA, Qualcomm, and AMD have the same IP across their product lines. Apple designs one IP and the same IP is used across their mobile and PC products. AMD designs and uses one IP in client and data center products. Their NPU IP has recently scaled in AI accelerators for data centers, PC silicon NPU, and embedded platforms. Qualcomm has their one IP design strategy once and implemented across

CHAPTER 5   SEMICONDUCTOR MANUFACTURING

all IoTs, mobile, PC, and all other segments. All these companies get the goodness of a single design and verification team for all their products, which is a great way to keep up with the product timelines. For example, having multiple CPU IPs for different product lines increases design and verification timelines and costs. Reuse of IP across has its advantages besides cost. Testing all the product segment scenarios on a single IP makes them more robust and efficient in a few design revision cycles.

Performance Per Dollar

Performance per dollar gives a clear metric of the IP efficiency to the unit price. Product managers can have many other metrics, but this is a must to evaluate the efficiency of the products being produced every generation and over competition. Product managers aim to deliver great products generation over generation. But the product's greatness should also consider the price factor so customers are willing to pay the right price for the products.

Consider the following. A CPU1 with a 1000 multi-thread score on an industry-valued benchmark costs $30, and a next-generation CPU2 with a 1200 score on the same benchmark costs $40. There is a 20% increase in performance at a 33% higher cost. Of course, there is only one benchmark as an example here, but it is important to get these numbers for a few key performance indicators of the serving segment and take a geomean or average of numbers. So, 20% more performance at a 33% higher price gives an estimate that performance per dollar is higher for CPU2 and has room for improvement. It is not always necessary to have an equal ratio of performance per dollar every generation. But the idea is to enable product managers to assess the reasons behind it, and if they are acceptable to their customers so the product can be sold at a price they are willing to pay.

The same performance per dollar can be derived for competitors to evaluate the value proposition of the products against competition, which

CHAPTER 5 SEMICONDUCTOR MANUFACTURING

helps is product pricing, promotion, and placement. This evaluation can be done on an actual benchmark performance or at a theoretical IP performance level, which can be done at the early stages of product planning.

Consider an NPU designed for delivering 50 theoretical TOPS built using TSMC's 3nm and has a die area of about 20 mm^2 with an overall die around 200 mm^2 in which this NPU is placed along with CPU, GPU, memory, and other units of SoC. Consider TSMC's 3nm wafer that looks like salami from which dies are formed) costs about $20,000, and because of the cutting-edge 3nm, the yield can be lower than usual mature nodes, consider the yield rate to be 50%. So, a typical-size wafer can produce about ~300 good dies.

> Wafer price = $20,000, good dies produced with 50% yield on 3nm = ~300
>
> The price of each die = $20,000 wafer price/300 good dies = ~$66 per die.
>
> An NPU delivering 50TOPS is 10% of the total die size, so $6.60 is the total cost of the NPU.
>
> In this case, performance per dollar for NPU is a TOPS per dollar, which is 50 TOPS/$6.6 = ~7.5 TOPS per dollar.

To assess performance per dollar to a competitor, consider a competitor using the same process node that delivers 45 TOPS with the same 20mm2 area of NPU. Then, the competitor's performance per dollar will be ~6.8, which is ~10% lower. These could be some potential ways to access performance per dollar on dies. For NPUs, it's TOPS; for GPU, it could be FLOPS; for CPU, it could be IPC or based on an actual application performance measured across all computers. This metric could be very helpful for B2B semiconductor product vendors like NVIDIA, Intel, AMD, and Qualcomm, which work with OEMs to produce end products. OEMs can access performance per dollar as a metric to assess each semiconductor product vendor's offering and negotiate pricing accordingly. Competitive product management metrics like these help product managers be on top of things if these metrics are part of the roadmap as a starting point.

Security

Security in semiconductor manufacturing is a critical concern due to the strategic importance of semiconductors in consumer electronics, defense, telecommunications, and critical infrastructure. Since PCs hold almost all the customers' electronic data, securing and ensuring customers feel safe about the security of their data is a critical value proposition of a PC product. Ensuring the semiconductor's security involves setting priorities from design and fabrication to supply chain management and final deployment like design security, fabrication security and taking innovative measures using AI to enable secure products.

A product manager's critical responsibility is to ensure architects design products with security in mind. Besides having functional features, the IP design should implement secure design principles from the initial stages to prevent vulnerabilities. Safeguarding intellectual property (IP) to prevent theft and unauthorized use is critical in ensuring the success of semiconductor products throughout their life cycle. Design and verification engineers use secure computer-aided design (CAD) tools that incorporate security features and can detect potential vulnerabilities, making the task easier. To prevent unauthorized access using cryptographic keys and other sensitive data during the design process, encrypting sensitive design data to avoid hacking into the IP are key focus areas for product managers.

CHAPTER 5   SEMICONDUCTOR MANUFACTURING

Product companies should use trusted and certified foundries to manufacture chips that reduce the risk of tampering and IP theft with proper SLA (service level agreements) signed. Ensuring the integrity of materials and components entering the manufacturing process is critical. Although product managers have little control over this, they can leverage SLAs and certifications. The SLAs and certifications should ensure fabrication facilities implement robust security protocols within the manufacturing process, including regular audits and inspections. Additionally, incorporating anti-tamper features into the chips themselves, such as sensors that detect physical tampering attempts, are added measures to be sure.

After fabrication, engineering samples received in the initial testing phase should ensure comprehensive testing to detect any anomalies or malicious alterations in the chips. Ensuring the firmware and software used in conjunction with the hardware are secure, like OTP (one-time programmable) and up-to-date encryption standards. A test plan with end-to-end data security cases must run on the engineering samples with a random seed generation–based testbench. Product managers can check the progress on the regression dashboard. These dashboards are usually maintained by the verification leads which gives a ratio of the number of tests failed to the total test run at each IP and full product level.

Besides testing, companies should establish a secure supply chain with verified suppliers, distributors, and methods for authenticating and verifying chips before deployment, such as digital certificates or physical unclonable functions (PUFs). Finally, continuously monitoring and managing the security of semiconductor devices throughout their life cycle, including updates and patch management.

Artificial intelligence is gradually becoming a critical aspect in any industry, redefining how things were done traditionally. Internally, a model can be made of the data collected over the years on security-related issues and trained on a neural network or a transformer. Deploying these

AI models to detect anomalies and potential security threats in real time during various stages of the manufacturing process can be beneficial in the long run. Artificial intelligence via incremental model training can attain the ability to evaluate any new issues found recently or older issues detected over the years. Using AI model-based verification that can update itself with the new scenarios to keep up with the new threats is the future of security.

Overall, Security in semiconductor manufacturing is challenging and requires a comprehensive approach to address risks at every stage, from design to deployment. The semiconductor industry can significantly mitigate security risks by implementing secure design practices, using trusted and secure fabrication processes, ensuring post-fabrication integrity, and using emerging technologies. Ongoing collaboration between industry, academia, and government agencies is essential to stay ahead of evolving threats and to ensure the resilience and trustworthiness of the global semiconductor supply chain.

Summary

Semiconductor manufacturing is a critical component of semiconductor product design for performance and power efficiency. There are many decisions that a product manager must make like deciding monolithic or MCM and choice of process technology. Additionally, the decisions in binning help with accurate product positioning and help get more economic value on the manufactured SoCs per wafer.

CHAPTER 6

The CHIPS Act of 2022

Out of clutter, find simplicity. From discord, find harmony. In the middle of difficulty lies opportunity.

—Albert Einstein

The CHIPS and Science Act of 2022[1] is legislation aimed at revitalizing the semiconductor industry in the United States through substantial federal investment to support semiconductor manufacturing companies. The United States produced close to 40% of the world's semiconductor supply in the 1990s, gradually due to the increase in offshore manufacturing in recent years that 40% has slipped to just 12%. Taiwan-based (TSMC) produces more than 60% of the world's supply of semiconductors and more than 90% of the most advanced chips as of 2023.[2]

---

[1] https://www.whitehouse.gov/briefing-room/statements-releases/2022/08/09/fact-sheet-chips-and-science-act-will-lower-costs-create-jobs-strengthen-supply-chains-and-counter-china/

[2] https://www.economist.com/special-report/2023/03/06/taiwans-dominance-of-the-chip-industry-makes-it-more-important

CHAPTER 6   THE CHIPS ACT OF 2022

The CHIPS Act was signed to address the critical supply chain and manufacturing vulnerabilities and aims to mitigate increasing global competition in semiconductor design and manufacturing in the United States. According to the US government, the Act allocates $52.7 billion in funding for semiconductor research, development, and manufacturing. The funding includes grants, subsidies, and incentives designed to encourage the construction of new semiconductor fabrication facilities (fabs) and expanding existing facilities within the United States. The CHIPS Act is aimed to bring back the United States' technology leadership, lower costs in semiconductor manufacturing and make the United States the leader in manufacturing advanced chips.

The CHIPS Act emphasizes providing resources for cutting-edge research in semiconductor technology and fostering technological innovations required to advance in areas such as advanced lithography, which help the transition to smaller process nodes like 5nm, 3nm, and 2nm that offer better performance and energy efficiency. Innovation in silicon photonics, quantum computing, AI, and other emerging fields rely on advanced semiconductor technologies. By supporting domestic manufacturing capabilities and technological innovations, the CHIPS Act aims to enhance US national security, economic competitiveness, and the resilience of the semiconductor supply chain besides positioning the United States as a leader in the global semiconductor market.

The Impact of the CHIPS Act

The CHIPS Act is one of the key political factors that impact the global technology industry, the US economy, and national security in the future. Let's discuss the factors listed in Figure 6-1.

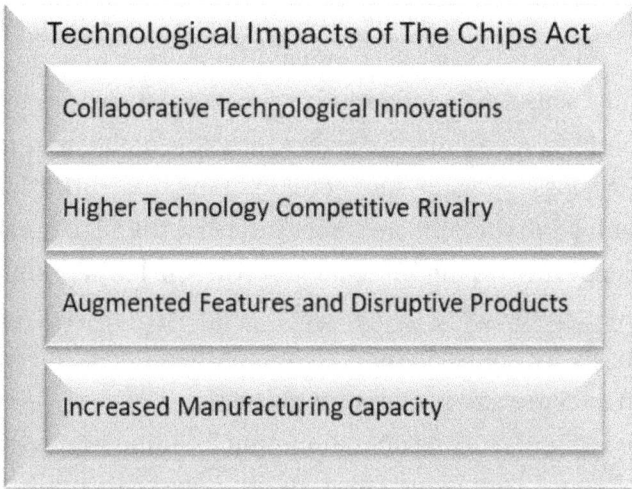

Figure 6-1. Technological impacts of the CHIPS Act

Technological Impacts

The CHIPS Act provides financial incentives for manufacturing companies, Research and development for advanced chips, and increased capacity in fabrication facilities to support domestic semiconductor production. The funding for research and development could foster collaborations among manufacturing companies and academic institutions to accelerate technological advancements.

With more companies like Intel, TSMC, and Samsung competing against each other directly within the same geographic location, it improves competitive technology and price offerings in the long term. This competitive rivalry strengthens the transistor and material technologies innovations for delivering advanced cutting-edge process nodes at a competitive price.

CHAPTER 6   THE CHIPS ACT OF 2022

As discussed, transistor technology impacts the two main KPIs in making competitive SoCs derived from cutting-edge semiconductor manufacturing. This dependency on cutting-edge process technology for leadership performance shifts the economic value of the product heavily on the country possessing the semiconductor manufacturing leadership. By strengthening the US semiconductor industry, the CHIPS Act returns technology leadership to the United States with the latest products designed and manufactured domestically. This Act ensures US national security with secure domestic semiconductor manufacturing critical for defense with a secure and resilient supply chain.

Expanded manufacturing operations and building new facilities increase the capacity to manufacture cutting-edge semiconductor devices. Enabling its reach to other electronic device segments like TVs, cameras, and hospital equipment, which otherwise would have been seen only in a data center, mobile, and PC segments due to capacity constraints.

Adopting cutting-edge lithography techniques, such as extreme ultraviolet (EUV) lithography across semiconductor products, increases augmented features and disruptive products in the technology industry. Some examples are the revolution in the medical industry with advanced treatments and vaccines, fully autonomous driving vehicles with advanced features and wearables and phone features than what is seen today.

Therefore, TSMC, Samsung, GlobalFoundries, and Intel play critical roles in the global semiconductor landscape with their unique strengths and strategic focuses discussed earlier. The CHIPS Act is aimed to enhance their capabilities further, driving innovations.

Economic Impacts

Most of the leading semiconductor fabless design companies, such as data center, mobile, and PC client devices, outsource their semiconductor manufacturing outside of the United States to TSMC in Taiwan, for example, AMD, Apple, Qualcomm, and NVIDIA. As of July 2024, one US dollar equaled 32.49 new Taiwan dollars. The transition of these manufacturing facilities into the United States incurs higher costs initially due to exchange rate dynamics to set up and run the manufacturing facilities. This leads to increased cost of goods sold (COGS) on the semiconductor devices until the facilities reach economies of scale to deliver incremental manufacturing benefits. Although the latest technology is priced premium and manufacturing companies receive funding, the CHIPS Act impacts the margins of these fabless companies for a short term until economies of scale are achieved. In the long term, this Act aims to enhance manufacturing capabilities within the United States, leading to more efficient and cost-effective production processes and enabling higher yields and lower defect rates in semiconductor wafers in the United States.

High-tech employment in the United States will increase, further improving the US economy. This unleashes new market development opportunities for fabless design companies to position disruptive products and services in the high-tech user base with a higher willingness to pay, as shown in the Figure 6-2.

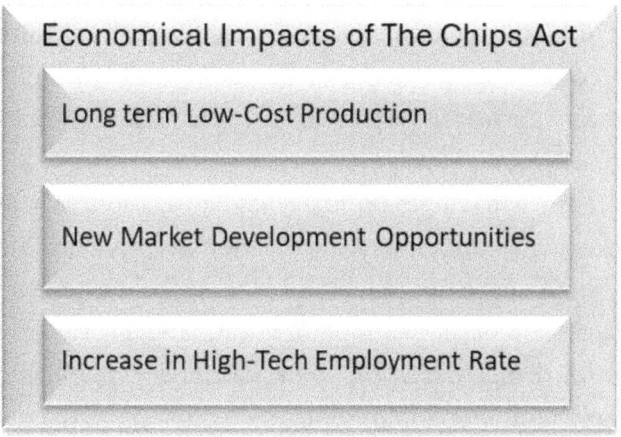

Figure 6-2. Economic impacts of the CHIPS Act

Other Impacts and Challenges

The global semiconductor industry is highly competitive, and other nations may continue investing heavily in their capabilities, maintaining the competitive pressure. The competitive pressure may impact global trade dynamics as other countries might take initiatives to support their domestic semiconductor product capabilities, such as SMIC semiconductor manufacturing companies in Mainland China.

Due to the CHIPS Act, global semiconductor device companies may face supply chain and regulatory challenges to support their products globally with potential geographical restrictions and regulations.

Role of Product Managers and Management

With the CHIPS Act in effect, the manufacturing capacity will expand gradually in the United States over the next few years. Semiconductor product companies should explore new partners for back-end assembly, testing, and device packaging that best fit their global and domestic strategy. Not just fabless companies, manufacturers should also explore more cost-effective methods to expand capacity in the United States than pursuing foundry partnerships globally to provide better value to their customers in the United States.

Manufacturers with single-point design, fabrication, sort, assemble, test, and packaging solutions services of heterogeneous multi-die domestically would have unique differentiation and advantage. A successful expansion of semiconductor manufacturing capacity requires companies to work together across their partner ecosystem, including foundries, semiconductor equipment, intellectual property, design services, fabless companies, system manufacturers, and application developers. As Intel owns its design manufacturing services and

CHAPTER 6   THE CHIPS ACT OF 2022

significantly expands its capabilities with the IDM2.0 strategy, Intel can fully leverage the benefits of the CHIPS Act if executed on plan IDM2.0. On the other hand, Samsung also differentiates with logic and memory end-to-end design and manufacturing capabilities.

Semiconductor product companies need to define their global strategy as the CHIPS Act comes with its pros and cons for product companies operating globally. Companies that design chips and use their foundries to manufacture, like intel and samsung, may need to consider new partnerships to comply with the CHIPS Act's geographical restrictions. This applies to fabless companies that design their chips but outsource manufacturing, like Apple and NVIDIA. The product managers should implement a SWOT analysis specific to semiconductor manufacturing with the CHIPS Act, make amendments to the product strategy with collaboration from other ecosystem partners, and take the best possible approach to operate globally. This could include new mergers and acquisitions, partnerships, and collaborations to strengthen their global market presence.

As the semiconductor industry has become essential to geopolitical security, governments globally may take initiatives to support their domestic manufacturing like the United States. This would threaten the current semiconductor design companies as the countries want to be independent in semiconductor designs, not just its manufacturing, to avoid dependency on the United States. Semiconductor fabless design companies should consider rebalancing strategies to overcome the geographic restrictions and provide more value to the customers globally.

Enhanced manufacturing capabilities and cutting-edge technology, such as performance and performance per watt and enhanced quality control, are great for differentiating products in the global market today. The CHIPS Act highlighting the advantages of domestically produced chips is also a key differentiator in the future. To achieve this, semiconductor product companies must develop a global market strategy that balances domestic manufacturing with strategic international partnerships. The aim should be to remain competitive on a global scale while leveraging the benefits of US-based production that brings the benefits of the CHIPS Act. Product managers, along with management, should fully assess their corporate strategy to determine how they can operate globally with leadership product differentiation and comply with geo-based restrictions.

The CHIPS Act is an interesting opportunity to influence and accelerate a new revolution in the technology industry and a challenging role for product managers to make critical decisions to design and position a competitive product in the global markets at the best price. The fab and fabless companies like Apple, AMD, Intel, NVIDIA, and Samsung already have unique advantages. With the CHIPS Act, product managers can make a global strategy by leveraging their existing unique advantages to make their products achieve continuous success.

Just-in-Time Manufacturing

To provide a best-priced product, factors like when a product gets manufactured contribute a lot to the overall product pricing. To deliver a product cost-efficiently to the customers, some methodologies can help product managers lower COGS in a highly competitive market like PCs. The methodologies like the popular Just-in-Time (JIT) semiconductor product development aimed at improving efficiency and reducing waste in the semiconductor manufacturing process. The idea of JIT mainly focuses on aligning production schedules closely with customer demand so companies can optimize their supply chain to reduce inventory costs and respond more quickly to market dynamics.

The JIT is implemented by initiating production of the products based on actual customer orders rather than forecasts to minimize the risk of overproduction and unsold inventory, adding holding costs. This timely production is only possible with flexible manufacturing facilities to quickly switch between different products to meet changing demands and an efficient production process.

JIT, with flexible and efficient manufacturing facilities, can lower production costs by holding needed inventory, accelerating the development and delivery of new products in response to dynamic market demands, and meeting customer requirements promptly. Many companies are implementing JIT in their manufacturing process. Dell Computer's JIT model takes a build-to-order approach and is considered a classic example of JIT in the technology industry. Dell implements JIT by assembling computers followed by shipping only after an order is placed, which minimizes inventory and helps respond quickly to customer needs. Apple implements JIT on higher configuration systems with larger memory and storage. Apple starts assembling these customized configurations after an order is placed.

Manufacturing companies like TSMC and Intel also implement JIT principles balancing the need for efficiency with the complexities of semiconductor fabrication. JIT semiconductor product development aims to create a highly efficient and cost-effective manufacturing process by closely aligning production with demand to minimize inventory. JIT can reduce production costs and improve responsiveness, but this approach requires careful management of potential challenges in supply chain risks and demand volatility. There are a few considerations, like leveraging advanced planning systems with AI to intelligently determine nontrivial risks and close supply chain collaboration, and semiconductor companies can effectively implement JIT principles to enhance their competitive edge. With the CHIPS Act 2022, manufacturing is tied to geographical location, so single-point manufacturing to implement JIT globally might be challenging.

CHAPTER 6   THE CHIPS ACT OF 2022

Summary

Political and economic factors like the CHIPS Act and global industry dynamics influence product managers' strategic decision-making to have a successful product life cycle. Now that you know more about semiconductor manufacturing, the next step is to assemble these manufactured SoCs into the customer products, such as PCs or smartphones, after thorough testing by OSATs. The assembled and tested semiconductor packages are given to OEMs for manufacturing PCs and smartphones and shared with channel partners for sales. The next chapter looks at OSATs, OEMS, and channel partners.

CHAPTER 7

OEMs and Channel Partners

This chapter discusses the final steps in semiconductor SoC-based product manufacturing with OEMs, which occurs before a product is sent to channel partners for retail market distribution. The aim is to explain an OEM's contribution to the semiconductor product developmental flow so that product managers can better understand it and leverage a successful product execution.

As semiconductor chips are designed, developed, and manufactured, they must be assembled into the final consumer products such as PCs and smartphones. These consumer products are manufactured by the OEMs (original equipment manufacturers), who are responsible for procuring and assembling the manufactured semiconductor products and other required components. OEMs can be part of a semiconductor product company, such as Apple, or an individual entity, such as Dell Lenovo. Before OEMs access the semiconductor chips for product integration, semiconductor product managers must ensure the manufactured semiconductor wafers are cut, packaged, tested for functionality, inspected for quality, and assembled for easy integration by the OEMs. These services are offered by OSAT (outsourced semiconductor assembly and test) facilities. OEMs can procure the semiconductor chips from OSAT facilities to manufacture the consumer products and distribute them to the retail channels to market them to the consumers, as shown in Figure 7-1.

CHAPTER 7   OEMS AND CHANNEL PARTNERS

This chapter discusses OEM methodologies and the role of semiconductor product managers in ensuring seamless product delivery to end users with channel partners.

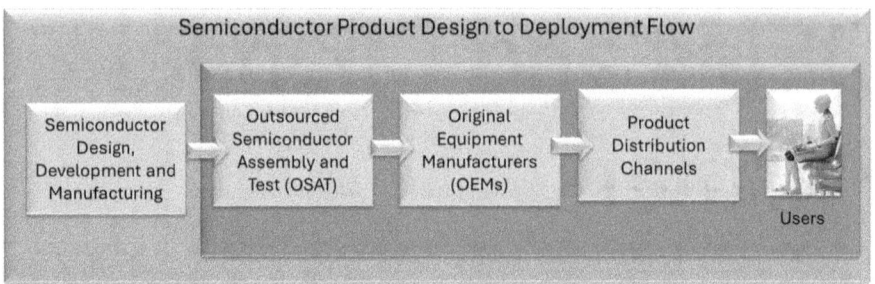

Figure 7-1. *Typical semiconductor product design to deployment flow*

OEMs

OEMs play an important role in assembling semiconductor chip packages into end user products. The assembly process involves several detailed steps to ensure that the final product is functional, reliable, and meets the required specifications. Figure 7-2 shows an overview of the typical process OEMs follow to assemble semiconductor chip packages such as SoCs, discrete GPUs, memory, and other critical components into end-user products such as PCs and smartphones.

CHAPTER 7 OEMS AND CHANNEL PARTNERS

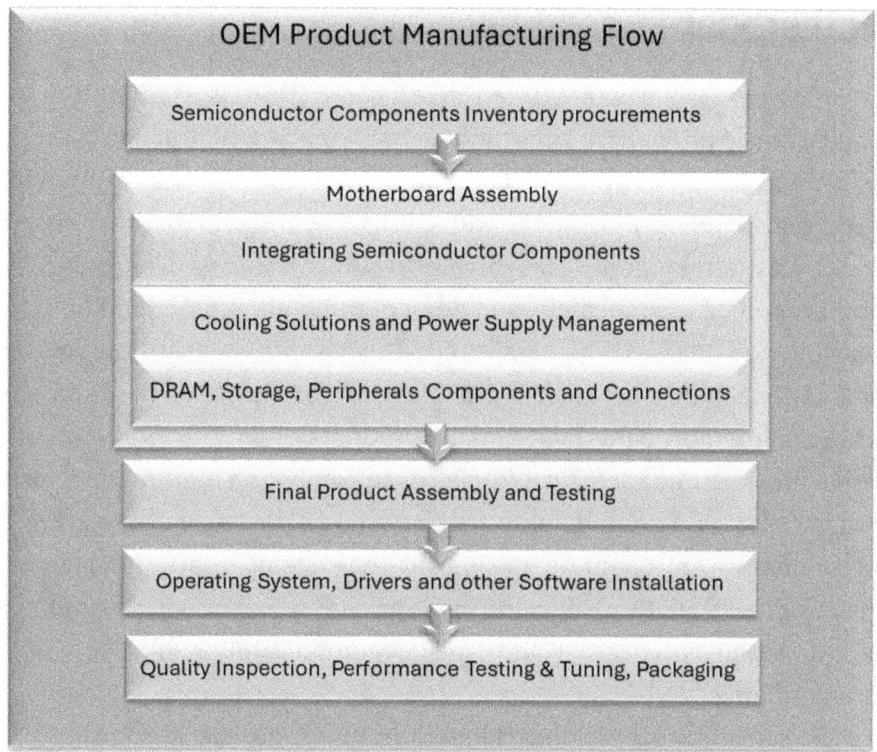

Figure 7-2. *A typical OEM product manufacturing flow*

OEMs receive semiconductor chip packages, such as SoCs, CPUs, GPUs, and memory chips, from semiconductor design companies like Intel, AMD, NVIDIA, and others through OSATs. Upon receiving the components, OEMs also perform quality and reliability checks to ensure the received packages meet the required standards. The packages are passed on to manufacturing using a systematic multi-step approach, as shown in Figure 7-2, such as motherboard assembly, final product assembly and testing, operating system, driver and other software installation, final quality inspection, performance testing, and packaging before they are shipped to channel partners or the customers directly. Let's discuss the various steps involved in manufacturing semiconductor consumer products.

CHAPTER 7   OEMS AND CHANNEL PARTNERS

Motherboard Assembly

A *motherboard* is the main printed circuit board (PCB) in a computer (known as a *logic board* in smartphones), serving as a central hub that connects and allows communication between all the different components of the system. It houses the SoCs with CPU, GPU, NPU, media, and other blocks, chipsets, random access memory (DRAM), storage devices and interfaces, display connectors, and other peripherals required for PC or smartphone functions. The motherboard also provides expansion slots for additional hardware, such as graphics cards, network cards, sound cards, and memory cards based on the product design. The motherboard's design and features are critical to a PC or smartphone's performance, size, compatibility, and expandability, making it one of the most important components in any computer or smartphone system. Product managers must work with OEMs to meet the motherboard requirements to supply the compatible SoC package and provide required cooling solution configurations.

The SoC packages are placed into the appropriate socket on the motherboard, and a thin layer of thermal paste is applied to the SoC to facilitate efficient heat transfer between the semiconductor SoC and its cooling solution. DRAM modules are inserted into the designated memory slots on the motherboard, ensuring they are properly seated and locked in place. The other components, such as cooling solutions, wirings and cables, storage, and power supply units, are installed and assembled. The assembled motherboard is secured in the PC or smartphone case to be tested for functionality.

Final Product Assembly and Testing

The assembled PC or smartphone is powered on to perform an initial check of the hardware, known as a *power-on self-test* (POST), using diagnostic tools followed by a BIOS setup (basic input/output system)) to test the functionality of all components. OEMs can configure the system settings such as boot order, DRAM and SoC operating frequencies as applicable. At this stage, semiconductor product managers must collaborate with the OEMs to execute a full suite of DFT tests with extensive load conditions to ensure the system meets stability, performance, and regulatory requirements.

Operating System, Drivers, and Other Software Installation

PCs and smartphones undergo chosen operating system installation, such as Android, iOS, Windows, and Linux, onto the primary storage device. Other necessary drivers, utilities and application software are installed per the consumer segment specifications or typical requirements. At this stage, commercial PCs are installed with device management software and updates to ensure the PC meets the business security requirements. However, recently, businesses have been able to securely manage devices using remote installation of security and device management software due to advances in security solutions.

Quality Inspection, Performance Testing and Tuning, and Packaging

The OEMs conduct a final inspection to ensure all components are properly installed and functioning. Benchmarks and performance tests are run to verify the system meets performance standards. At this stage semiconductor product managers can update any drivers, firmware, or other software to ensure the system is tuned for target consumer segments meeting the target performance. Finally, PCs or smartphones are packaged with protective materials to prevent damage during shipping, along with manuals, warranty information, and any additional accessories. The packages are sent to channel partners or directly to the end customer depending on the OEMs supply chain methodology.

Channel Partners

OEM channel partners such as Best Buy, Costco, Amazon, Walmart, and others are essential for expanding the reach, customization, and support of OEM products. They add significant value by tailoring solutions to customer needs, managing distribution, and providing localized expertise and support. Product managers must ensure the sales and marketing teams collaborate effectively with OEM and channel partners for technical support, product messaging and other marketing efforts required to generate awareness and help communicate the product's value to the consumer market. Effective OEM and channel partnerships and collaboration help product managers build brand awareness and recognition using effective go-to-market and pricing strategies required to build a sustainable customer base for long-term success.

Summary

OEMs meticulously assemble components into PCs, ensuring high quality, reliability, and performance. This involves precise component installation, effective cooling solutions, robust power supply management, thorough testing, and careful packaging. In summary, product managers can collaborate with OEMs and other component partners to deliver semiconductor consumer products that meet the diverse compute and functional needs of consumers and businesses. The assembled products are either shared with channel partners or sold in the retail market directly by OEMs.

This chapter and previous chapters discussed the competitive product strategy development, semiconductor product life cycle, SoC architecture, manufacturing, and assembly into end consumer products. By understanding these insights, product managers can plan and manage the semiconductor products effectively through implementing successful long term product roadmaps with objective targets and performance management to meet those targets throughout the semiconductor life cycle.

The next chapter discusses performance management.

CHAPTER 8

Performance Management

If you can't measure it, you can't improve it.

—Lord Kelvin

If you can't measure it, you can't manage it.

—Peter Drucker

Usain Bolt was the fastest person on the earth as he finished a 100-meter run in 9.58 seconds in 2009, and the record still holds until today.[1] The time Usain Bolt took to finish a 100-meter run was lower than other competition participants, confirming him as the fastest man on earth. Measuring the participants' time to finish a 100-meter run is a *performance measurement.* A 100-meter run represents the category of compete and time represents the unit of measure to indicate the measure of competitiveness. Similarly, every competition has a set of rules and categories for the comparison and units of measure.

---

[1] As of 2024

CHAPTER 8   PERFORMANCE MANAGEMENT

How did he become the fastest person on earth? Usain Bolt broke the 9.77^2 seconds record set by Asafa Powell in the 100-meter run in 2006 and set a record of 9.69 seconds to finish the 100-meter run in 2008. He then set an all-time new record of 9.58 seconds in 2009, beating his 2008 record. The process of measuring and improving performance continuously is known as *performance management.* Usain Bolt worked hard to beat the 9.77 seconds to set another winning record. He then continuously improved to beat his own record. Performance management helps set the KPI targets to be competitive and manage performance relative to the company's prior products and external competitors by continuous improvements in performance, as shown in the Figure 8-1. This chapter discusses the performance management strategies and executing performance management across the semiconductor product development life cycle.

---

[2] Source https://en.wikipedia.org/wiki/2007_World_Championships_in_Athletics_%E2%80%93_Men%27s_100_metres

CHAPTER 8   PERFORMANCE MANAGEMENT

Figure 8-1. *Performance management and measurement*

In the semiconductor industry, performance management needs to be implemented strategically, given the broader scope of the semiconductor products in the industry. For example, Apple develops tablets, laptops, and desktops using the same or scaled M series SoCs. As semiconductor hardware is the building block of the technology industry with numerous possibilities, product managers should take a strategic approach to performance management to deliver tailored customer-centric products and stay ahead of the competition. This systematic and strategic performance management approach ensures that product managers expand their reach into various semiconductor product segments by carefully scaling, controlling, and managing the factors influencing performance.

CHAPTER 8   PERFORMANCE MANAGEMENT

Product Performance Management Strategy

Design is not just what it looks like and feels like. Design is how it works.

—Steve Jobs

Semiconductor products are positioned with differentiated product capabilities serving various customer needs. Their market positioning depends on the extent of their capabilities and the value they deliver to the various user segments. For example, a casual PC user laptop is manufactured using a 15/28-watt SoC to serve the needs of a typical PC user. On the other hand, enthusiast gamer PCs are manufactured using a 45-watt or higher SoC to meet the gaming compute requirements. Product managers can scale the capabilities of the SoC to meet the different computing needs and serve most user segments for higher revenue and market share. To effectively control and scale these SoC capabilities, product managers should implement a strategic product performance management approach that systematically monitors, measures, and optimizes the semiconductor product's performance to ensure it aligns with the market requirements.

The product performance management strategy should integrate various aspects of product management, performance analytics, and strategic planning to ensure that semiconductor products meet their performance, quality, and reliability targets. The performance management strategy also helps product managers to clearly differentiate and manage the product's capabilities tailored to the user segment needs, such as gamers casual users in the PC industry. Additionally, this approach helps ecosystem partners like ISVs to deliver tailored solutions to reach various users according to their needs. For example, Adobe Premiere has Rush and Pro application versions to support different user needs in the content creation space. Given the complexity and fast-paced nature of the semiconductor industry, a robust performance management strategy is crucial for maintaining competitiveness and driving innovation.

CHAPTER 8   PERFORMANCE MANAGEMENT

Implementing a Product Performance Management Strategy

Implementing a product performance strategy involves several key steps to ensure that products meet or exceed expectations in terms of quality, reliability, and performance. This approach is particularly critical in the semiconductors industry, where the complexity and precision of products require meticulous planning and execution.

Consider a stock exchange server implementation, the critical requirement to implement a server setup is its time sensitivity. The server should enable real-time stock information to be shared with the users with minimum delay. The hardware setup into these servers must be implemented to deliver higher data processing speeds.

Another example is a database management system, the critical requirement for successful implementation of database management is its longevity and reliability to hold the data accurately for a longer period with considerably decent data processing and retrieval speeds. The setup might slightly use slow performing semiconductor products but demands a highly reliable and enduring compute and memory management. These are some generic examples of implementing semiconductor product performance management strategies tailored to the user segments.

The performance management strategy aims to clearly define the performance characteristics of the semiconductor devices needed to meet or exceed the users' expectations while providing competitive performance. It also helps product managers define the products' clear short term and long-term performance capabilities as a framework to deliver continuous product improvements. The framework ensures each product revision enhances the user experience with innovation and pushes the boundaries of technology using a strategic performance management approach. The strategy can be implemented at the semiconductor product on the SoC level or the device level.

Let's discuss this on the system-on-chip—or SoC—level.

CHAPTER 8   PERFORMANCE MANAGEMENT

SoC-Level Performance Management Strategy

Companies like Intel, AMD, and Qualcomm design IPs such as CPU and GPU and integrate the IPs to form SoCs to serve mobile, PC, IoT, networking, server, automation, and other categories. Within these categories, for example, in the PC category, user segments are further divided into two types: consumer and commercial PC user segments. Within those two user segments, various product SKUs are differentiated by the computer and other system-level needs of the users like gaming, productivity, and content creation in various form factors like tablets, laptops, and desktops. Therefore, typical semiconductor IP and SoC design must be implemented to offer scalability and flexibility to serve as many SoC categories as possible to capture the maximum value in the semiconductor market. The broader SoC performance management is implemented with scalable performance, power, and area (PPA) characteristics to suit various customer segments.

The scalability mainly depends on the flexibility to control the SoC's PPA. Achieving an optimal balance among these three factors is essential to gain a competitive advantage and deliver efficient SoC performance. The performance of the SoC is determined by the frequency and area by scaling IP core count integration into the SoC. At the same time, the architecture of the individual IPs remains the same across the categories. Additionally, frequency is also dependent on the power directly responsible for the heat generated by the SoC. The heat generated must be managed using cooling systems as the thermal design power (TDP) increases in the SoC categories. For example, a 15W TDP might not necessarily need a cooling system, while 28W, 45W, and higher TDP SoCs need a cooling system to avoid thermal throttling, resulting in unwanted performance characteristics. Therefore, core count (area), performance (frequency, voltage), and TDP are the key scaling factors in the performance management of the SoC.

CHAPTER 8 PERFORMANCE MANAGEMENT

As shown Table 8-1, leading semiconductor SoC design companies like Intel and AMD differentiate the SoC scaling performance, power, and area. The scalability of the SoC is a PPA function using dynamic voltage and frequency scaling (DVFS) and core count scaling as main parameters. Therefore, the performance management strategy of the SoC to serve most product categories is possible by scalable and managing its performance, power, and area to meet the customer requirements and deliver efficiency, reliability, and longevity of the semiconductor products.

Table 8-1. *Examples of SoC Scalability to Serve Various User Segments*

SoC Examples	CPU Core Count	Graphics Core Count	Default TDP
AMD Ryzen™ 9 PRO 8945HS	8	12	45W
AMD Ryzen™ 7 PRO 8840U	8	12	28W
AMD Ryzen™ 7 PRO 8845HS	8	12	45W
Intel® Core™ Ultra 7 165U	12	4	15W
Intel® Core™ Ultra 7 165H	16	8	28W

Let's examine the implementation of PPA analysis for performance scaling using an example. Consider the two SoC examples shown in Figure 8-2. Example 1 has each core IP of CPU, GPU, and NU scaled six times to implement a 6-core CPU, GPU, and NPU. Each core is set to an operating frequency of 1 GHz to deliver certain SoC performance. To deliver the same SoC performance, another possibility is to cut the number of cores to half and double the frequency of the cores, as shown in example 2. Example 1 has more area, comparatively less power, and thermal density than example 2. The area of the SoC in example 2 is half, and the frequency is scaled to 2x using voltage scaling. Although example 2 seems to be a better implementation, there are higher power and thermal density

CHAPTER 8   PERFORMANCE MANAGEMENT

product managers must deal with. Therefore, PPA[3] analysis ensures that the final SoC product meets the specifications for power consumption, performance, and chip area derived from the product roadmap, which is crucial for the device's efficiency, cost, and overall functionality.

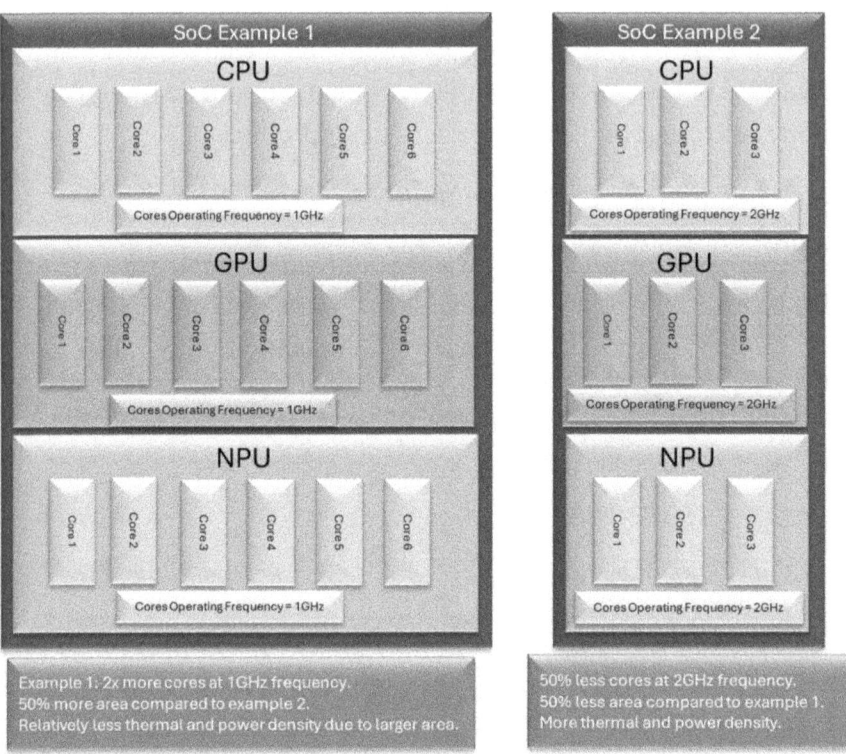

Figure 8-2.* SoC PPA scaling example*

By this stage, product managers can scale the PPA of the SoC using the dependent parameters to deliver SoCs to as many user segments as possible. Now, there is a mechanism to take a tailored approach to product performance management in terms of different SoC offerings. But what

---

[3] https://semiengineering.com/knowledge_centers/eda-design/definitions/ppa/

performance targets do these SoCs require to be competitive, and what is the framework for continuous improvements? To get the performance targets, the product manager should take a competitive intelligence-based product roadmap approach discussed in the next chapter.

While the targets are acquired from competitive intelligence and product roadmap, another key aspect of performance management strategy is to outline a framework for continuous performance management of the SoC. The performance management framework can be defined by dividing the SoC performance into basic, differentiating, and augmented performance areas[4]. This feature categorization is possible with market research and knowledge of the innovations in the technology industry. Product managers must develop a deep comprehension of the real-time technological advancements in the industry, which can influence the performance of the SoC. For example, consider a SoC with basic performance characteristics executed by CPU and GPU functionalities like at least meeting the competitor's performance, supporting USB, camera, and others. Supporting differentiating characteristics like the SoC delivers x% higher performance, CPU and GPU delivers y% higher performance, and z% higher performance per watt than any available competitors and prior-generation SoC in the market. It also supports a few augmented characteristics like hardware ray tracing, optimized shader pipelines for high-quality image resolution, and others, as shown in Table 8-2.

---

[4]https://www.researchgate.net/profile/Muhammad-Tanveer-27/publication/ 267798158_Marketing_Mix_Not_Branding/links/59c8f2db458515548f3d9b3e/ Marketing-Mix-Not-Branding.pdf

CHAPTER 8   PERFORMANCE MANAGEMENT

This performance characterization framework of SoC into basic, differentiated, and augmented helps drive continuous improvements to the SoC, driving generational advances and innovations, as shown in the Figure 8-3. The best part of implementing this framework is that it feeds into the market positioning of the SoC with clear competitive differentiation in the marketplace, Figure 8-4 shows an example of the Apple's SoC-level performance positioning in the market. Product managers can follow this progressive product performance framework to drive the long-term vision of the semiconductor products. The industry started microcontroller design with bit-by-bit arithmetic calculations, and today, there are 64-bit CPUs running trillions of operations per sec. This progression is possible through the continuous implementation of a progressive performance management strategy by the product managers with vision, innovation, and generational performance improvements.

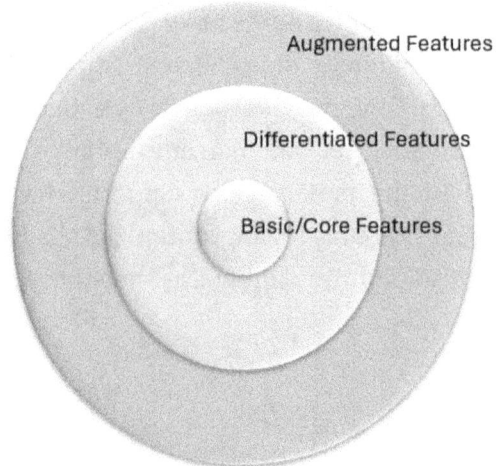

Figure 8-3. *An example of product feature categories*

CHAPTER 8   PERFORMANCE MANAGEMENT

Figure 8-4. An example of Apple's SoC-level performance positioning in the market

Table 8-2. Example of the SoC Performance Management Framework

Types of performance characteristics	Description
Basic Performance Characteristics	With basic performance characteristics executed by CPU and GPU functionalities like at least meeting the competitor's performance, supporting USB, camera, and others
Differentiating Performance Characteristics	The SoC delivers x% higher performance, CPU and GPU deliver y% higher performance, z% higher performance per watt than any available competitors and prior-generation SoC in the market
Augmented Performance Characteristics	SoC supports advanced characteristics, for example, hardware ray tracking, hardware guided scheduling, optimized shader pipelines for high-quality image resolution, and others

CHAPTER 8   PERFORMANCE MANAGEMENT

System-Level Performance Management Strategy

System-level performance management involves optimizing the entire system's performance, including hardware components (like SoCs, memory, and I/O devices) and software components (like operating systems, firmware, and applications). This strategy ensures that all parts of the system work together efficiently to meet competitive performance goals while maintaining power efficiency, reliability, and scalability.

Consider an example of a content creator user segment within the consumer PC category. The top few applications used by content creators are Adobe, DaVinci Resolve, Black Magic, and Final Cut Pro the features in these applications are developed by the ISVs (independent software vendors) in collaboration with hardware design product managers. These software vendors aim to help content creators with tools to create content like movies and videos. The basic features are simple editing capabilities like merging a set of videos, while the differentiating features could be changing the background of the entire video by a simple step and augmented features could be voice assistance. These factors help develop and improve the system's economic value in the market for the entire system. The system-level performance management demands a collaborative effort of semiconductor product managers, other ecosystem partners, and ISVs to bring valuable features and user experiences at the system-level.

Therefore, semiconductor product managers should have a feature co-design relationship with application developers and other ecosystem partners. Hence, the new semiconductor device has more hardware capabilities and enhanced and augmented user application capabilities across various ISVs to be competitive in the end-user market segments. Like the SoC performance management framework, system-level performance management should also implement a system-level performance management framework for continuous improvements and market leadership of the system. The collaborative features should be categorized as core,

CHAPTER 8 PERFORMANCE MANAGEMENT

differentiating, and augmented across various use cases like productivity, content creation, and gaming for effective performance management of the PC, as shown in the Table 8-3.

Table 8-3. Example of Feature Categories

Types of features	Description
Core/Basic features	Basic features a product should be able to deliver. Example: calculator, camera, Notepads, supporting basic video editing capabilities like merging a set of videos on a PC software
Differentiating features	Features that provide faster and easy implementation of existing features Example: Macs can isolate a subject from its background throughout a 4K video using Final Cut Pro with just a tap
Augmented Features	Disruptive and unique capabilities to improve the user experience of the product. Example: Background changing flexibility in the notepad

The division of product features into these three categories ensures the product has the necessary characteristics to succeed in the highly competitive market across various use cases. Therefore, system-level performance management is a comprehensive approach that involves optimizing the interaction and efficiency of all system components into basic differentiated and augmented features for clearly defining the system's value proposition. By implementing this framework of system-level performance management, product managers can ensure that the system meets competitive standards while maintaining power efficiency, scalability, and reliability. Additionally, the system differentiation and augmented features are the key contributors to the system demand generation in the market, increasing the brand value for long-term success, Apple system level performance positioning as shown in the Figure 8-5.

CHAPTER 8 PERFORMANCE MANAGEMENT

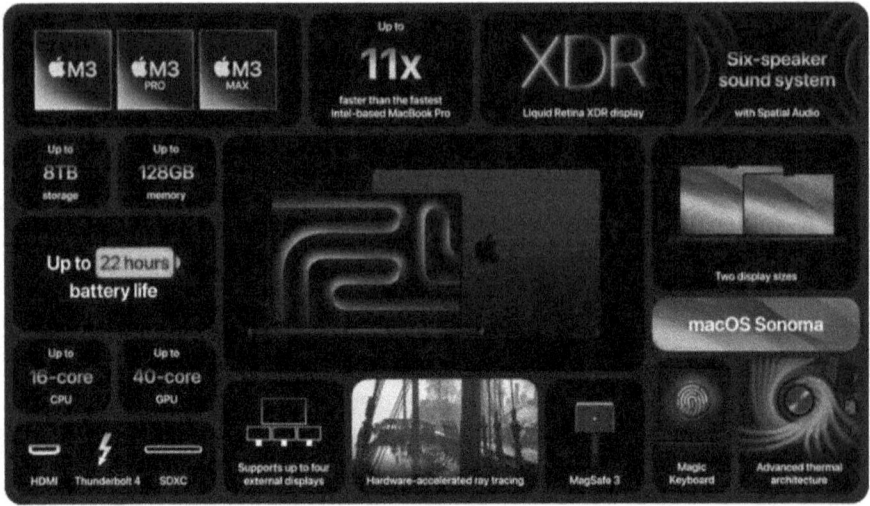

Figure 8-5. *An example of Apple MacBook Pro system-level performance positioning in the market with M3 series SoCs*

The ideal approach to performance management is combining the SoC and system-level performance management frameworks to efficiently manage the end-to-end performance of semiconductor products. Continuous monitoring and optimization using a unified framework help product managers to quickly adapt to changing workloads and user requirements, ensuring sustained system performance over time.

An example of how a unified semiconductor performance management framework can be implemented is shown in Figure 8-6. Consider SoC at its generation 1 aimed at a user segment, say content creation with certain performance on applications like Premiere Pro to deliver at IP level (CPU/GPU/NPU/media, etc.). It can deliver x% higher performance on an existing application compared to the available competition or deliver x% more performance at the same power, add a new feature to the applications to increase capabilities of content creators like one tap background and subject isolation in a video. The second generation can improve existing feature performance and implement a

CHAPTER 8 PERFORMANCE MANAGEMENT

new disruption feature through innovation, followed by generation 3, simplifying the disruption at a higher performance, and these SoCs deliver leading performance over the available competitors, followed by innovation and simplifying existing methods to improve efficiency and performance. The example implements SoC and a system-level performance management framework.

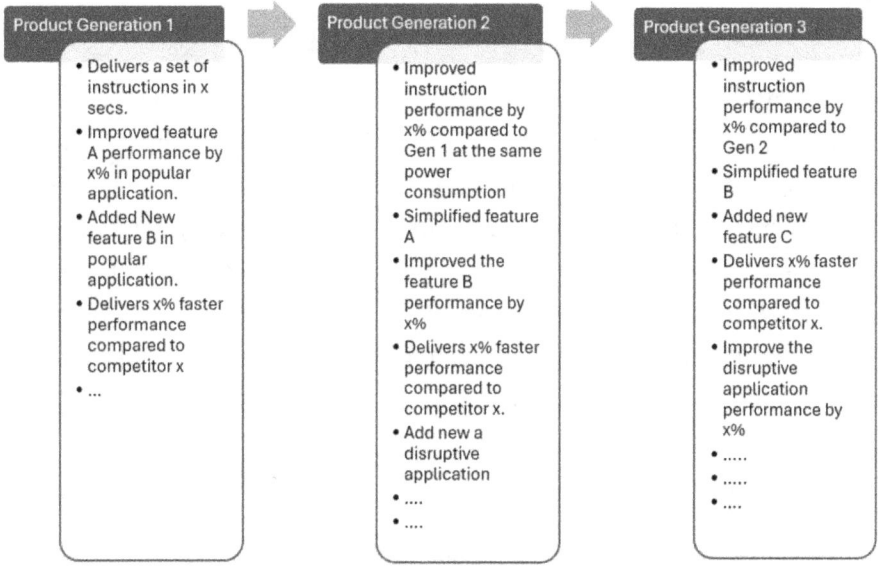

Figure 8-6. Progressive product roadmap performance strategy from IP to end product level

The product performance management strategy framework helps deliver meaningful performance to the users and enhances the capabilities of the target user segment generation over generation. The same approach can be followed in different SoC segments like commercial, data center, mobile, and PC. The idea is to keep improving, innovating, and moving forward, keeping competition as one critical pillar to compare your product's performance in a highly competitive environment like PC.

CHAPTER 8   PERFORMANCE MANAGEMENT

The product performance management strategy is implemented using a performance management and measurement process which helps product managers to take a systematic approach to control and manage the performance of the semiconductor products across the product life cycle. Let's discuss the performance management.

Product Performance Management

Performance management helps product managers execute the performance management strategy effectively by managing and monitoring the performance across different stages of product development, as shown in the Figure 8-7. It helps to ensure the product execution is progressing as planned across different stages and the product is delivered with a competitive advantage in the market. Performance management also helps infuse product improvements and set new targets for the products in the future roadmap based on continuous learning along the way.

Figure 8-7.   Significance of performance management

The key aspect of performance management is performance measurement, which helps product managers quantify measurements like performance, power, security, reliability, and others with a systematic methodology to collect performance data with metric selection units of measure selection so it is reproducible for manageability. Therefore, Performance management and performance measurement complement each other to help product managers effectively manage performance. Performance management focuses on continuously improving product KPIs relative to competition and its own. On the other hand, performance measurement focuses on systematically collecting, analyzing, and reporting data to assess the effectiveness and efficiency of activities and outcomes. Together, they provide a comprehensive approach to helping product managers achieve and maintain high performance of the products for sustained long-term success.

Specific to semiconductors with complex product life cycles, performance management helps product managers set competitive KPI targets during the planning phase, ensuring the SoC design and manufacturing meet those planned KPI targets. Optimize design for scalability and flexibility to deliver a broader range of semiconductor products like PC SoC, mobile SoC, and data center hardware. Ensure the reliability and longevity of semiconductors through stress testing and monitoring for corner cases. It helps product managers ensure regulatory and standard compliance is met and implemented with a customer value-differentiated go-to-market strategy. As a result of implementing performance management across these phases, product managers can identify timely risks to develop a mitigation plan using either firmware or software updates. It also feeds this learning into a continuous product improvement roadmap. Performance management can only be effective with reproducible, systematically defined performance measurement methods to help product managers make data-driven decisions.

CHAPTER 8   PERFORMANCE MANAGEMENT

Stages in Performance Management

The performance, power, and other KPIs can be improved or managed if measured systematically and ensure different user segments' needs are met. The tradeoffs associated with it are managed effectively. Managing or improving performance and power is dependent on performance measurements. Measuring performance and power over the actual customer's use case metrics is key to ensuring the product is valued by the customers. Therefore, as shown in Figure 8-8, performance management can be divided into IP and SoC level pre-silicon and post-silicon, device and system-level, and customer-facing features and use cases where both software and hardware performance can be managed in a customer-centric approach. It is important for product managers to uplevel and map the pre-silicon and post-silicon performance management metrics and KPIs to the device-level features. These device-level features help product managers quantify and continuously improve the SoC to deliver more or enhanced features to the customers through architecture improvements. The uplevel mapping also helps discover a clear product value proposition, which is useful in implementing a go-to-market strategy. Due to the complex design, development, and manufacturing phases, the performance measurement and management of semiconductor products across their life cycle is not a straightforward path. Product managers should implement a systematic approach to measure and manage performance in the pre-silicon and post-silicon phases of the semiconductor products to effectively manage risk and product progress in the competitive market dynamics. The performance management needs to be implemented as pre- and post-silicon performance measurement phases to have more control over the semiconductor product life cycle. The reason for treating pre- and post-silicon performance measurement phases differently is due to the distinct methods employed in the performance measurements in both phases. In the design phase, the performance measurement is done using EDA tools in a complete software environment. On the other hand,

CHAPTER 8   PERFORMANCE MANAGEMENT

post-silicon performance measurement is implemented in labs with actual SoC connected with various performance monitoring setups and integrated environments, as shown in the Figure 8-9. The skills and technologies utilized in both phases of performance management demand a separate and systematic approach to semiconductor performance measurement and management.

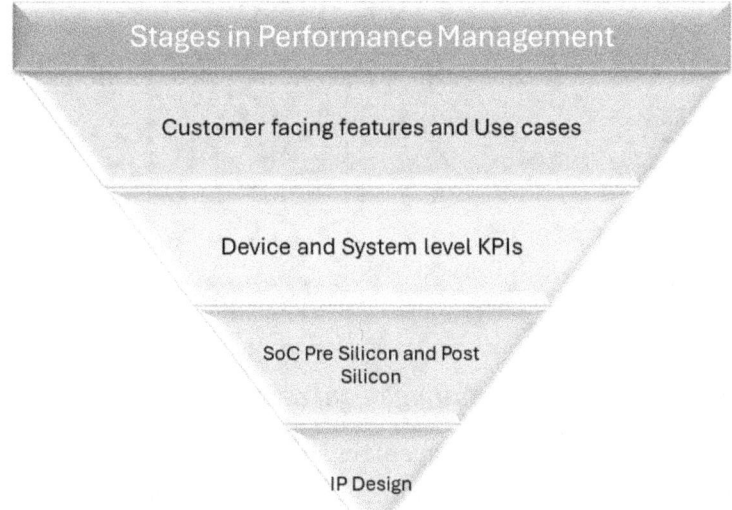

Figure 8-8. *Stages in performance management*

CHAPTER 8 PERFORMANCE MANAGEMENT

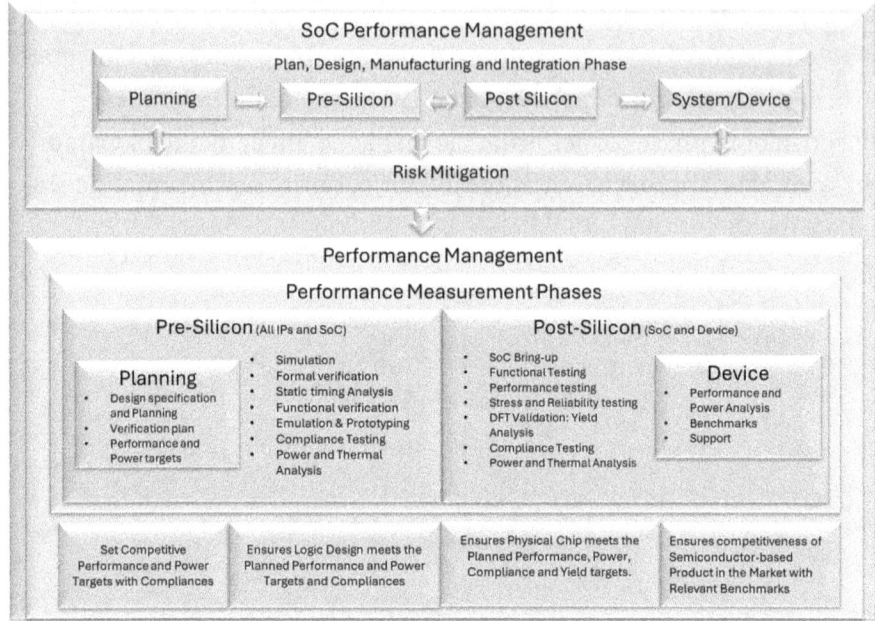

Figure 8-9. Performance management and measurement steps

From the performance management strategy framework and competitive product roadmap, product managers can define the product requirements documents from which silicon design specifications are drafted for IPs and integrated SoC. These design specifications are implemented and developed in pre-silicon phases. The performance is measured and managed using systematic and reproducible methods to implement a robust design, as shown in the Figure 8-10. The pre-silicon performance management is followed by post-silicon performance management. The actual semiconductor products are measured for performance characteristics to manage risk and ensure the semiconductor is functionally competitive as planned. After the post-silicon performance measurements are complete, to ensure the reliability, performance, power, and functionality of the semiconductor product, the next stage is to implement a device-level performance measurement with benchmarks to implement a performance-based go-to-market strategy and support the semiconductor products until they reach end of life (EOL).

CHAPTER 8   PERFORMANCE MANAGEMENT

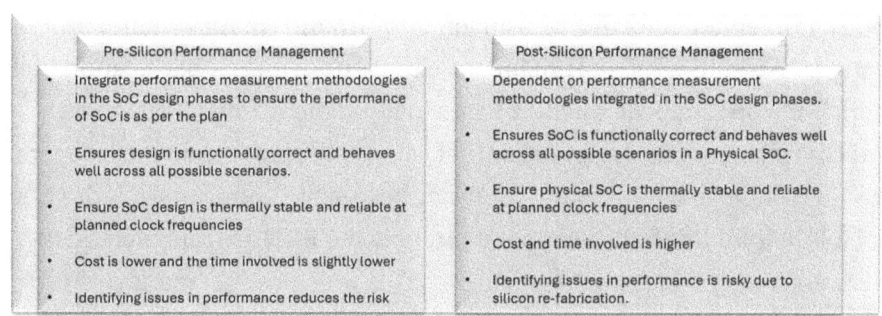

Figure 8-10. Significance of pre-silicon and post-silicon performance management

The previous chapters defined the various factors and KPIs contributing to the PC SoC competitiveness associated with individual component IP and SoC architecture, manufacturing technology and power efficiency. The next phase is to measure these competitive performance characteristics so the product managers can make data-driven decisions across the product design, development, and manufacturing phases to appropriately define product positioning and a risk mitigation plan if needed. Let's discuss end-to-end semiconductor performance management.

Pre-Silicon and Post-Silicon Performance Measurements

A semiconductor product planned with specific design specifications and architecture variables shall deliver certain characteristics across pre-silicon phases to meet the KPI targets. For example, CPU IPs' timing and logic functional characteristics are measured to ensure they meet the clock speed KPI targets with stability in pre-silicon performance management. This characteristic measurement analysis, with the help of hardware, firmware, software design, and verification engineers help product managers in effective product management.

CHAPTER 8   PERFORMANCE MANAGEMENT

To implement effective pre-silicon performance management, product managers, with the help of engineers, should draft a clear verification plan for pre-silicon and post-silicon phases to meet the various KPI targets and compliance. This is not to say that semiconductor product managers should technically know simulation synthesis and timing analysis data. But it is helpful for them to understand how the KPIs are represented in the pre-silicon phases and post-silicon. This way, product managers can better manage a product across complex and highly technical phases. This also helps product managers to have meaningful conversations with engineers for effective risk management when needed. If any performance impact risks are identified during these phases, an engineering change order or change requests can be discussed with technical subject matter experts to make appropriate amends to the design. The aments should be thoroughly analyzed to mitigate the associated performance risks without any other negative impacts. Since product managers are CEOs of the product, it would be wise to know the risk associated with technical details at the impact level at the least so decisions can be taken timely and appropriately. Table 8-4 gives a high-level overview of some of the critical pre-silicon and silicon performance management methods that help product managers for effective performance management.

Table 8-4. *Pre-Silicon and Post-Silicon Performance Measurement Methods*

Measurement types	Description
Simulation measurements	Engineers use software simulators to verify if the logic design behaves as per the design specification document derived from the product requirements document. **Simulation Tools**: Synopsys VCS, Cadence Incisive, Mentor Graphics ModelSim

(continued)

Table 8-4. (*continued*)

Measurement types	Description
Formal verification measurements	Another method for engineers to verify the logic design is using mathematical methods to prove the correctness of the design. This method of verification tests the designs for all mathematically possible scenarios. **Equivalence Checking**: Compare the simulated design with the synthesized transistor gate-level design to ensure they are functionally equivalent. **Property Checking**: Use formal methods to verify whether certain properties hold true for the design, such as the following. Assertion properties: for example, enable read-only if the buffer is full. Safety properties include no deadlocks or unwanted signal behavior in logic. **Formal Verification Tools**: Cadence JasperGold, Synopsys Formality, Mentor Graphics Questa Formal
Static timing analysis (STA) measurements	Engineers simulate the design at the clock-cycle level to ensure correct timing and sequencing. These measurements help assess the signal propagation delays and whether the design is functioning correctly at the planned clock speed. STA Tools: Synopsys PrimeTime, Cadence Tempus, Mentor Graphics TimeQuest

(*continued*)

Table 8-4. (*continued*)

Measurement types	Description
Emulation and prototype measurements	Engineers use hardware emulators to run the design near-real-time, allowing for more extensive and complex testing scenarios; for example, mapping the design onto an FPGA to validate its functionality and performance in a hardware-like environment for end-to-end validation, or using virtual platforms to create virtual models of the hardware and system to simulate the design in a software environment. **Emulation Platforms**: Cadence Palladium, Synopsys ZeBu, Mentor Graphics Veloce **FPGA Prototyping Tools**: Xilinx Vivado, Intel Quartus, Synopsys ProtoCompiler **Virtual Prototyping Tools**: Synopsys Virtualize, Cadence Virtual System Platform
Power and thermal Analysis measurements	**Power Estimation:** Engineers use simulation and analytical tools to estimate the design's power consumption under different operating conditions. **Thermal Analysis:** Engineers assess the thermal behavior of the design to ensure it operates within safe temperature ranges.
Bring up measurements	Engineers implement physical testing involving Power consumption and functionality of the early chip samples.

(*continued*)

CHAPTER 8   PERFORMANCE MANAGEMENT

Table 8-4. (*continued*)

Measurement types	Description
Functional testing measurements	Ensure the chip functions correctly within the final product, like SoC, after integrating all the component-level IPs. **Integration Testing:** Integrate the chip into the system (e.g., a smartphone or computer) and test its interactions with other components. **End-to-End Testing:** Perform tests that simulate real-world usage scenarios to ensure the system meets overall functional and performance requirements
Performance testing measurements	Engineers perform tests to ensure the chip delivers stable performance across different use cases.
Stress and reliability testing measurements	Engineers conduct stress tests to ensure the chip's reliability over its expected lifetime. This includes burn-in, thermal cycling, and electrostatic discharge (ESD) testing.

(*continued*)

Table 8-4. (*continued*)

Measurement types	Description
Yield analysis measurements	Engineering assessment to analyze and improve the manufacturing yield. **Process Optimization:** Adjust the manufacturing process to reduce the occurrence of defects and improve yield. **Defect Analysis:** Identify and classify defects found during testing using design for testability (DFT) and design for debuggability (DFD) measurements like built-in self-tests, joint test action group (JTAG) scans, scan chains, test pointers utilized in **Wafer Testing (Wafer Sort):** Test the silicon wafers before dicing them into individual chips. This involves probing each die to check for basic functionality and performance. **Die Testing:** Perform tests on individual dies after they are separated from the wafer but before they are packaged. **Package Testing:** Test the packaged chips to ensure they meet all functional and performance requirements.

Most of these measurements are possible due to continuous innovation and improved capabilities provided by electronic design automation (EDA) and other tools. The one key thing product managers must ensure for effective performance management is implementing the DFT and DFD approach.

DFT and DFD

Before getting into the details, why do product managers have to care about these performance measurement methods?

Let's take an example of the modern car driving experience: drivers do not always pay attention to when the car needs to be serviced or when it is low on tire pressure. The system in the car self-identifies the issues, like when the engine needs servicing or tires need air, using visual identifiers of the issues for the drivers to attend to. Otherwise, drivers would most likely know the car is low on air until the air is too low to drive or can get the engine serviced only when the car breaks down, which is costly and strenuous to the car driver. Therefore, the built-in system's capabilities to identify these issues in time and let the owner know makes modern car ownership a hassle-free user experience. This build-in system analysis is possible by ensuring the car system is designed with testable factors embedded into the system design to implement timely automatic checkers like tire pressure and engine health.

DFT (design for testability) is a crucial methodology in semiconductor design and development in modern semiconductor devices. It aims to make testing and diagnosing integrated circuits, individual IPs, and SoCs easier in post-silicon performance management. The primary goal of DFT is to ensure that the design includes features that facilitate efficient and effective testing during the manufacturing process and throughout the product's life cycle. While DFT is for testability, the DFD (design for debuggability) is implemented for debugging features that help identify and isolate faults during the development and post-silicon stages. DFD focuses on providing visibility into the internal operations of the SoC design, like trace buffers and access points, to easily diagnose and fix issues in post-silicon performance management.

DFT and DFD help to identify and fix the issues before the product release and help maintain the quality, reliability, and longevity of the SoC's continued success. Some DFT and DFD methods can be integrated to implement intelligent diagnostics and issue fixing. This area is a continuously improving segment of the electronic industry to aid efficient electronics design and development with innovations and intelligent features. Product managers must

CHAPTER 8   PERFORMANCE MANAGEMENT

use the latest DFT and DFD technologies and methodologies for implementing a robust design for efficient performance management from design to EOL of the SoCs, as shown in the Table 8-5 and Table 8-6.

Table 8-5. *Examples of Few DFT Methods for Performance Management*

DFT Techniques	Description
Scan design	Integrating scan chains into the design allows for the sequential scanning of test patterns into the flip-flops and capturing the test responses.
	Implementing the boundary scan using the JTAG standard provides a means to test the interconnections and the functionality of the SoC.
Built-in self-test (BIST)	Incorporating self-testing mechanisms within the chip to test the logic circuits automatically
	Embedding test circuits within memory blocks to verify memory functionality and identify faults
Test point insertion	Adding control points to stimulate specific parts of the circuit during testing
	Adding observation points to monitor specific signals and enhance test coverage
Fault simulation	Using fault models such as stuck-at, transition, and bridging faults to simulate potential defects and verify the effectiveness of test patterns
	Generating test patterns that target specific fault models to ensure comprehensive fault coverage

Table 8-6. Examples of DFD Techniques in Performance Management

DFD Techniques	Description
Debug ports	Real-time debugging and diagnosis using dedicated ports on SoC
Debug registers	Special registers that provide diagnostic information
Trace buffers	Capture and store trace data for debugging and behavioral analysis
On-chip instruments	Embedding instruments like performance counters and logic analyzers for debugging and monitoring
Triggering Mechanisms	To capture specific events or conditions for debugging
Diagnostic software	Software tools that interact with the SoC to provide a comprehensive debugging environment

The performance measurement techniques discussed are categorized as pre-silicon and post-silicon. Pre-silicon measurements are done using EDA tools, which gives more control over performance management as it is easy to fix the design within the EDA tools. Once the performance management reaches the physical product stage, the performance is measured on the manufactured SoC. The control is limited to the debugging and testing capabilities of the SoC and is highly risky as it is associated with time and cost. Therefore, product managers should ensure a high focus on design performance measurement in the pre-silicon stage with robust verification and validation plans with the help of engineers. Also, ensure implementation of DFT and DFD techniques to ensure robust post-silicon performance management with appropriate risk management methods.

CHAPTER 8   PERFORMANCE MANAGEMENT

Once the semiconductor is out of the design and development phases in the pre- and post-silicon phases, the SoC gets integrated into a full system like a PC, mobile, or data center setup to provide its full performance benefit. Although the system or device-level performance management is still post-silicon, it is more complex as the system level adds other dependency factors to the performance management. Therefore, product managers should approach device- or system-level performance management differently. Let's discuss the SoC system device-level performance management.

SoC System Performance Measurements

The SoC system performance measurements are critical to ensure that the SoC meets the required specifications and operates efficiently under different conditions as per the performance management strategic framework discussed earlier. Performance measurements in this stage provide insights into various aspects of the SoC's functional operation, such as speed, power consumption, thermal behavior, and overall efficiency. These insights are critical for implementing performance management at the SoC level and optimizing the performance relative to other SoCs. In the product development life cycle, these measurements are the source of final performance optimizations at the SoC system level to deliver a competitive system in the market.

The performance measurements at the SoC system determine the quality of the semiconductor in terms of performance efficiency, reliability, and security. These measurements help define the go-to-market plans and launch of the SoC systems, comparing the measurements to competition and prior-generation SoC systems.

CHAPTER 8   PERFORMANCE MANAGEMENT

In the pre-silicon and post-silicon performance measurements, the product managers deal with indirect performance measurements like simulation timing, signal propagation, logic functionality, and BIST, which contribute to the system-level performance but do not exactly quantify the value it means to the SoC system users. The performance measurements at the SoC level help product managers quantify the performance of the SoC system at the user experience level. Therefore, these measurements give product managers a view into the SoC system market positioning and allow managing the SoC performance to deliver competitive performance. After the performance optimizations are completed and rigorously tested to ensure safety, security, reliability, and longevity, the SoC system is ready to be launched by the product managers with a go-to-market strategy by using easy performance quantifiers for the customers to capture its value. The launch phase is followed by supporting the product, but the measurement methodology used at this phase would be similar until the SoC system reaches its EOL, as shown in the Figure 8-11. Therefore, this measurement phase is critical to the success of the product life cycle. Let's examine the performance measurement methodology at the SoC system level for efficient performance optimization by the product managers.

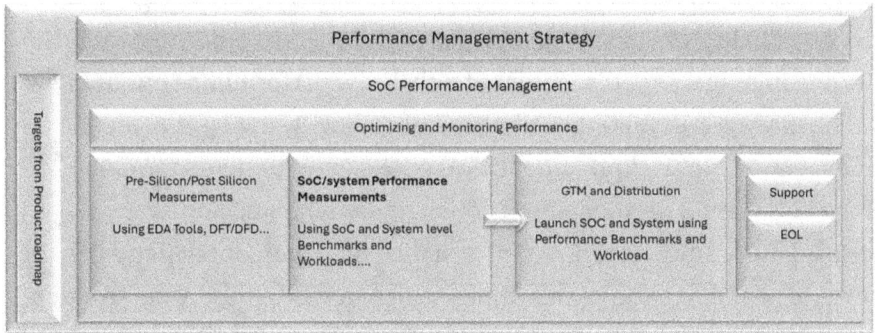

Figure 8-11. *SoC system performance measurement hierarchy*

CHAPTER 8   PERFORMANCE MANAGEMENT

The SoC system-level performance measurements methodology must be derived from the performance management strategy framework to ensure it is progressive and quantifies the SoC's core, differentiating, and augmented features. For example, since a PC is a generic computing device, the SoC system-level performance should be measured for typical PC application features like web browsing, gaming, productivity, and content creation. Then, these features and characteristics must be transformed into metrics that can be measured and reproduced under similar conditions. Therefore, a structured and comprehensive methodology to accurately reproduce the SoC system performance measurements is essential for ensuring that the final product meets its design goals and operates efficiently in real-world scenarios.

The first stage in performance measurements at the SoC system level is to identify the key performance contributors and indicators from IP to the SoC level and learn how these indicators are responsible for the overall SoC system performance. For example, The CPU instructions per cycle (IPC) and clock frequency are responsible for the web browsing experience on a PC or a mobile as the browsing is sensitive to the CPU's clock speed to process the web search. Product managers can optimize the CPU clock frequency based on the flexibility to scale the voltage using the VF curve to deliver a faster experience in the SoC systems. Importantly, product managers should note that only a few performance parameters can be managed at this stage of post-silicon SoC system performance management. Several pre-silicon and post-silicon design parameters of the SoC should be considered constant in managing SoC system performance. Therefore, SoC performance management depends on the strategic product planning roadmap, which decides the key parameters like transistor process technology, and pre-silicon and post-silicon fixed parameters of the SoC design. As a result, product managers can use SoC performance measurements to optimize its performance using voltage, frequency to scale, and software parameters to ensure the SoC targets are met in different customer segments and feed the additional performance learning updates to the future SoC product roadmap.

As discussed in the architecture section, the basic elements of CPU, GPU, and NPU performance like clock speed, IPC, FLOPS, TOPS, throughput of a compute engine, latency of a task or memory, power consumption, TDP are a few metrics to measure the performance of the IPs and SoCs. Performance management can be implemented at the microarchitecture level, enhancing the internal design of CPUs, GPUs, or other IPs, such as improving branch prediction, increasing the width of instruction decode pipelines, and optimizing cache hierarchies for faster data throughput, which can improve the performance of the IP like improved core performance, similar performance consuming less power. Table 8-7 shows the KPIs to measure to improve the performance and power at the IP to SoC level. These KPIs provide measurable and quantifiable SoC parameters to manage the delivery as many SoCs in the market tailored to meet different customer needs. For example casual PC users with a 15W SoC, enthusiast gamers with a 45W SoC, and professional content creators with a 60W SoC and so on with various compute configurations.

Table 8-7. SoC KPIs

SoC KPIs	Description
Clock speed (GHz)	The speed at which the compute unit, like CPU, GPU, and NPU, is running for faster workload performance
Instructions per cycle (IPC)	Enhancing the internal design of CPUs and GPUs, such as increasing the number of cores, improving branch prediction, and optimizing cache hierarchies
Throughput	Leveraging parallel processing capabilities in multi-core and many-core architectures
Latency	Enhancing memory hierarchy for better data routing
Power consumption	Reducing the size of transistors (e.g., from 10nm to 7nm) to fit more transistors on a chip, leading to better performance and efficiency
TDP	Implementing effective cooling systems to prevent thermal throttling
FLOPS or TOPS	Scaling the IP blocks
Compiler or application runtime	Updating drivers and firmware and optimizing software to take full advantage of hardware capabilities
Application feature performance	CPU, GPU, NPU, and SoC-based performance at the application level (e.g., web browsing performance)

The next step is to standardize the performance measurements of these metrics using a fair benchmarking approach to ensure the performance measurements are reproducible accurately by the internal and external stakeholders such as engineering teams, ecosystem partners, technology press and community, and customers when measured on any SoC. The standardization of performance measurements ensures the performance of the SoC is communicated with assurance for anyone to

CHAPTER 8 PERFORMANCE MANAGEMENT

reproduce and evaluate the performance and user experience of the SoC system. The semiconductor product managers do not necessarily have to implement the benchmark development. The technology industry has a set of standard performance benchmarking instructions that continuously increase the standard of benchmarks to verify the performance of the SoC system. These benchmarks are available at the IP level, SoC level, and system level to help users make purchase decisions, and product managers compare the performance of the SoC system with prior generations and competitors. These benchmarks measure performance on an application's existing instructions and available features and help with the market positioning of the semiconductor products. For example, AMD Ryzen PRO 8400[5] compared Intel Core Ultra 7 155H to position itself as a better performing SoC using benchmarks like Geekbench and Procyon 3DMarks.

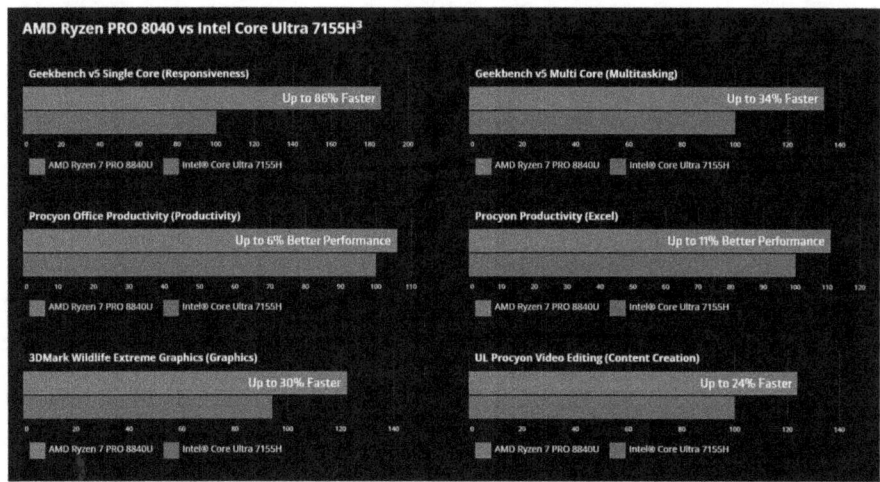

Figure 8-12. An example of benchmarks used in market positioning of SoCs (For reference only, not to compare)

---

[5] Source: https://www.amd.com/en/products/processors/laptop/ryzen-for-business.html as of August 25 2024

CHAPTER 8   PERFORMANCE MANAGEMENT

While basic and differentiating features are evaluated using existing benchmarks. The disruptive and augmented features do not have industry benchmarks ready; the product managers must collaborate with benchmarking institutions for new benchmark development to make it part of the performance measurement standards or implement augmented features in user applications to show the enhanced user experience delivered by the SoC to the users. Let's talk about benchmarks.

Benchmarks

Checking a peck of rice is enough to evaluate if the pot of rice is cooked.

— An ancient Indian proverb

Benchmarks are standardized tests used to evaluate the performance of SoC designs into quantifiable and measurable metrics. They provide a consistent and repeatable way to measure and compare the capabilities of different SoCs as a medium of competition. In highly competitive market environments, benchmarks are critical in defining a systematic and adaptive measurement methodology to evaluate the SoC system's capabilities as a neutral platform to guide the industry to compare different solutions.

Product managers should have clear objectives before selecting the benchmarks to compare to their competition. These objectives should self-identify the available industry benchmarks to best represent the performance of the SoC system. Therefore, before getting started on benchmarks, the product benchmarking strategy should be developed, which involves several key steps to ensure the benchmarks are relevant, accurate, and useful for the intended purpose. For example, semiconductor companies want to compare hardware capabilities like clock speed, IPC, and component TOPS/FLOPS. In contrast, software

CHAPTER 8   PERFORMANCE MANAGEMENT

companies want to compare the application's performance, like rendering speed or memory required for a feature, to other competitive software.

Benchmarking performance evaluation in semiconductor products like PCs can be at individual SoC component levels, overall SoC levels, and the entire system level. It involves running a set of standardized tests on hardware and hardware and software layers to evaluate the performance of the architecture and system. The following are some of the different types of benchmarks used for evaluating the performance metrics and optimizations relative to other SoCs.

- Microbenchmarks test the architectural elements at the SoC and IP levels.

- Synthetics benchmarks are tests designed to simulate a specific type of workload at the IP or SoC levels.

- Real-world benchmarks that use real applications or workloads measure performance at a product, SoC, or IP level.

Other unofficial benchmark workloads are not part of any benchmarks but represent a valid use case scenario of the target user segment. For example, the speed at which an application's code gets compiled while developing an application or how long a user can stream a video using applications like Netflix, YouTube, and other applications on a PC without recharging.

The key role for product managers is to identify the right benchmarks and application usages from a micro, synthetic, real-world benchmark, and user applications categories shown in Table 8-8 in text reference that best represent their SoC capabilities according to the performance management strategy. The next step is to monitor the performance of benchmarking tools and methodologies to ensure they remain relevant and accurate to the fast pace of development and changing features of the applications. The benchmark versions also need to be up to date before

CHAPTER 8   PERFORMANCE MANAGEMENT

they are tested. Generally, benchmark institutions and vendors maintain websites with version notifications, and when a benchmark is launched, there are notifications on the version updates when applicable.

Table 8-8. *Types of Performance Measuring Methodologies*

Types of Benchmarks	Significance	Examples
Microbenchmarks	Focuses on specific aspects of performance metrics	Memory latency, I/O throughput, or cache performance
Synthetic Benchmarks	Simulates a specific type of workload	Examples include 3DMark for GPUs, Geekbench for CPUs, and SPECrate for general CPU performance
Real-World Benchmarks	Uses real applications or workloads to measure performance	For example, rendering a video in Adobe Premiere or running a game like Baldur's gate.
Application usage without an official benchmark representing a customer	Represents a valid use case scenario of the target user	For example, how long a user can stream a video using applications like Netflix, YouTube, and other applications on a PC without having to recharge.

Let's look at the types of benchmarks.

CHAPTER 8 PERFORMANCE MANAGEMENT

Microbenchmarks

Microbenchmarks are essential tools for understanding the performance characteristics of individual hardware components. They provide valuable insights that can guide optimizations and improvements in hardware design and software development. As the name suggests, microbenchmarks are specialized tests that evaluate specific, low-level micro aspects of performance in SoC components like CPU instructions, memory access patterns, I/O operations, and latencies. Paired with profiler tools that help to analyze the behavior of operations, microbenchmarks can provide significant information on areas for performance improvement. These benchmarks are idle for accessing granular performance aspects like the architecture of specific hardware IP or analyzing integrated SoC components during the developmental stage to verify the progress relative to set targets. These benchmarks also come in handy in analyzing discrepancies in hardware behavior as they can report low-level characteristics, as shown in the Table 8-9. They are usually run in a controlled environment to minimize external hardware and software influence, providing clear insights into the performance characteristics of the measured semiconductor component.

Product managers can manage specific performance targets at the SoC subsystem level by modeling external scenarios required to achieve full system performance targets and tracking progress using these microbenchmarks at different stages. This divide and conquer method to achieve full system performance targets gives more control to product managers to build the SoC with predefined IP level targets. SoC is complex hardware integrated from multiple IP components. Microbenchmarks help measure the performance characteristics of the building blocks with precise, low-level information that identifies any issues in time to fix or prepare for risk management if the issues cannot be fixed.

Table 8-9. *Advantages of Microbenchmarks*

Advantages	Description
Focus and	Microbenchmarks target specific hardware features or operations, such as IPC, memory latency, cache performance, or branch prediction efficiency.
Easy to run	They are usually lightweight and run quickly, making it possible to isolate and measure the performance of specific components without significant interference.
Detailed Insights with Precision	Offers detailed and precise measurements for specific hardware components, which can be critical for diagnosing performance issues and help hardware designers and software developers optimize specific parts of the system for best performance and power.

To conclude, microbenchmarks can be run at individual IP component levels of an SoC to access semiconductor IP and an application capability for efficient performance management. Some areas where microbenchmarking comes in handy are accessing CPU, GPU, NPU, media subsystem performance, memory and storage performance, and networking performance. Table 8-9 shows examples of microbenchmark utilization.

CPU Microbenchmarks

The CPU microbenchmarks evaluate the CPU performance at its microarchitecture level to assess its capabilities in efficiently executing general-purpose computing. The generic KPIs to evaluate CPU performance are mentioned in Table 8-10. Product managers can measure the CPU microbenchmarks to manage the performance of the KPIs along with profilers by identifying performance improvement opportunities from its architectural behavior. Many CPU microbenchmarks are available to precisely measure the low-level KPIs in the open source ecosystem.

CHAPTER 8 PERFORMANCE MANAGEMENT

However, it is important to prefer the ones that get the data directly from the registers that store this information rather than proxy tools, which give data with a high margin of error. Therefore, product managers should aim for design/verification teams to have dedicated microbenchmarks and profilers built for their design to track the performance and power accurately. The benchmarks give the performance data, and profilers reveal behavior characteristics to achieve the microbenchmark performance like time spent on a set of instructions. Therefore, both benchmarks and profilers help in efficient performance management. There are many CPU microbenchmarks and profiling tools available from third-party vendors like HWiNFO, LMbench, CoreMark, LINPACK, SPEC CPU, and proprietary performance and power profilers like EMON (Intel) and Instruments (Apple).

Table 8-10. *Examples of CPU Microbenchmarks Performance Metrics*

Types of performance metrics	Description
Instructions Per Cycle (IPC)	Helps to access core performance per clock
CPU Pipeline Throughput	Helps access core instruction and data efficiency
Branch Prediction accuracy and efficiency	
CPU cores frequency ramp up for ST and MT workloads	
Power consumed per single and multi-core	TDP characteristics
CPU core utilization and multi-core behavior	Helps to access the best way to implement workloads
CPU Core L1, L2 and L3 Hit and Miss rates	Helps to access CPU wait time to get the data from caches impacting ST and MT core performance
Memory Bandwidth	Helps to access CPU bandwidth utilization per different types of workloads

CHAPTER 8   PERFORMANCE MANAGEMENT

GPU Microbenchmarks

GPUs GPUs are accelerators for general-purpose parallel[6] instructions. The microbenchmarks for GPU report the performance characteristics of its microarchitecture like shader and tensor cores, and its memory utilization methodology. These benchmarks help product managers manage the GPU performance to achieve maximum utilization and assess its capabilities and limitations. Specifically for accelerators, the hardware capabilities and software programmability are key to optimizing for maximum GPU performance. Product managers should utilize the GPU microbenchmarks and profilers to manage the programmability and hardware capabilities. The programmability reveals information like how a workload is divided into SIMT instructions and handed to hardware to execute and the number of cores a program utilizes.

Table 8-11 shows a few examples of microbenchmarking metrics for GPUs. Similar to CPU microbenchmarks, it is important to prefer the ones that get the data directly from the registers that store the relevant information rather than proxy tools that give data with a high margin of error. Therefore, product managers should aim for design/verification teams to have dedicated microbenchmarks or profilers built for their design to track the performance and power accurately. There are third-party microbenchmarks for GPU like HWiNFO and Rodini and proprietary microbenchmarks and profilers like CUDAMicroBench.

---

[6] Single Instruction Multiple Threads

Table 8-11. Examples of GPU Microbenchmarks Performance Metrics

Types of performance metrics	Description
GPU core utilization	Provides insights on the throughput of the GPU for a given workloade
Kernel launch time	Launches latency measured in GPU time
GEMM FLOPS	Measures the GPU GEMM FLOPS for different float and int data types, with or without Tensor Core
Vertex processing capabilities	Helps programmers to define the structure and geometry of shapes, lines, and curves
Frequency of operation	Offers insights on theoretical limits of GPUs like FLOPs
Frame rate (FPS)	Measures how many frames the GPU can render per second in each
Resolution capabilities	FPS at various resolutions (e.g., 1080p, 1440p, 4K)
Thermal performance	Measures the operating temperature of the GPU
Power consumption	Indicates power used by the GPU, which is important for energy efficiency and thermal management
Memory Bandwidth	Measures the data transfer rate between the GPU memory and the GPU cores
Shader Performance	Evaluates the efficiency of the GPU's shader units

CHAPTER 8   PERFORMANCE MANAGEMENT

NPU Microbenchmarks

NPUs are accelerators for specific parallel instructions called MACs (multiply-accumulate) or MAD (multiply-add) operations. The microbenchmarks for NPU report the performance characteristics of its microarchitecture, like SIMT cores, and its memory utilization methodology for implementing MACs and MAD operations. Like GPU, hardware capabilities and software programmability are key to maximum NPU performance. Therefore, NPU microbenchmarks help product managers analyze the programmability and hardware capabilities for efficient performance management. The benchmarks and profilers reveal the execution of neural networks, transformer models, and diffuser models. Understanding this information helps product managers optimize the models for efficient execution by optimal SIMT cores, memory, and power utilization.

Table 8-12 shows a few examples of microbenchmarking metrics for NPUs. Like GPU microbenchmarks, it is important to prefer the ones that get the data directly from the registers that store this information rather than proxy tools that give data with a high margin of error. Therefore, product managers should aim for design/verification teams to have dedicated microbenchmarks and or profilers built for their design to manage the performance and power accurately.

Table 8-12. Examples of NPU Microbenchmarks Performance Metrics

Types of performance metrics	Description
MACs/MAD FLOPS/TOPS	Measure the NPU FLOPS/TOPS for different float and int data types
Accuracy	Evaluates the precision and correctness of the AI models running on the NPU, ensuring performance is not gained at the expense of accuracy
Throughput	Measures the number of AI operations or inferences the NPU can perform per second
Latency	Indicates the time it takes for the NPU to process a single inference or operation
Thermal Performance	Measures the operating temperature of the NPU
Power Consumption	Indicates power used by the NPU, which is important for energy efficiency and thermal management
Memory Bandwidth	Measures the data transfer rate between the NPU memory and the GPU cores

Other Microbenchmarks

Microbenchmarks for other hardware components in the SoC are also available, such as media blocks, memory controllers, and storage controllers, as shown in Table 8-13. The purpose of all the microbenchmarks is to evaluate the KPIs for individual SoC components, and the profiler reveals the utilization behaviors to manage the performance accordingly. Therefore, benchmarks and profilers effectively manage performance, and product managers should implement microbenchmarks and profilers at the register level to get accurate information.

Table 8-13. Examples of Microbenchmarks

Microbenchmarks	Test focus	Examples
Media Microbenchmarks	Media Encoder and decoder performance Memory efficiency	Example: AME benchmark
Memory Subsystem Microbenchmarks	Latency Bandwidth Cache Performance	Example: STREAM, Memtest86
Storage I/O Microbenchmarks	Read/Write Latency Throughput	Example: Iometer, FI/O
Networking Microbenchmarks	Latency Throughput	Example: Iperf, Netperf

Synthetic Benchmarks

The synthetic benchmarks help manage the performance of the SoC system using specific workloads and use cases, unlike KPIs in microbenchmarks. These benchmarks synthesize artificial scenarios that approximate real-world tasks but are controlled and repeatable. Synthetic benchmarks are designed to simulate a specific type of workload with repeatable patterns on an IP or SoC system; for example, 3DMark for GPUs, Geekbench, and SPECrate for CPU performance, and PCMark for SoC system-level performance.

These benchmarks execute simulated scenarios that may or may not be implemented in an actual application but can fully access the specific hardware under test. These benchmarks are popular in performance management and go-to-market advocacy to position the SoC as competitive. Technology press, social media influencers, and others use these benchmarks to access the capabilities of different SoC systems and influence the industry by giving SoC ratings based on the benchmark results. They provide a consistent and repeatable way to measure performance across different systems, facilitating fair comparisons.

These benchmarks execute specific workloads like gaming and AI performance. Therefore, it is important to pick the right benchmarks representing the SoC's target user segment. Some of the types of synthetic benchmarks available in the industry are shown in Table 8-14. These benchmarks are continuously updated with the latest trends in the industry, and new benchmarks are implemented in collaboration with SoC design companies. The synthetic benchmarks are available to evaluate performance on specific compute units like CPU, GPU, NPU, and SoC system-level specific tests like PCMark and SysMark.

Table 8-14. Examples of Synthetic Benchmarks Available in the Industry

Benchmarks	Components Tests	Types of Workloads
SPECrate	CPU single-core, multi-core performance	Integer and floating-point instructions
Cinebench	CPU single-core, multi-core performance	Sustained workload performance
	GPU performance (Cinebench GPU)	
Geekbench	CPU single-core, multi-core performance	Bursty workload performance
	GPU Performance (Geekbench GPU)	
	AI Performance (Geekbench AI)	

(*continued*)

CHAPTER 8 PERFORMANCE MANAGEMENT

Table 8-14. (*continued*)

Benchmarks	Components Tests	Types of Workloads
3Dmark Wild Life	GPU FPS performance in Shader, ray tracing	GPU throughput performance For different types of cores
GfxBench	GPU FPS performance	3D graphics performance
PCMark	System-level benchmark	Full SoC performance
SysMark	System-level benchmark	Full SoC performance
ML Commons	AI Performance	NPU neural network performance

Real-World Benchmarks

Real-world benchmarks measure the performance of a system using applications or workloads that represent the user behavior, like running actual applications and user scenarios to assess the system's performance under real operating conditions. This benchmark performance provides the most accurate representation of end users with reference to user interactions and other environmental factors. Product managers need to keep this benchmark performance as the priority in performance targets as they can reveal issues related to resource contention, I/O performance, and other factors that synthetic benchmarks might not capture.

Efficient performance management considers most of the real workload benchmarks available in the industry. Table 8-15 provides some examples of the real world. These benchmarks are also used by technology press and social media influencers to guide PC users.

CHAPTER 8   PERFORMANCE MANAGEMENT

Table 8-15. *Examples of Real-World Benchmarks Available in the Industry*

Benchmarks	Types of Workloads
UL-Procyon	Microsoft Office, Battery life productivity performance Stable diffusion and Computer vision AI models performance
Puget Bench	Content creation application use case scenarios in Adobe Photoshop, Adobe Premiere Pro, and After Effects
Gaming benchmarks	Cyberpunk 2077, Shadow of the Tomb Raider built-in benchmarks in Games

Conclusion

Knowing each benchmark type makes it clear that the critical ones are the real-world benchmarks as they determine the actual user's experience. Should product managers just focus on real-world benchmarks?

Delivering good customer experience in the generic computing market segments like PC and mobile is challenging as the conditions in real-world workloads are less controllable. Although real-world workloads are good for managing SoC performance, the path to delivering great performance on real workloads is best if it goes through micro and synthetic benchmarks to ensure the performance management is systematic and organized. It also helps to identify opportunities for performance improvement by studying the workload characteristics from real-world to synthetic to microbenchmark level with controlled conditions, as shown in the Figure 8-13.

CHAPTER 8   PERFORMANCE MANAGEMENT

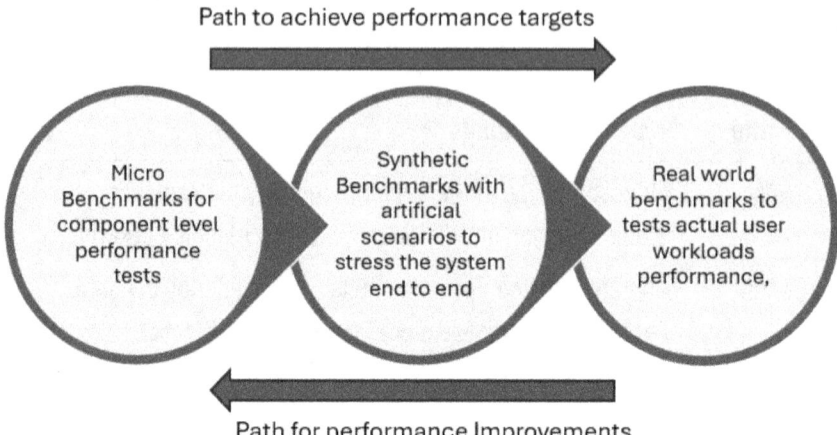

Figure 8-13. *Approach for performance evaluation to meet and improve performance*

Comprehensive performance management at the SoC system level should use a combination of microbenchmarks, synthetic benchmarks, and real-world benchmarks to get a full picture of system performance across different levels and scenarios. For example, A CPU-based real-world productivity workload performance must be managed by the KPIs from the microbenchmarks and synthetic benchmarks that stress the productivity KPIs along with profiler characteristics to manage performance on a real-world benchmark.

Therefore, product managers should implement an efficient SoC system performance management process by making a suite of benchmarks representing relevant categories of PC users. And manage the performance from individual low-level microarchitecture performance measured through microbenchmarks followed by synthetics benchmarks and finally to the real-world benchmarks and user applications.

New Benchmark Development

When implementing a progressive performance management strategy, product managers can manage the performance of basic and differentiating features using KPIs, existing benchmarks, and workloads. What about the augmented features? How can product managers manage these augmented features and characteristics for continuous improvement?

As technology advances, hardware and software capabilities improve significantly, and today, we have benchmarks to manage and evaluate performance per workload category like games, content creation, and productivity. This continuous need to evaluate the performance of emerging use cases and features forced the industry to develop a methodology for new benchmarks that represent emerging customer use cases. The new benchmarks are developed by different hardware or software companies collaborating. Or by an independent benchmark entity in collaboration with hardware companies to develop a benchmark that can assess the performance of the emerging use cases without bias. Collaboration is needed as each hardware design company can provide insights into their products' specific capabilities and features to ensure that benchmarks help evaluate the performance by effectively utilizing the SoC characteristics.

Therefore, product managers should strive to benchmark the augmented characteristics of the SoC for continuous improvement to stay competitive in the market. Benchmarks are key to product positioning and give customers a metric to evaluate their purchase decisions.

By being involved in benchmark development, product managers can validate that benchmarks are appropriately stressing and measuring the best performance on the hardware in ways that reflect real-world use cases. Therefore, product managers should aim to implement innovative use cases and workloads and have them benchmarked appropriately.

CHAPTER 8   PERFORMANCE MANAGEMENT

Go-to-Market Strategy

The performance management-based go-to-market strategy clearly defines and differentiates SoC performance capabilities like M3, M3 Pro, and M3 Max from Apple, Intel Core Ultra 5, 7, and 9 from Intel, AMD Ryzen 5, 7, and 9 from AMD. This is taking a good, better, best-performance scaleup approach to meet the various computing needs for PC user segments. This approach demands product managers to always adjust the good, better, and best SoC offerings based on the market needs by continuous monitoring to adapt to market dynamics and maintain a competitive edge, as shown in the Figure 8-14.

Apple M3 Series SoCs	Geekbench Single Core Performance Scores	Geekbench Multi Core Performance Scores
Apple M3 Max (16-CPU)	3070	21006
Apple M3 Max (14-CPU)	3011	18871
Apple M3 Pro	3024	14932
Apple M3	3023	11801

Intel 14th Generation SoCs	Geekbench Single Core Performance Scores	Geekbench Multi Core Performance Scores
Intel Core Ultra 9 185H	2393	12836
Intel Core Ultra 7 155H	2082	10356
Intel Core Ultra 7 165H	2403	10926
Intel Core Ultra 7 165U	2102	6360
Intel Core Ultra 7 155U	2314	9313
Intel Core Ultra 5 135H	2041	8248
Intel Core Ultra 5 135U	943	5923

AMD Ryzen 8000 series SoCs	Geekbench Single Core Performance Scores	Geekbench Multi Core Performance Scores
AMD Ryzen 9 8945HS	2763	14350
AMD Ryzen 7 8700G	2905	15894
AMD Ryzen 7 8700F	2727	13417
AMD Ryzen 7 8840HS	2579	11391
AMD Ryzen 5 8600G	2694	12328
AMD Ryzen 5 8645HS	2410	10274
AMD Ryzen 5 8640HS	2296	7889

Figure 8-14. Examples of performance-based SoC go-to-market strategy (for reference only, not to compare) (source: Geekbench.com August 2024)

Although in the modern world of the Internet, mobiles and PCs have become integral to everyone's life, not every electronic device user better understands semiconductor products. When I first told my mother I would work for a chip design company. She asked me, "Why does a company want to design a chip; isn't it dependent on the size and shape of the potato?" I had to tell her that a chip is a *semiconductor product* that goes into an electronic device.

Semiconductor product managers must meticulously craft the go-to-market strategy for successful commercializing semiconductor products and their systems from the end user's perspective. The strategy must define the semiconductor product's relevance in the competitive system market and establish brand recognition at the end-user level. The idea is to clearly communicate the unique value propositions of each SoC product to avoid customer confusion. This is a crucial process to the sustained success of semiconductor products, especially in the Windows PC ecosystem.

Unlike the Apple ecosystem, which designs SoCs and PCs to market directly to the end users, the Windows ecosystem takes a layered approach where Intel, AMD, and Qualcomm design SoCs. Operating systems are designed by Microsoft, Google, and SoC devices and manufactured by OEMs like Dell and HP. As a result, the economic value of the PC is distributed into these layers, and basic business instinct pushes these B2B and B2C companies to keep as much of the economic value as possible. Therefore, product managers must dynamically adapt to the competitive market with clear performance and feature differentiated value propositions of the offered SoCs by implementing effective marketing tactics and excellent customer support to the customers to establish SoCs brand recognition and achieve long-term market success. Shimano Industries, Salesforce, and Shopify are examples of established brands in B2B companies.

CHAPTER 8   PERFORMANCE MANAGEMENT

Support and EOL

Effective support and EOL management of semiconductor devices are crucial for customer satisfaction. Throughout the life cycle of a semiconductor device product manager should implement robust support mechanisms, which include technical assistance, firmware updates, and maintenance services to ensure that the products perform reliably and meet customer expectations until its EOL.

Especially in PC user segments like gaming, which tend to push the performance of the SoC by running it at overclocked speeds, need clear documentation on the procedure to overclock the CPU and memory. Clear technical guidelines and support documentation are critical to ensure the users implement the guidelines as needed to realize the additional performance benefits of overclocking. Product managers should also implement a mechanism to collect and analyze customer feedback to continuously improve the performance of the SoC in the future generation by taking a consumer-centric approach to the roadmap targets besides competition.

As the SoC system approaches its EOL, it becomes essential for product managers to strategically manage the transition to newer technologies. This involves clear communication with customers about the timeline and implications of EOL, providing options for upgrades or migrations to newer products, and ensuring that critical support and spare parts remain available during the transition period. For example, AMD implements a reusable motherboard socket to help its users easily upgrade to newer SoCs when needed. Proactive EOL management helps minimize disruption, maintain brand loyalty, and streamline the phase-out process, allowing product managers to focus resources on research and development for continuous innovation and developing next-generation semiconductor products and devices.

Summary

Performance management strategy clearly defines the SoCs objectives needed to meet or exceed the users' expectations while providing competitive performance. It helps product managers define the products' clear short term and long-term performance capabilities as a framework to deliver continuous product improvements. The framework ensures each product revision enhances the user experience with innovation and pushes the boundaries of technology using a strategic performance management approach.

The ideal semiconductor performance management combines the SoC and system-level performance management frameworks into one for efficiently managing the end-to-end performance of the semiconductor products. Continuous monitoring and optimization using a unified framework help product managers to quickly adapt to changing workloads and user requirements, ensuring sustained system performance over time.

To execute the performance management across the semiconductor development life cycle. The process can be divided into IP and SoC level pre-silicon and post-silicon, device and system-level, and customer-facing features and use cases where both software and hardware performance can be managed in a customer-centric approach. Although the system or device-level performance management is still post-silicon, product managers should also utilize benchmarks for post-silicon performance management. In highly competitive market environments, benchmarks are critical in defining a systematic and adaptive measurement methodology to evaluate the SoC system's capabilities as a neutral platform to guide the industry to compare different solutions.

Now that you better understand performance across the semiconductor development life cycle. The next step for product managers is to implement and plan a competitive semiconductor roadmap. The reason why the roadmap is, in the end, is because product managers

CHAPTER 8 PERFORMANCE MANAGEMENT

developing roadmaps should have a firm knowledge of the semiconductor life cycle, product strategy, architecture, power and performance management, and manufacturing information. These insights help product managers to implement roadmaps with competitive advantage wherever possible. Let's discuss the semiconductor roadmaps.

CHAPTER 9

Competitive Semiconductor Product Roadmaps

If you define the problem correctly, then you almost have the solution.

—Steve Jobs

Planning is as natural to the process of success as its absence is to the process of failure.

—Robin Sieger

How many of us make a grocery list before going on a grocery mission? Most of us, isn't it? Making a list of things to buy makes it easy to get everything we need and know when we can finish grocery shopping. In business management, planning and execution of the products demand a similar list. Product managers need a guide that outlines the product plan deliverables with clear and actionable elements to use a product roadmap successfully. A product roadmap outlines the full plan of the products to

CHAPTER 9   COMPETITIVE SEMICONDUCTOR PRODUCT ROADMAPS

help product managers set competitive targets, track the progress in the development phase and precisely know when products are ready to be launched. This chapter discusses the semiconductor product roadmaps with a path to implementation and secrets for building strong roadmaps for delivering competitive products.

A semiconductor product roadmap is a strategic tool that outlines the competitive product strategy plans for semiconductor products over a specific period with actionable objectives. It serves as a high-level guide for product development, helping align stakeholders, prioritize product features, communicate the product direction both internally and externally, and track progress. The guidance includes clear directions for innovation with objectives and deliverables to build value and trust with customers and partners. They help coordinate research and development activities and set realistic expectations for customers and partners. Roadmaps help provide a clear timeline for launching new products and features, enable companies to anticipate market trends, mitigate risks, and ensure that they consistently deliver value to their customers.

Defining Competitive Semiconductor Product Roadmaps

The roadmap begins with a clear articulation of the product vision, which describes the product's intended purpose, value proposition, and long-term objectives. Goals and key performance indicators (KPIs) are defined to measure progress and success in achieving the intended product vision. Usually, roadmaps are defined for five years so let's consider the timeline as five years. The best semiconductor product roadmap captures the KPIs for the semiconductor product elements, revealing cause and effect and giving a full view of the product's value. For example, adding 50% more CPU performance (cause) in the SoC improved PowerPoint editing features performance by x% (effect) and provided a complete view of the product's value proposition. Therefore, a product roadmap defines the KPIs from semiconductor SoC microarchitecture architecture to the end product level features facing customers. Once the product managers define the KPIs for the roadmap, the next step is to organize the roadmap following the competitive product strategy developed using the framework mentioned in the competitive product strategy chapter. Let's discuss the KPIs of the semiconductor product roadmap.

Roadmap KPIs

In the semiconductor industry, specifically in PC products, end-to-end product roadmap KPIs can be divided into six types, as shown in Figure 9-1. These six objectives are manufacturing technology, Individual SoC component features, SoC features, platform features, application features, and product features, which provide clear targets for executing the semiconductor product life cycle. Product managers should pair these six objectives with financial elements like cost and product pricing associated with these factors to capture the economic value of the roadmap products. These six objectives act as the foundational aspects of semiconductor products to ensure the roadmap products are systematically categorized with targets from design to product deployment.

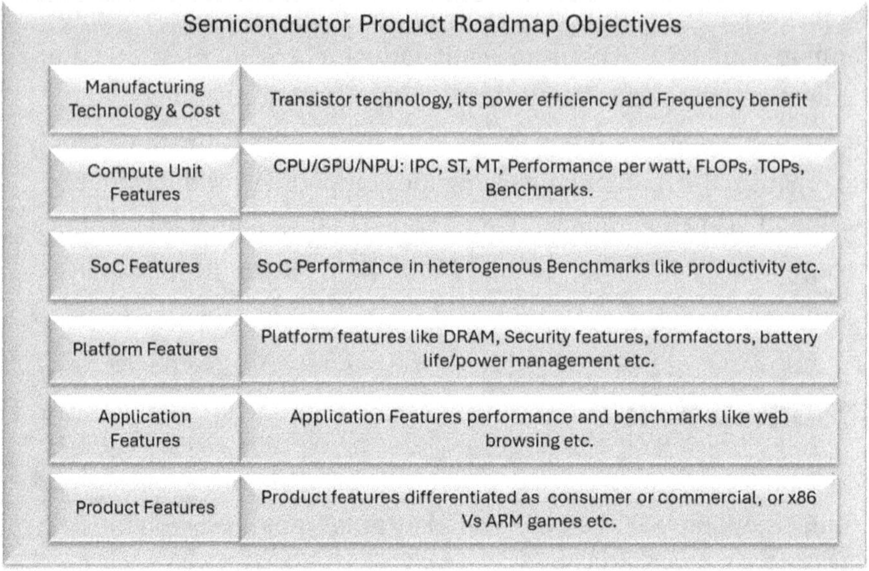

CHAPTER 9   COMPETITIVE SEMICONDUCTOR PRODUCT ROADMAPS

Semiconductor Product Roadmap Objectives	
Manufacturing Technology & Cost	Transistor technology, its power efficiency and Frequency benefit
Compute Unit Features	CPU/GPU/NPU: IPC, ST, MT, Performance per watt, FLOPs, TOPs, Benchmarks.
SoC Features	SoC Performance in heterogenous Benchmarks like productivity etc.
Platform Features	Platform features like DRAM, Security features, formfactors, battery life/power management etc.
Application Features	Application Features performance and benchmarks like web browsing etc.
Product Features	Product features differentiated as consumer or commercial, or x86 Vs ARM games etc.

Figure 9-1. *Semiconductor product roadmap objective categories*

Additionally, these six aspects of the semiconductor roadmap define structurally related elements interdependent and need to be clearly quantified with KPI targets in the five-year product roadmap to realize the impact. For example, The manufacturing process technology helps define the maximum frequency of the compute unit and SoC impacting the application level features like games. In an open PC ecosystem like Windows, capturing all six in a roadmap is challenging as the dependencies are distributed across other stakeholders. However, it would be ideal if product managers could maintain this end-to-end level of roadmap view to get a hint of the semiconductor products end-user value. Now that the KPIs for semiconductor products have been defined, the next step is to organize the roadmap that fits the product strategy. Let's discuss organizing product roadmaps.

CHAPTER 9   COMPETITIVE SEMICONDUCTOR PRODUCT ROADMAPS

Organizing Product Roadmaps

Product managers determine KPI targets to measure progress and track the success in achieving the product vision. The roadmap should be organized into strategic focus areas or segments that align with the product strategy. For example, premium, mainstream and entry consumer SoCs are one product line in the PC industry. Each segment can represent a broad area of SoC functionality for a particular customer group the product manager aims to address. The product roadmap should also include a timeline that outlines when specific SoCs are planned for launch. For example, yearly or once in two years. This timeline can be divided into quarters, months, or other relevant time intervals based on the product life cycle phases like product release candidate and volume production, and other stages.

Semiconductor SoC launches can be planned with a preferred cadence with new or revised products, usually called generations. For example, consider the premium SoC in the consumer PC segment that launches a new SoC every year. Then, the year 1 SoC can be named generation 1, year 2 is generation 2, and so on. Each generation of SoCs should align with the product strategy and provide incremental value to users with a competitive advantage with basic, differentiated, and augmented product features. For example, new generation SoC can be 25% higher in gaming or CPU performance than the prior generation and available competition. The future generations' KPI targets are usually acquired through projections or scenario modeling of the planned features of the SoCs. The modeling or projections must be based on the current product learnings and optimization outlook to keep the KPI targets data-driven as much as possible. For future competitor products, product managers can utilize information using competitive intelligence gathered through investor documents, publicly available data, technology conferences, and technology press updates. Projections are discussed more later in this chapter.

CHAPTER 9   COMPETITIVE SEMICONDUCTOR PRODUCT ROADMAPS

The key aspect of the roadmap is that the KPIs should be compared to the prior generation SoCs and the competition to enforce continuous improvements to the SoCs and stay ahead of the competition. A product roadmap should also be flexible and adaptable to changes in market conditions, customer needs, and internal priorities. The roadmap should be regularly reviewed and revised based on new information, changing priorities, and lessons learned from previous launches. Product managers should broadly communicate revised roadmap updates to ensure that all stakeholders are informed of the product direction and take input or feedback as necessary. Feedback from customers, users, and internal stakeholders is essential for refining and updating the product roadmap over time. Figure 9-2 shows an example of the semiconductor product roadmap with KPIs compared to prior generation and competitor SoCs.

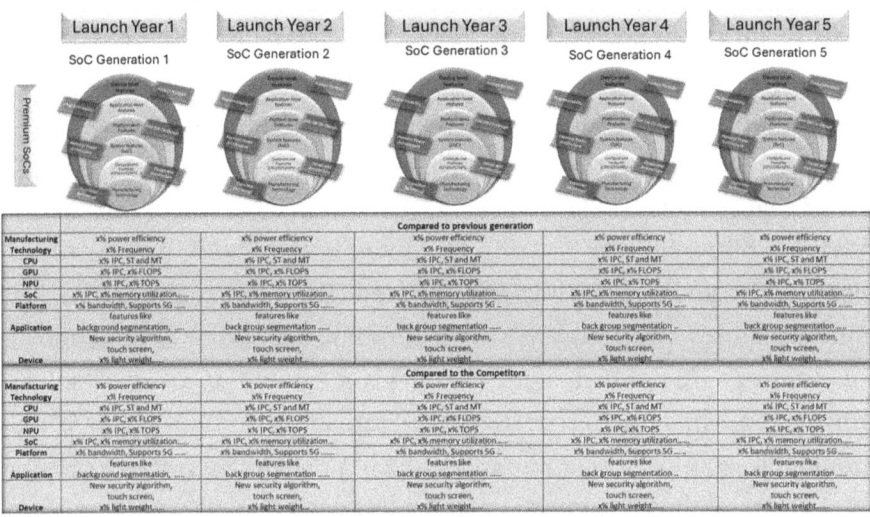

Figure 9-2.   Example of a semiconductor product roadmap

CHAPTER 9   COMPETITIVE SEMICONDUCTOR PRODUCT ROADMAPS

A Path to Achieve Product Roadmap KPIs

Product managers should understand the underlying KPI dependencies to achieve the product roadmap KPIs. KPI dependencies refer to the factors influencing the six-product roadmap KPIs and provide a path for product managers to achieve KPI targets successfully. A few critical semiconductor product roadmap KPI dependencies are transistor technology, SoC and subsystem architectural choices, memory and power architectural choices, HW-SW and system co-design approaches, programmability, and product portfolio choices, as shown in Figure 9-3. These factors can be within the product manager's internal team's expertise or dependent on external stakeholders and ecosystem partners capable of impacting the execution of the product roadmap KPI targets. For example, user application programmability depends on the external ISV developer ecosystem.

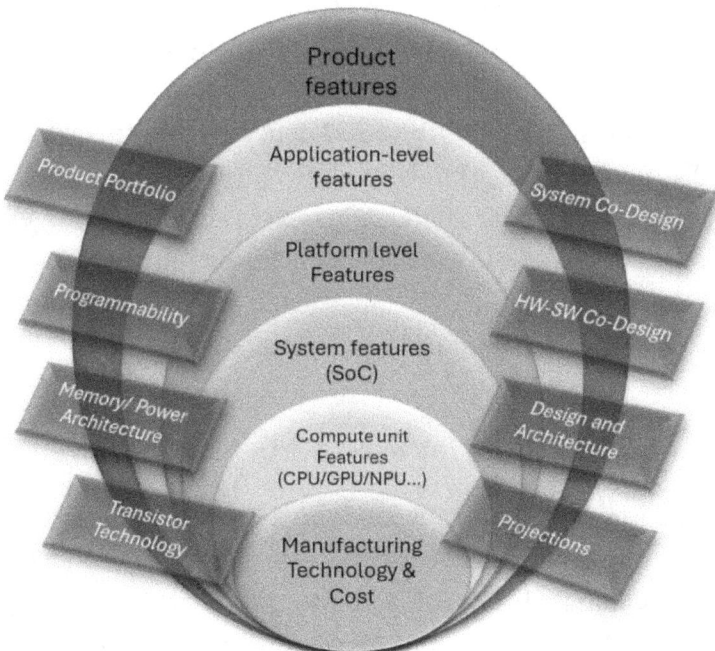

Figure 9-3. Competitive semiconductor product roadmap dependencies

Product managers working with these dependencies can realize that they can influence more than one KPI and reveal how one KPI dependency can impact or be impacted by another, creating an interdependency effect. Therefore, defining a path to achieve product roadmap KPIs in semiconductor product roadmap is a complex task. However, understanding these dependencies and their implications can help product managers choose an optimal achievable path that best fits the strengths.

As shown in Figure 9-3, the semiconductor manufacturing technology is dependent on the transistor technology, compute unit features are dependent on manufacturing technology and design/architecture of the CPU/GPU/NPU compute units, which contributes to the complete SoC features along with the choice of memory and power architecture. These SoC features influence the platform features by utilizing design methodology, for example, either HW-SW co-design or HW-guided quality of service. These platform-level features help user application development using the programmability, and finally a well-defined product portfolio helps to deliver computing needs based on the customer segments. Therefore, these KPI dependencies are highly integrated. Product managers must analyze and assess the dependencies, flexibility, and limitations to set the right path to achieve KPI targets in the roadmap. Let's discuss these KPI dependencies and other crucial indirect dependencies such as competitive intelligence, projections for future SoCs and secret to strong semiconductor product roadmaps.

Process Technology

Semiconductor manufacturing depends on the transistor technology for frequency and power efficiency of the semiconductor products. Fabrication companies like TSMC and Intel provide transistor technology input elements. Product managers can get the frequency, voltage, and power efficiency targets to design a SoC by working closely with manufacturing companies.

CHAPTER 9   COMPETITIVE SEMICONDUCTOR PRODUCT ROADMAPS

The process technology has a higher influence on cost, the advanced process node wafer and yield impact is higher on the semiconductor product costs. While achieving the KPIs targets, product managers should ensure the cost of the semiconductor product is also competitive along with performance and features. If monolithic chip design is costly, disaggregated chips can be a good choice for being cost-effective. The latency risk associated with disaggregated multi-chip modules (MCM) can be traded off using advanced on-chip interconnect packaging technologies such as 2D and 3D interposers. These advanced packaging technologies reduce the latency penalties on semiconductor products, yielding benefits with disaggregation design choices. However, product managers must evaluate their decisions best for their product strategy as both MCM and monolithic can sometimes become equally costly due to advanced transistor and interposer technologies.

Product managers should compare the SoCs performance and power efficiency derived from the manufacturing technology to prior generations and competitor products to get insights into the performance differentiation acquired due to transistor technology. This becomes important if there are very few advanced transistor technology manufacturers. For example, In the modern semiconductor industry dynamics, TSMC is the preferred manufacturer of top semiconductor design companies like Qualcomm, Intel (as of July 2024), AMD, Apple, and NVIDIA. The products from all these competitors have the same advantages gained using the same process technology nodes. In these circumstances, the product managers should not just rely on the process advantages for product differentiation but explore other KPIs, such as SoC, and features architecture to improve the value of the products in the roadmap. Let's discuss the architecture and design dependencies on the semiconductor product roadmap KPI targets.

CHAPTER 9   COMPETITIVE SEMICONDUCTOR PRODUCT ROADMAPS

Design and Microarchitecture

The advanced transistor technology goodness feeds into defining the desired performance and efficiency in the semiconductor products. Although transistor technology is critical, it is not the only aspect of developing a competitive semiconductor product. SoC design methodology and the CPU, GPU, and NPU compute unit's microarchitecture significantly contribute to the performance and efficiency of the semiconductor products to be competitive. For example, consider the three real-world SoCs competing against each other, as shown in Table 9-1 for reference, and their CPU single thread (ST) performance as measured by Geekbench 6.[1] The three SoCs are from top semiconductor design companies, and by looking at the performance scores and frequency of the CPU core in this example, the competitor C CPU running at 4.83GHz delivers a lower single core score than the competitor A running at 4.05GHz frequency. The competitor B CPU, although it uses the same 4nm process technology, operates at a lower frequency but still can deliver competitive performance as competitor C runs at a higher frequency.

Table 9-1. CPU Performance as Measured by Geekbench 6 (for reference only)[2]

Geekbench 6 Benchmark	Process Technology	CPU ST Scores	Frequency
Competitor A CPU (Apple)	TSMC 3nm	3203[3]	4.05 GHz
Competitor B CPU (Qualcomm)	TSMC 4nm	2792[4]	4.01 GHz
Competitor C CPU (AMD)	TSMC 4nm	2841[5]	4.83 GHz

---

[1] Results taken from Geekbench.com
[2] Results as of Aug 2024
[3] https://browser.geekbench.com/v6/cpu/7315121
[4] https://browser.geekbench.com/v6/cpu/7306177
[5] https://browser.geekbench.com/v6/cpu/7315652

Recall that CPU ST performance = Instructions/program *instructions/cycle* CPU clock cycle speed (frequency).

Competitor A is executing instructions faster, even at lower clock speeds, than competitor C to deliver higher performance by implementing efficient microarchitectural and architectural design. Therefore, architecture and microarchitecture play a major role in the performance of the semiconductor besides process technology and higher frequencies.

Product management defining targets for the KPIs on the roadmap should have microarchitecture improvements besides just frequency and efficiency of process technology. Semiconductor microarchitecture defines the implementation of the instruction set architecture (ISA) on hardware and contributes to the speed at which the instructions are executed. Microarchitecture optimization can be implemented at many levels of instruction execution, such as the pipeline structure, specialized instruction execution units, branch prediction mechanisms, memory hierarchy and various other features that determine the performance efficiency of the processor. The following are some examples.

- **Instruction-level parallelism**: The microarchitecture determines how instructions are executed in parallel within the IPs data and instruction pipeline architecture. Features like superscalar execution, out-of-order execution, and speculative execution can improve performance by maximizing instruction throughput.

- **Memory hierarchy**: The microarchitecture defines the structure and organization of the memory hierarchy, including caches and memory controllers. Efficient caching mechanisms, prefetching strategies, and memory access optimizations can reduce memory latency and improve system performance.

- **Pipeline structure:** The pipeline depth, branch prediction accuracy, and other pipeline-related features impact instruction throughput and latency. A well-designed pipeline minimizes stalls and latency and maximizes instruction throughput.

- **Specialized instruction execution units:** Microarchitectures often include specialized execution units for tasks such as floating-point arithmetic, vector processing, or cryptographic operations. These units can accelerate specific workloads and improve the product's performance.

A well-designed microarchitecture takes advantage of the capabilities offered by the underlying transistor technology, while efficient subsystem design enables the implementation of sophisticated microarchitectural features. Together, they define semiconductor products' performance, power efficiency, and scalability. Product managers should carefully determine the strengths of the preferred ISA and microarchitecture per the needs and set the microarchitectural improvement targets in the product roadmap to achieve compute unit KPIs. It is not easy to improve performance through microarchitectural changes alone, as these improvements require resilience to try numerous innovative techniques with an exploratory mindset. The other way to approach this could be to exploit the existing ISA implementation by continuously improving the existing techniques. For example, AMD implemented AVX512 instruction support in their latest PC CPUs to double the vector size to get higher performance compared to earlier implementations of AVX256 instructions.

Memory Architecture

In addition to the microarchitecture of the individual subsystems like CPU/GPU/NPU, the architecture of SoC can also be optimized for achieving higher KPI targets. Increasing the memory bandwidth of

CHAPTER 9   COMPETITIVE SEMICONDUCTOR PRODUCT ROADMAPS

DRAM, system cache density, and memory controller optimizations on SoC improve the performance of CPU, GPU, and NPU using higher memory speeds that support faster data transfer rates. However, the performance upgrade is achievable only on bandwidth-bound workloads and capabilities of the subsystems to leverage the higher data transfer rates. AI-based workloads like large language models (LLMs) are usually compute and memory bound, so adding advanced matrix multiplications instruction support like advanced matrix extensions (AMX), and wave matrix multiply accumulate (WMMA) along with higher bandwidth enhances AI performance on CPU, GPU, and NPU respectively. Product managers should weigh the trade-offs and decide which one works best.

The evolution of memory technology has been significant to the computing capabilities of the semiconductor industry. The introduction of several high speed and power-efficient technologies (e.g., double data rate (DDR), low power double data rate memory (LPDDR), high-bandwidth memory (HBM), and high-speed peripheral component interconnect express (PCIe) data speed) has significantly contributed to enhancing semiconductor product capabilities in the technology industry. Semiconductor product managers can utilize these memory technologies as per the needs to enhance the performance of the SoCs to meet the high computing needs and maintain the competitive edge in the modern technology industry. For example, AMD implemented 3D V-Cache to increase performance by providing higher data transfer capabilities to the CPU subsystem. NVIDIA implements a high-speed communication bidirectional link to scale and improve multi-GPU data transfer speed and performance using a direct GPU-to-GPU interconnect called NVLink.

For competitive performance comparison and positioning against competitor products, product managers should know the differentiation of the underlying microarchitecture and technology differences among ARM, x86, and RISC-V on user applications for sustainable long-term product positioning and advocacy. On the other hand, if the performance

CHAPTER 9   COMPETITIVE SEMICONDUCTOR PRODUCT ROADMAPS

is lagging compared to competitor products in the early roadmap scenario planning. Product managers knowing the different architectures help root cause the performance discrepancies, thereby providing an opportunity to make amends to the microarchitecture, memory architecture and software as needed. Therefore, comprehending the design principles, features, and implementations specific to each architecture helps product managers to learn and push the performance envelope of the product architecture higher and higher for continuous improvements and identify challenges early.

As stated in the first chapter, semiconductor products are the building block of the technology industry. These building blocks depend on user applications developed on top of the semiconductor hardware layer to realize the full potential of the semiconductor products. End of the day, the feature performance and the user experience are the tangible way to realize the value of all semiconductor products. To summarize, when semiconductor product managers increase the raw hardware performance using advanced process technology, system architecture, and subsystem microarchitectures. This raw performance needs to be converted to user application performance and efficiency for end-user experience and enhanced product capabilities. For example, adding 20% more performance on the CPU through microarchitecture and advanced process technology can potentially increase the performance of games by 20%. However, there is a possibility that the game software may not be effectively utilizing the SoC hardware for improved performance. Product managers should also focus on knowing how applications are utilizing the hardware and assess if the hardware or the software layer needs improvements. Therefore, another way to increase performance and achieve roadmap KPIs is to optimize software layers and applications to use the hardware capabilities effectively.

Semiconductor hardware product capabilities limit the possibility to optimize the software. In other words, software is limited by the hardware capabilities. For example, consider hardware as the swimming pool and software applications as the swimmer shown in Figure 9-4; the size of the pool limits the swimmer's swimming distance.[6] As semiconductor hardware and application software depend on each other, the ideal way to approach achieving KPI targets by the product managers is through a HW-SW co-design.

Figure 9-4. *An example emphasizing the strengths and weaknesses of software and hardware*

HW-SW Co-Design

Hardware-software (HW-SW) design refers to the process of concurrently designing a system's hardware and software components to meet specific performance, power, and cost objectives or designing hardware

---

[6] Photo generated using AI with prompt: Photo realistic cartoon athletic swimming in a big swimming pool with a full view of swimming pool

architecture based on the software application requirements. This approach recognizes the close interaction between hardware and software in modern computing systems and seeks to optimize the semiconductor and application design together rather than separately. This approach ensures the semiconductor hardware architecture, and improvements are tailored to the needs of software applications and utilize the semiconductor products to their maximum efficiency.

For example, Apple usually follows a pattern[7] in their product launches and software service releases. They roll out a preview of the operating system/programming capabilities and new software features in their yearly held WWDC with beta's available to developers to get their hands on it and later release hardware products with the latest software/operating system (OS) services. Apple ensures the new Apple products are ready with enhanced software user applications leveraging the incremental hardware improvements before they release the new Apple products.

The Advantages of HW-SW Co-Design

HW-SW design requires close collaboration between product managers, hardware engineers, software developers, system architects, and other stakeholders to achieve the desired system-level objectives. It involves trade-offs between hardware and software complexity, performance, power consumption, and cost and often requires iterative refinement to achieve optimal results. However, this method achieves the desired results with numerous advantages, as shown in the Figure 9-5 to build semiconductor products competitive edge. The following describes some of the advantages.

---

[7] Observation based on the Apple M1, M2, and M3 SoC launches and macOS releases

CHAPTER 9 COMPETITIVE SEMICONDUCTOR PRODUCT ROADMAPS

- **Reduces product time to market**: Overall development time is shortened by designing hardware and software in parallel. Products can be brought to market faster, which is critical in competitive industries. It helps product managers determine the partitioning between hardware and software, deciding which tasks are implemented in hardware and software.

  For example, if a product manager, for any reason, chooses not to support a feature at the hardware level, like ray tracing or systolic executions, the support can be made available through software capabilities. The software has the power to bridge most of the hardware limitations but at the expense of some trade-offs. Product managers can choose software routes for short-term roadmap competitiveness until the features can be supported at the hardware level. The important part of supporting new features at the software level first is it helps with key learnings on hardware requirements so a better hardware support can be designed to ensure a continuous performance improvement cycle.

- **Improved performance and efficiency**: HW-SW co-design gives product managers two choices of optimizations, either using hardware or software to improve the performance and efficiency of an application when product managers must prioritize features to implement. For example, critical algorithms can be implemented in hardware for speed, while software handles more flexible parts.

- **Enhanced product quality**: Early validation and testing of the integrated hardware-software system reduces the chances of bugs and defects, leading to higher product quality and reliability.

- **Cost efficiency**: Optimizing the balance between hardware and software can reduce the need for expensive hardware resources, leading to cost savings in the final product.

Figure 9-5. Advantages of HW-SW co-design

- **Flexibility and scalability**: HW-SW co-design enables the implementation of scalable and flexible semiconductor products by balancing the workload between hardware and software, where software updates can extend functionality without requiring hardware changes and vice versa.

Overall, the HW-SW co-design approach helps product managers create more efficient and optimized semiconductor products and systems by considering hardware and software interfaces as an integral part of the performance efficiency process. For short-term and long-term product roadmap KPI targets, product managers can rely on implementing HW-SW co-design to achieve a competitive advantage across the semiconductor product user segments. This approach in an open ecosystem like Windows PC requires close collaboration and stakeholder engagement to fully utilize the benefits of HW-SW co-design. However, this approach may help optimize SoC or platform-level performance. There is another co-design approach that helps design the entire product using a system co-design approach to enhance the entire product's performance. It combines HW-SW and other system peripheral dependencies such as DRAM frequency which can be sorted by working with memory technology vendors like Micro, Samsung, and SK Hynix. Utilizes higher storage IO data transfer speeds, better battery and power management, power delivery techniques and connectivity to the system to attain optimal system performance and user experience of the entire product. Let's discuss system co-design.

System Co-Design

System Co-Design in the semiconductor industry refers to the collaborative and integrated process of concurrently designing the entire system's hardware and software components. This approach ensures the development of end-to-end products like smartphones and laptops are implemented using optimal SoCs, memory subsystems, peripherals, and interfaces to meet the user segment's system performance, power and functionality requirements. Product managers should collaborate with ISVs, OEMs, and other peripheral hardware suppliers to define the overall system requirements to meet the customer segments' functional requirements to achieve a successful system co-design approach based on KPI targets.

CHAPTER 9   COMPETITIVE SEMICONDUCTOR PRODUCT ROADMAPS

For example, if a generation 1 device with a set of features delivers ten hours of battery life, product managers working on generation 2 devices with new features should ensure at least ten hours of battery life to avoid regressing the system capabilities to the users. Product managers can upgrade the battery size if the performance-to-power ratio is not balanced at the SoC level. Hence, generation 2 products maintain or provide better battery life than previous generation products. Ideally, the best approach would be to ensure new features can be capitalized appropriately for the new user experience so system co-design choices like bigger battery size don't affect the overall product margin but act as an incremental revenue stream.

Microarchitecture optimizations, along with HW-SW co-design and system co-design collectively, are ideal to enhance the performance and efficiency using the available resources to ensure the semiconductors deliver maximum economic value and maintain a competitive edge in the market. This can be possible when product managers embrace a close collaboration approach with stage holders right from the product roadmap KPI target assessment stage to stay ahead of the competition and maintain dominance in the market. While these are all the knobs to twist and turn for achieving and setting competitive KPI targets on the product roadmap, the scope of these knobs is dependent on the programmability of the semiconductor product and software applications, as shown in Figure 9-6. In simple terms, programmability is like a remote to a TV. The TV could have 4K resolution supporting Netflix, Amazon Prime, Xfinity, Peacock, and many other applications and capabilities. The only way to realize its value by the users is through a remote controller and its ability to specify the instructions to help navigate to realize the full potential of the TV as per the user's needs. Like channel shifts, volume, and other settings, including other required information on buttons so users can use the TV system at its potential. Let's discuss programmability.

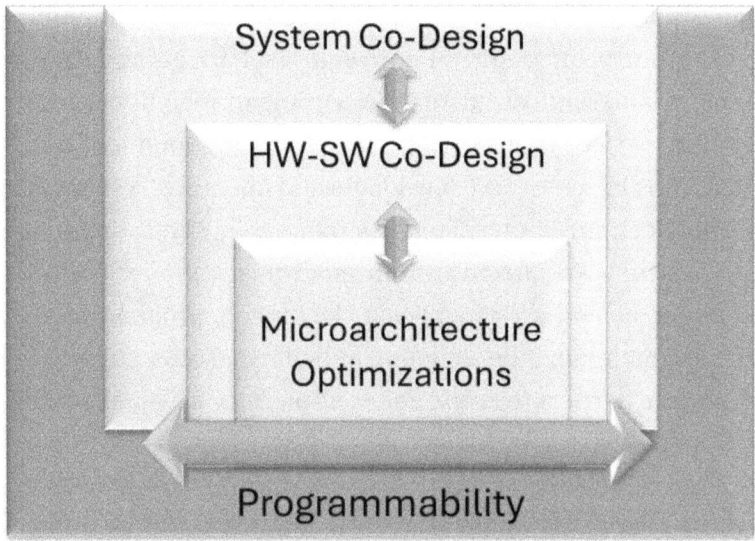

Figure 9-6. *Programmability dependency on semiconductor design*

Programmability and Developer Tools

Programmability in semiconductor products refers to the ability of these products and devices to be configured, reconfigured, or programmed by the semiconductor design product managers, ISVs, and end users as per their needs. Programmability is the essential aspect of semiconductor product management for product managers to track, update, and improve, similar to the semiconductor products. The drivers and APIs[8] for the developer ecosystem and supporting operating systems to increase the user base in the hardware ecosystem are critical to driving leadership in the industry. For example, NVIDIA's leadership in the GPU market is attained by unmatched programmability support using compute unified design architecture (CUDA) and other tools besides GPU hardware.

---

[8] API Application programmable interface

CHAPTER 9   COMPETITIVE SEMICONDUCTOR PRODUCT ROADMAPS

Semiconductor product managers must embrace a broader mindset and focus beyond semiconductor hardware level drivers and APIs to ensure end-to-end semiconductor device programmability. As shown in Figure 9-7, the various layers in semiconductor programmability, from drivers and APIs to ecosystem developers and operating systems, shape end-user application features. This programmability and support ensure their APIs and tools are effectively utilized to create new experiences and features at the end customer level. The broader programmability support helps maintain differentiation and manage ecosystem challenges like competitive barriers to entry. For example, along with APIs, drivers, and developer tools, Apple has iOS, iPadOS, macOS and other operating systems per product line to efficiently use semiconductor hardware resources based on the product usage. Therefore, programmability is a key aspect to integrate into a product roadmap, it helps product managers to guide the long-term strategy of a semiconductor product, influencing decisions around product development, market positioning, and technological innovation.

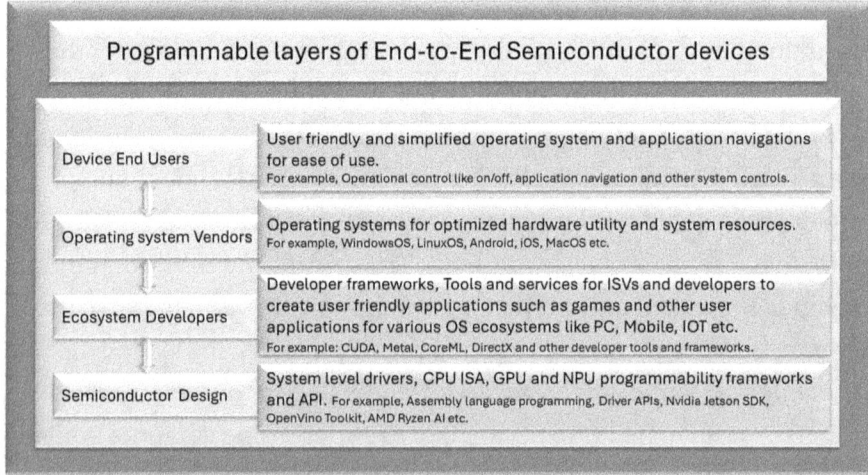

Figure 9-7. Programmable layers of end-to-end semiconductor devices

A product roadmap that emphasizes programmability can ensure that the products meet current demands and are capable of evolving with future technological advancements. For example, Generative AI models can run on existing semiconductor products with programmability support, thereby increasing the value of the semiconductor products further. As part of building programmability strengths, product managers must make decisions to choose from different programmability frameworks such as open source, proprietary, or a mix of open source and proprietary to differentiate against competition.

Open Source and Proprietary Frameworks

The programming frameworks in the semiconductor product ecosystem are divided into open source, proprietary, and hybrid (a mix of open source and proprietary), as shown in the Table 9-2. These proprietary, open source, and hybrid programming frameworks provide the tools and libraries needed to develop software for specific tasks or hardware platforms.

Table 9-2. Examples of Programmability Frameworks

Framework	Type	Supports
Open CL	Hybrid	CPU, GPU, and others
SYCL	Open Source	CPU, GPU, and others
Open GL	Open Source	GPU
Vulkan	Hybrid	CPU, GPU
ROCm	Open Source by limited to AMD GPUs	GPU
CUDA	Proprietary to NVIDIA GPUs	GPU
DirectX	Proprietary to Microsoft Windows Platforms	GPU
Metal	Proprietary to Apple Ecosystem	GPU

CHAPTER 9   COMPETITIVE SEMICONDUCTOR PRODUCT ROADMAPS

An open source framework can be shared over web developer communities like GitHub and lets anyone access the source code and help distribute tools to develop applications through open source license to any ISVs or developers to implement application solutions on compatible semiconductor products across various platforms. For example, consider open source GPU programming frameworks like OpenCL and OpenGL, available on any compatible GPUs. These frameworks can be used to develop user applications like game content creation on cross-platform GPUs. The open source frameworks can be accessible by free license access through governing authority and are usually free of charge, encouraging innovation through collaboration. Besides promoting innovation, open source frameworks have various advantages like flexibility, customization, and community support, as shown in Figure 9-8. However, due to the nature of open source, where anyone can access, modify, and customize the source code, these frameworks may possess security threads to the developed applications.

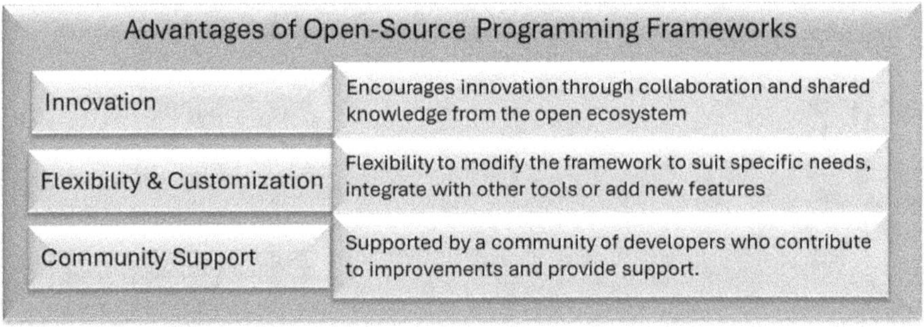

Advantages of Open-Source Programming Frameworks	
Innovation	Encourages innovation through collaboration and shared knowledge from the open ecosystem
Flexibility & Customization	Flexibility to modify the framework to suit specific needs, integrate with other tools or add new features
Community Support	Supported by a community of developers who contribute to improvements and provide support.

Figure 9-8. *Advantages of open source programming frameworks*

On the other hand, proprietary programming frameworks can be shared as part of the semiconductor product toolchain or as part of ISV platform solutions. For example, CUDA and Metal are the proprietary programming frameworks available through NVIDIA and Apple semiconductor products, respectively. At the same time, Microsoft DirectX

CHAPTER 9   COMPETITIVE SEMICONDUCTOR PRODUCT ROADMAPS

is a proprietary framework available to developers on any semiconductor products to implement solutions across Windows platforms. The proprietary frameworks are well secured and provide feature upgrades to the developers with continuous improvements with extensive support, as shown in Figure 9-9. However, the innovation in proprietary programming frameworks is limited to the vendor's research ability and capabilities.

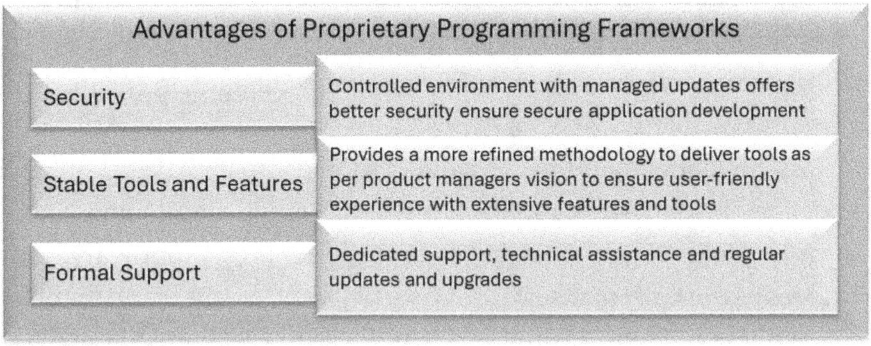

Advantages of Proprietary Programming Frameworks

Security	Controlled environment with managed updates offers better security ensure secure application development
Stable Tools and Features	Provides a more refined methodology to deliver tools as per product managers vision to ensure user-friendly experience with extensive features and tools
Formal Support	Dedicated support, technical assistance and regular updates and upgrades

Figure 9-9. Advantages of proprietary programming frameworks

A hybrid framework uses a mix of open source and proprietary frameworks. Product managers must evaluate the best choice of programming framework suitable to gain or maintain a competitive advantage in the market. Specifically, software capabilities are not very strong in most semiconductor design companies. However, making hardware and software capabilities the key strengths of implementing semiconductor products and proprietary programming frameworks is ideal. For example, NVIDIA's strong GPU architecture, paired with NVIDIA's programming frameworks, makes it a leader in modern parallel computing. However, to offset the software strength, product managers can take an approach similar to AMD, where the ROCm framework is made open source but is only available on their GPUs. This helps AMD continuously improve the ROCm framework through community support and all the advantages of the open source framework. This semiconductor

CHAPTER 9   COMPETITIVE SEMICONDUCTOR PRODUCT ROADMAPS

product-specific open source programming framework approach helps enhance the semiconductor product competitive advantage in the market. This can help product managers enhance the application development capabilities through continuous framework innovation and upgrades by leveraging larger ecosystem community strengths. However, product managers must not leave the framework development entirely on the open ecosystem but take a mid-way approach to leverage the ecosystem to gain software expertise. Additionally, product managers must take measures to establish framework security by enforcing strict guidelines to ensure the framework is stable and secure.

The semiconductor product roadmap should also include the optimal programmable framework approach that suits product development strategy by evaluating the pros and cons of open source, proprietary, and hybrid framework approaches.

Regardless of choosing proprietary, open source, or hybrid framework approaches, semiconductor product managers should implement an efficient programmable framework that delivers higher performance using optimal compute and memory resources and efficient power consumption by proactively considering hardware-specific features and constraints along with the software components of the system such as OS kernels, device drivers, middleware, and application software suitable for the target semiconductor hardware platform.

For example, NVIDIA developed a proprietary CUDA software framework and tools for developers to program applications that deliver optimal performance on NVIDIA hardware, making it a leader in parallel computing. NVIDIA states, "CUDA is a programming language for the hardware and the hardware that runs the programming language." NVIDIA designed the CUDA programming framework to match what the hardware can do and adjust the hardware to be more programmable. The framework approach to execution is highly parallelized, as shown in Figure 9-10. A single image can be broken down into many blocks, so they can be executed with maximum compute hardware utility with optimal memory usage.

Figure 9-10. An example of CUDA framework processing an image (source: Nvidia GTC 2022)

Competitive Intelligence

Competitive intelligence in semiconductor product management is as important as any other business seeking to maintain or improve its competitive position by systematically collecting and analyzing data on competitors and the market through public information and ethical sources. Semiconductor product managers can make informed roadmap decisions that enhance the competitive position, anticipate challenges ahead, and seize potential opportunities if possible.

The goal is to assess the competitive landscape and develop product roadmaps that gain a competitive edge. The information revealed during technology conferences, product launch presentations, patent publications, investor meetings, SEC filings, IDC surveys, testing publicly available competitor products, and other legitimate sources provide valuable competitive intelligence for product managers to leverage in defining or updating the product roadmaps.

CHAPTER 9   COMPETITIVE SEMICONDUCTOR PRODUCT ROADMAPS

Competitive intelligence is not only gathering and analyzing information on competitor products but also understanding the implications of the competitor's product strategy and its impacts on market trends and customers. It is more like knowing competitor product managers' long-term and short-term vision of the product and analyzing its impact on the market trends. As innovations and a forward-thinking approach drive the technology industry, the products have the power to shape the customer and market behavior. For example, if I ask my niece to help me with a math calculation, he simply suggests I use a calculator on my phone. Therefore, the information gathered through sources should be viewed in terms of the value the competitor products are creating in the market and to the customers. With this value comparison information handy, product managers can implement competitive product roadmaps to deliver better or higher-value products than competitors, ensuring a customer-centric approach. The comparison gets challenging with the open ecosystem like Windows PC and Android mobile, for semiconductor product managers to assess the end customer value in such a complex ecosystem. The challenge is worth taking to implement a customer-centric approach for long-term success. On the data center and enterprise side, semiconductor product managers can collaborate with other B2C product managers to seek their feedback and long-term customer solutions vision while evaluating the competitor's strategy to develop a robust semiconductor product roadmap.

The customer-perceived product value over competitor product features paired with timely competitive intelligence helps product managers set appropriate competitive product roadmap KPI targets. The targets can be set to offset the competitor's strategy's short-term or long-term implications.

CHAPTER 9   COMPETITIVE SEMICONDUCTOR PRODUCT ROADMAPS

Projections

Projections in a product roadmap refer to the anticipated timelines, features set, milestones, and KPI targets executed in semiconductor development and the evolution of a product line over time. These projections are critical for aligning the efforts of different teams within a company, managing resources, and setting expectations with stakeholders, including customers, partners, and investors. The feature projections outline the future SoC or subsystem features and KPIs introduced with its launch. Features could include adding programmable features, enhancements to existing functionality, or introducing new technologies measured through benchmarks and application use cases.

Product managers must ensure projection models are developed entirely through data and learned assumptions that can be backed by facts to ensure educated and data-driven projections of future products. This can be possible by thoroughly comprehending underlying dependencies through sensitivity analysis of the factors contributing to the PPA and KPI targets. The dependencies such as microarchitecture, process technology, memory bandwidth and latency, TDP, and semiconductor area (cost) associated with the product must be modeled to derive data-driven KPI target projections, as shown in Figure 9-11.

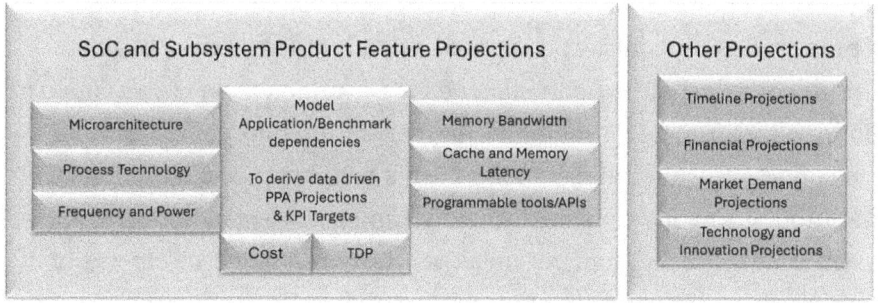

Figure 9-11. An example of feature and performance projections

CHAPTER 9   COMPETITIVE SEMICONDUCTOR PRODUCT ROADMAPS

The educated assumptions and sensitivity data-driven projections help product managers get the KPI modeling better with incremental learnings and identify any risks associated with the model projections. However, the assumptions of the model need to be scenario-based, and it is ideal for product managers to do multi-scenario modeling and be prepared for the risks associated with mitigation plans. These scenario-based modeling inputs and outputs should be added to the competitive product strategy development framework to develop a robust product strategy with a long-term competitive product roadmap.

Besides roadmap product features, product managers must project the launch timeline, financials, demand, and technology trends to ensure the roadmap products are executed seamlessly and meet their targets respectively for sustainable success in the marketplace. Once the product KPIs are projected, for example, if there are premium, mainstream, and entry SoCs as part of the product roadmap with certain KPIs. Product managers need to position those SoCs in the market by choosing a strategic self-cannibalization strategy with incremental revenue through a robust product portfolio structure. Let's discuss the product portfolio.

Product Portfolio

The product portfolio in semiconductors products refers to the range of product lines specifically designed and tailored for supporting the various compute and functional needs of the targeted user segments. The semiconductor SoCs for segments like server and data center, gaming and content creators, workstations, casual consumer, and commercial PCs, mobile, and IoTs can be designed using a single generation of IPs by scaling the SoC integration as per the compute requirements of each segment. The portfolio typically includes various types of SoCs,

CHAPTER 9   COMPETITIVE SEMICONDUCTOR PRODUCT ROADMAPS

memory chips, discrete graphics processors, chipsets, and other essential components that power and enable the functionality of semiconductor products in each segment.

Consider Apple's product portfolio[9] on personal computing as an example. As shown in Table 9-3, Apple designs a generation of CPU, GPU, NPU, and other peripheral component IPs and scales these IPs to various integrated SoCs sizes such as A series, M series, M Pro Series, M Max series, and M Ultra series with an increase in compute and functional capabilities respectively. The vast product portfolio with tailored compute SoCs serves multiple PC and mobile customer segments paired with a pricing strategy to have a deliberate healthy product cannibalization. Moreover, similar compute SoC in different form factor offerings serve customers with personalized device choices without compromising system performance. In Apple's case, Apple entirely makes product portfolio decisions due to its end-to-end ecosystem integration. Product managers in the open semiconductor ecosystem, such as Windows, Android, and cloud/enterprise semiconductor infrastructure providers, must make product portfolio decisions in collaboration with stakeholders and manage the semiconductor product (SoC) portfolio accordingly through the product roadmap.

---

[9] Data derived from Apple.com as of August 2024

CHAPTER 9   COMPETITIVE SEMICONDUCTOR PRODUCT ROADMAPS

Table 9-3. Apple Mobile and PCs Product Portfolio as of August 2024

Product Lines	Silicon Series	Form Factors
Apple iPhone	Apple A series chips	Mobile
Apple iPad	Apple A series chips	Tablets
Apple iPad Mini	Apple A series chips	
Apple iPad Pro	Apple M series chips	
Apple iPad Air	Apple M series chips	
Apple MacBook Air 15"	Apple M series chips	Laptops
Apple MacBook Air 13"	Apple M series chip	
Apple MacBook Pro 14"	Apple M, M Pro, and M Max series chips	
Apple MacBook Pro 16"	Apple M Pro and M Max series chips	
Apple iMac	Apple M series chip	All-in-One Desktop
Apple Mac Mini	Apple M and M Pro series chip	Desktops
Apple Mac Studio	Apple M Max and M Ultra series chips	
Apple Mac Pro	Apple M Ultra series chip	

To maintain and decide on a robust product portfolio product roadmap, semiconductor product managers have to thoroughly study the market, technology trends, user behaviors, and preferences along with their compute needs to maintain a tailored product portfolio in consumer electronics and differentiate the product portfolio as needed to ensure flexibility and price advantage. In contrast, enterprise and data center portfolios should be based on the application requirements, such as latency for stock management and endurance for data management. The product portfolio should ensure a robust supply chain so that customers can access the entire product portfolio. Let's discuss the supply chain.

CHAPTER 9   COMPETITIVE SEMICONDUCTOR PRODUCT ROADMAPS

OEMs and Supply Chain

The semiconductor product portfolio depends on original Equipment Manufacturers (OEMs) for production if semiconductor products are designed for open ecosystem devices and the supply chain for their distribution. Besides helping to build a strong semiconductor product portfolio, OEMs and distribution channels ensure the entire product portfolio is available to the users easily. Semiconductor product managers can collaborate with OEMs and channel partners for efficient production like Just-in-Time and distribution with support documentation, customer support, end of life (EOL), and product refresh process. This process requires product managers to closely collaborate with OEMs on design wins to accurately make demand and supply estimates and long-term projections with risk-mitigating strategies to address product delivery and management. While this may be early to think of during product roadmap planning, it helps product managers proactively think of these scenarios in modeling financial estimates to better control the semiconductor product development life cycle. Large companies like Intel, AMD, Qualcomm, and others have established a standard process in collaboration with OEMs and channel partners to efficiently deliver the SoCs to produce and deliver products. For example, Dell Technologies has mastered the Just-in-Time product assembly and distribution methodology for cheaper distribution. Similarly, Apple implements a build-to-order (BTO) methodology to assemble a product only after confirming a customer order.

Product managers implementing semiconductor roadmap planning should proactively consider feature planning, competitive KPI targets, dependencies, launch timelines, customer segments, and product portfolios with appropriate supply chain methods until the product's EOL. This end-to-end process can be figured out early in the roadmap planning stage utilizing competitive product strategy developed using the competitive product strategy development framework.

CHAPTER 9   COMPETITIVE SEMICONDUCTOR PRODUCT ROADMAPS

The Secret to Strong Product Roadmaps

Approaches to defining semiconductor SoC product roadmaps, methodologies for organizing long-term roadmaps, various product objectives with clear KPIs, and dependencies of those KPIs to find the best approach for competitive product KPIs are all factors that help product managers to prepare a long-term actionable semiconductor product strategy with clear objectives, targets to guide internal teams, external stakeholders, and their customers to deliver a successful product. The product managers should organize regular reviews and monitoring of the information from development teams, market dynamics and stakeholders to ensure the roadmap is adaptable with necessary updates to ensure competitive advantage.

To create a strong product roadmap, product managers should embrace a strong product vision that can create and capture customer value with a flexible execution strategy. This strong product vision with implementation flexibility ensures product managers adapt to the changing market dynamics, learn from past experiences, collaborate with other ecosystem partners, and innovate new technologies to create a valuable product with a competitive edge in the market. Product managers can follow a two-step framework approach[10] (see Figure 9-12) to build strong roadmaps. The first step is to explore new technologies that fit the product vision, and the next step is to improve and exploit existing technologies and methodologies to continuously create customer value.

---

[10] https://journals.aom.org/doi/abs/10.5465/AMJ.2006.22083026
  Henrich R. Greve, "Exploration and exploitation in product innovation," *Industrial and Corporate Change*, Volume 16, Issue 5, October 2007, Pages 945–975, https://doi.org/10.1093/icc/dtm013

CHAPTER 9　COMPETITIVE SEMICONDUCTOR PRODUCT ROADMAPS

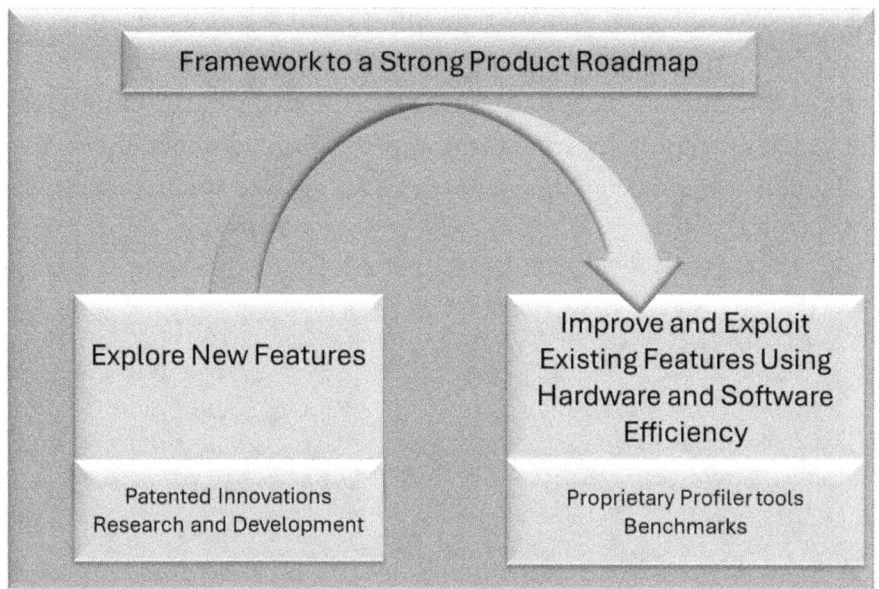

Figure 9-12. A strong product roadmap framework

Product managers must focus on innovating new technology features by investing in research and development resources that fit the product vision and simultaneously focus on improving and exploiting the invented features in future product generations. This cycle must continue to beat your product's value every generation with consistent growth above the competition. Consider an example scenario as shown in Figure 9-13. With a vision to continuously improve the SoC value in user applications, a product manager innovated new features such as GPU ability to support ray tracing and CPU ability to accelerate AI operations using AMX implementations. This is the first part of exploring ideas in which a product manager has to analyze multiple research and development innovations and implement the ones that add value to the customers. In the example, Ray tracing features help gamers and content creators to develop realistic scenes in moving lights and shadows to enhance the user experience in multimedia. AMX accelerates the AI operations such as faster facial or

CHAPTER 9   COMPETITIVE SEMICONDUCTOR PRODUCT ROADMAPS

object recognition. Exploring for right innovations relevant to increase the value of the products is the first step. This value-based exploration must be followed by continuous improvements and exploring existing innovations. The secret is to repeat both these steps in every product generation of the semiconductor product in the roadmap for strong continuous growth.

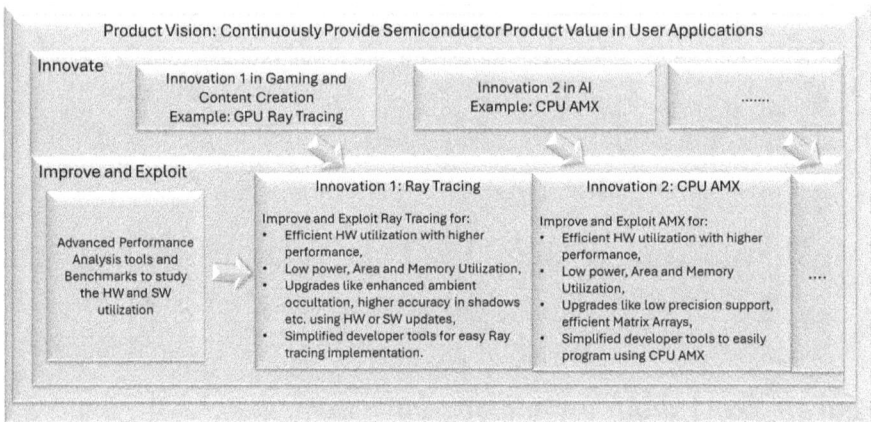

Figure 9-13. *An example of implementing a two-step product roadmap framework*

Improving and exploiting must be implemented using advanced performance analysis tools and benchmarks that help study the hardware and software behavior to find opportunities to improve and exploit. The performance analysis tools act like mirrors, revealing the hardware and software's current behavior and patterns to realize bottlenecks and improvement opportunities. The performance analysis tools also can drive innovative features to solve existing bottlenecks. The two successful semiconductor companies, NVIDIA and Apple, have a vast set of proprietary performance analysis tools to profile the various SoC application dependencies and their behaviors to help continuous improvement and innovation, as shown in Figures 9-14 and 9-15.

294

CHAPTER 9   COMPETITIVE SEMICONDUCTOR PRODUCT ROADMAPS

Therefore, the secret to strong roadmaps is exploring, improving, and exploiting features, while performance analysis tools are the secret to strong product roadmap implementation.

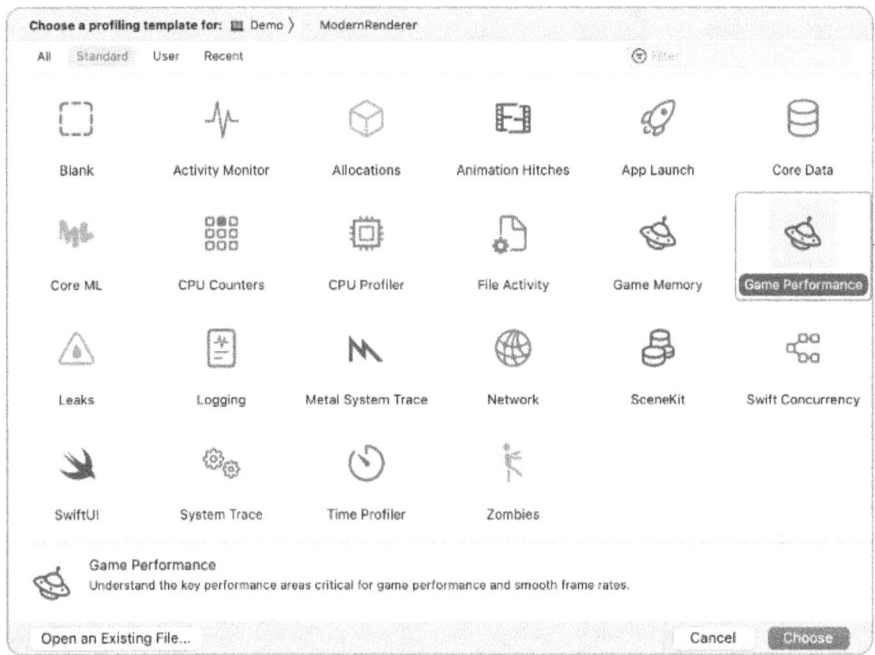

Figure 9-14. *NVIDIA performance analysis tools (source: NVIDIA.com)*

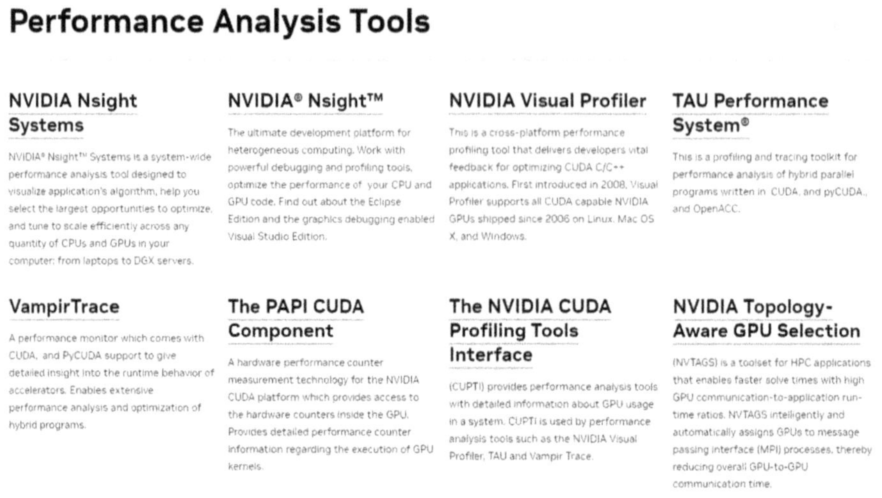

CHAPTER 9   COMPETITIVE SEMICONDUCTOR PRODUCT ROADMAPS

Performance Analysis Tools

NVIDIA Nsight Systems
NVIDIA® Nsight™ Systems is a system-wide performance analysis tool designed to visualize application's algorithm, help you select the largest opportunities to optimize, and tune to scale efficiently across any quantity of CPUs and GPUs in your computer: from laptops to DGX servers.

NVIDIA® Nsight™
The ultimate development platform for heterogeneous computing. Work with powerful debugging and profiling tools, optimize the performance of your CPU and GPU code. Find out about the Eclipse Edition and the graphics debugging enabled Visual Studio Edition.

NVIDIA Visual Profiler
This is a cross-platform performance profiling tool that delivers developers vital feedback for optimizing CUDA C/C++ applications. First introduced in 2008, Visual Profiler supports all CUDA capable NVIDIA GPUs shipped since 2006 on Linux, Mac OS X, and Windows.

TAU Performance System®
This is a profiling and tracing toolkit for performance analysis of hybrid parallel programs written in CUDA, and pyCUDA, and OpenACC.

VampirTrace
A performance monitor which comes with CUDA, and PyCUDA support to give detailed insight into the runtime behavior of accelerators. Enables extensive performance analysis and optimization of hybrid programs.

The PAPI CUDA Component
A hardware performance counter measurement technology for the NVIDIA CUDA platform which provides access to the hardware counters inside the GPU. Provides detailed performance counter information regarding the execution of GPU kernels.

The NVIDIA CUDA Profiling Tools Interface
(CUPTI) provides performance analysis tools with detailed information about GPU usage in a system. CUPTI is used by performance analysis tools such as the NVIDIA Visual Profiler, TAU and Vampir Trace.

NVIDIA Topology-Aware GPU Selection
(NVTAGS) is a toolset for HPC applications that enables faster solve times with high GPU communication-to-application run-time ratios. NVTAGS intelligently and automatically assigns GPUs to message passing interface (MPI) processes, thereby reducing overall GPU-to-GPU communication time.

Figure 9-15. *Apple performance analysis tools (source: Apple.com)*

Summary

The semiconductor product roadmap seems to be a complex task. But following a systematic methodology, product managers can ensure the roadmap is defined and organized, capturing competitive KPI targets based on product strategy, market trends and competitive intelligence. In addition to defining the KPI targets, product managers should also define the path to implementing and achieving the set KPI targets through a thorough grasp of the KPIs and their dependencies. Paired with strong collaboration with stakeholders and partners to align on clear objectives which are communicated, reviewed, and revised regularly to adapt to the dynamics in the industry. Product managers can help define a robust and competitive product roadmap for execution by leveraging two-step roadmap frameworks to explore, improve, and exploit and using advanced performance analysis tools. This roadmap helps product managers enter the development cycle with clear objectives and targets leading to successful product launches. Product managers can utilize concepts to define and execute the semiconductor product's life cycle for market success. Additionally, AI can be a valuable tool for product managers to further develop effective product management methodologies in semiconductor performance management, manufacturing, and other areas. Let's discuss how AI can impact semiconductor product management.

CHAPTER 10

AI in Semiconductor Product Management

In the modern AI technology marketplace, each user has to be treated as a unique segment with a demanding personalized product experience revolutionizing semiconductor product management.

—Sultana Begum

The introduction of generative AI has transformed the technology industry into a new era of possibilities. Traditionally, typical information procurement was based on Google or other search engine tools built on an algorithm to gather data from the web. For example, the ChatGPT is positioned as a single entity that knows everything in every possible area. It was trained on diverse data sources, including books, websites, research papers, and other publicly available content. This training allows it to generate ethical and rational responses based on a broad understanding of language, knowledge, and concepts. It's as if you have someone by your side who knows everything and is ready to always assist you, as shown in Figure 10-1. Let's discuss the importance and impact of AI on semiconductor product management.

CHAPTER 10   AI IN SEMICONDUCTOR PRODUCT MANAGEMENT

Figure 10-1. *Generative AI possibilities*

AI Transformation in Semiconductor Product Management

Like ChatGPT in information search, AI transforms semiconductor product management by enhancing efficiency, reducing costs, and enabling data-driven decision-making. From planning roadmaps to design, development, and manufacturing to EOL, AI can help develop powerful tools and algorithms to optimize every stage of the semiconductor product life cycle. Embracing AI in product management helps stay competitive and paves the way for innovation and long-term success in the dynamically evolving semiconductor product industry.

AI in Product Development Life cycle

In R&D, AI-driven analysis can help identify new materials, processes, and HW-SW architectures by analyzing vast amounts of scientific data, accelerating innovation in semiconductor technology and user applications. AI-driven algorithms can optimize semiconductor designs by predicting the performance of configurations and combinations such as core count, throughput, latency, memory bandwidth, frequency, and others to select the best option to meet the KPI targets. This helps product managers to significantly reduce the data modeling, roadmap implementation and design cycle time with improved product performance. Supervised and unsupervised Machine learning models can learn from historical data to predict how a new design behaves and reveal potential bugs, reducing the need for scenario-based manual testing and meeting delivery deadlines. AI tools can generate innovative semiconductor architectures by exploring a vast design space more efficiently than traditional methods in complex integrated SoCs with billions of transistors. AI can also assist product managers in tracking product design and development processes with data-driven and granular details for effective design management.

Product managers can implement AI-driven dynamic pricing algorithms by continuously analyzing market conditions, competitor pricing, and supply-demand elasticity. Additionally, AI models can predict manufacturing and development costs based on prior market data. AI models get more accurate pricing and budgeting as the datasets get bigger and broader. Similarly, product managers can use AI algorithms to analyze market trends, customer behavior, and historical sales data to forecast demand more accurately. This streamlines inventory management and helps predict when a semiconductor product reaches the end of its life cycle based on consumer sales data, technology trends, and market conditions.

AI-powered decision tree models support product managers with actionable insights for data-driven decisions in real time by synthesizing and analyzing multiple data sources such as customer feedback, market demands, and technological advancements. Product managers can decide on timely product upgrades or new features, ensuring the product line remains competitive.

Product managers can leverage AI tools in each stage of the semiconductor product's life cycle for better control and data-driven decision-making. Additionally, the automated tools help improve and exploit the existing product implementation, fostering operational excellence. Now that you know more about AI in product development, let's discuss how AI impacts consumer market trends and user experience, demanding more AI applications and solutions from electronic product users.

AI Use Cases

The AI use case market is divided into cloud, enterprise, and client, similar to generic computational use cases. In my opinion, AI use cases bring a huge update to the way things were traditionally implemented. Let's consider Google's search engine example. Traditionally it used a search engine algorithm to list the top-rated websites from which users must manually procure information. With ChatGPT and other LLMs, summarizing and procuring information became simpler. Traditionally, to create a movie or music or write an email, users have manually started designing each character's identity, writing musical notes and rhythms, and emails from scratch, where as with generative AI models the images, music, and text generation has become easy to help users be more creative. This is a huge leap forward for AI driver consumer application technology.

CHAPTER 10　AI IN SEMICONDUCTOR PRODUCT MANAGEMENT

For enterprise businesses, AI models help automate numerous redundant tasks fostering the industry to innovate and push the boundaries of technology while exploiting redundant tasks with AI. The industrial product development and many other open universal scene description (OpenUSD)-driven use cases implemented using digital twins to learn and develop precise products and services as planned help many businesses to improve marketplace product offerings.

Therefore, AI has revolutionized every segment of the technology industry. Accurate climate and weather predictions optimized agricultural practices, faster research and development studies in medicine and many other industries have seen a huge uplift in the way things were implemented traditionally and empowering human capabilities. However, with great power comes great responsibility. These AI platforms (cloud/enterprise/client) and their implementations must be secure and appropriately implemented using guardrails to avoid unwanted results and consequences. As semiconductor is the basis of any technological advancement, AI is also heavily driven by the semiconductor products that execute these AI use cases across cloud/enterprise and client platforms. There is a huge competition in semiconductor product companies to deliver tailored semiconductor hardware to increase the performance of AI use cases. AI adds another competitive edge to the already competitive semiconductor product market. From a hardware point of view, accelerators like CPU, GPU, and NPU are popularly utilized for AI execution. The AI competition in the semiconductor industry is intensifying as every company strives to leverage AI to gain a competitive edge. Let's briefly discuss AI competition.

CHAPTER 10   AI IN SEMICONDUCTOR PRODUCT MANAGEMENT

Competition in AI

The AI competition in the semiconductor industry is multifaceted, involving advances in hardware, software, design, manufacturing, and end-user use cases. Product managers must integrate AI into their product management strategies and continuously innovate AI-driven technologies to stay ahead of the competition for sustained success. As AI solutions and innovations continue to evolve, the competitive dynamics intensify and lead to faster innovation and the emergence of new leaders across all the semiconductor industry elements. Product managers must aggressively implement SWOT analysis and focus on gaining strength by collaborating with or acquiring other companies that complement the AI implementation to increase the competitive advantage.

The current competition landscape can be divided into an open source pre-trained model generation such as Llama, Mistral, Gemma, Phi, and many others transformer architecture LLMs (large language models), multimodal Mamba models, convolutional neural networks, variable autoencoder for diffuser models and many other models are a starting point to begin the development of AI use cases. These models help developers implement use cases like chatbots, content creation applications, AI-driven productivity apps, augmented shopping, and autonomous driving. The models are trained on different datasets with different capabilities and hardware requirements. Product managers must plan to implement hardware configurations such as compute TOPS and memory bandwidth configurations to meet the needs of the AI models.

The next step is to ensure a robust programmability framework is available to ensure the developers can implement IA solutions to empower the ecosystem, such as Windows OS, macOS, and others. Product managers' collective implementation of hardware and programmability support ensures a strong foundation for AI competitiveness, as shown in Figure 10-2. For example, NVIDIA implemented Tensor cores and TensorRT runtime for efficient model training and deployment of AI

CHAPTER 10   AI IN SEMICONDUCTOR PRODUCT MANAGEMENT

models on their hardware. Like generic GPU programmable solutions, AI can also be implemented in open source, proprietary and hybrid methods. Product managers must pick the implementation that fits their product strategy.

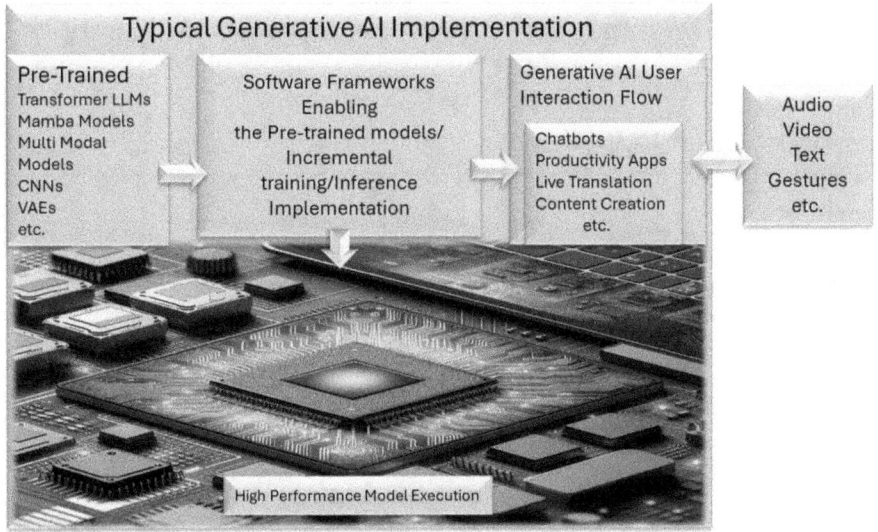

Figure 10-2. Typical implementation of generative AI

Programmable frameworks such as Copilot Runtime or ONNX Runtime from Microsoft and Core ML from Apple, Triton Inference Server, TensorRT from NVIDIA, OpenVINO from Intel, and RyzenAI from AMD are some of the popular AI frameworks in the AI developer space. On the other hand, Llama.cpp, PyTorch, and TensorFlow are open source frameworks to deploy LLMs and other models on compatible semiconductor products, as shown in Table 10-1. AI is a fast topic and is dynamically changing the competitive landscape of the semiconductor product industry. Semiconductor product managers must implement semiconductor products for faster AI performance.

CHAPTER 10   AI IN SEMICONDUCTOR PRODUCT MANAGEMENT

Table 10-1. *Examples of AI Software Frameworks*

	NVIDIA Corp.	**Apple Inc.**	**Intel Corp.**	**AMD Corp.**
Software Frameworks Examples	CUDA, TensorRT	Core ML, MLX	OpenVINO, DirectML	RyzenAI, DirectML
Open Source Frameworks	Llama.cpp, TensorFlow, PyTorch…			

Summary

The scope of what artificial intelligence can offer in bringing efficiency to the existing processes and future innovations has become huge with the introduction of generative AI, which can be a huge advantage to product managers to bring competitive, innovative features with faster turnarounds in timelines.

Conclusion

This book began by discussing the importance of product managers and their key roles in making product management successful in advanced technology-based semiconductor product life cycle processes. Competitiveness is an important element in product management, and losing the competitive edge can cause successful companies to lose their market share and get out of business. Windows phones and BlackBerry phones eventually failed for not implementing competitive product management. Windows phone never succeeded but BlackBerry fell from a dominant market position for missing the implementation of effective competitive product management. To conclude, the key is to not just think about competition but keep competition as one key input in all product management decision phases to continuously improve product quality by continuous innovation and scalability to provide great customer service at a great price with competitive differentiation.

Competition played a significant role in driving the technology industry forward with revolutionary trends such as the evolution of single semiconductor transistors to an SoC with billions of transistors executing trillions of operations. With such advancements, the modern evolution of the PC industry implemented semiconductor systems on chips with CPU as a central processing unit and other accelerator compute units like GPU and NPU along with other SoC peripherals to executive current compute applications delivering great performance and user experience. The typical PC user segment categories are consumer and commercial. Windows and Apple ecosystems play dominant roles in positioning their products in the PC industry, leveraging their strengths and challenging each other.

CONCLUSION

Product managers must create the social and economic value for their semiconductor products to succeed in the marketplace. The product manager's role gets challenging in creating and capturing higher economic value in open ecosystems such as Windows, where multiple stakeholders collectively work to capture the maximum portion of the economic value of their products. To succeed, product managers should understand the competitors in depth for long-term sustainability using scenario-based modeling combining business objectives and SWOT analysis to define a product management life cycle framework.

The semiconductor product management life cycle is a rigorous exercise of continuous collaboration and evaluation of trends with various ecosystem partners at all stages of the life cycle. The role product managers play is very critical in each phase of the semiconductor product development cycle to ensure the products keep up with market needs, collaborate, negotiate, and make sure the partners across all the stages keep competitive analysis as a key factor. The semiconductor product life cycle typically has planning, design, and development stages in which there are substages such as design methodology, tape-in, tape-out, sample testing, and product release before the semiconductor products undergo full-volume manufacturing. Manufacturing facilities send the packages to original equipment manufacturers (OEM) for product assembly and delivery. Product managers need to ensure regulatory and standard compliance are met across the stages of the semiconductor product management life cycle.

The architecture of semiconductor SoC in PC and smartphone segments is typically divided into a CPU GPU, NPU, media encoder and decoder, system memory, network connectivity, and other peripherals required to support the use cases. PCs have different form factors, such as desktops, laptops, all-in-ones, tablets, and so forth. CPU architecture depends on the instruction set architecture such as x86, ARM, and RISC V. The three ISA implementations have advantages and disadvantages for product managers to choose them appropriately to meet their product strategy. CPU IPs are scaled in terms of CPU cores, and the performance is mainly measured as a single-core multi-core. The cores are divided into performance cores, medium cores, and efficiency cores to deliver higher performance and power efficiency as needed by the workloads. Some KPIs to track on the CPU are clock speed, IPC, single-core and multi-core performance, and performance per watt. GPU and NPU are accelerators to complement the CPU in specific parallel tasks such as AI and graphics. Some KPIs for GPU and NPU are TOPs/FLOPs, throughput, pipeline efficiency, and performance per watt. Collectively, these compute units are integrated to address various compute needs of the PC and smartphone customer segments.

Power is a critical component for product managers to focus on to implement low power SoC so that the battery life of the PCs and smartphones is longer. While designing SoCs, product managers have to implement power management, although it adds to the design complexity. This complex task can be accomplished by a well-thought-through approach and making the right choices applicable to the design, starting from SoC and platform planning, execution, manufacturing, and OEM assembly of a PC to meet the required performance and power targets. The power management starts with choosing the right transistor threshold voltage, deciding the operating voltage and frequency, and SoC power supply and delivery management. Individual IP power can be managed with meticulous dynamic and leakage power management by setting limits to dynamic power and clock gating or power gating methods. To simplify the power management from small IP components to large SoCs and the entire device, power management states are defined to give hardware and software more flexibility. The advanced process technologies ensure higher frequencies are achieved at low power consumption. Innovating advanced silicon material techniques to lower the leakages allows for lower operating voltages without significant power loss.

CONCLUSION

When fabless companies finish design to enter production, the handouts to manufacturing companies are in the form of tape-out and masks containing the blueprint of the chip. The blueprint is sent to the manufacturing company, the design is fabricated, and individual dies are sorted to filter out nonfunctional dies. The good dies are assembled and tested for power and performance characteristics which eventually end up in the OEM warehouse.

In a perfect Moore's law world, having a monolithic SoC design would be a great choice given transistor count doubles on die every two years to almost double SoC's capabilities. However, technological progress has slowed compared to the needs of the industry in the last few years. A disaggregated MCM method emerged to offset some of its effects. Besides Moore's law, the cost of multi-die chips can be lower than large monolithic dies as there is a higher yield percentage on small dies than single large die. It is not necessary that monolithic is always the cost-aggressive solution. Combining packaging costs and the complex multi-die manufacturing process can also increase costs. Product managers must evaluate the pricing of their product vs. the relevant competition at a given timeline to determine the manufacturing design strategy.

Intel, TSMC, and Samsung are dominant semiconductor manufacturers in the industry. The CHIPS Act is aimed to enhance their capabilities further, driving innovations and shifting the manufacturing leadership back to the United States. However, the global semiconductor industry is highly competitive, and other nations may continue to invest heavily in their capabilities, maintaining the competitive pressure. The competitive pressure may impact global trade dynamics as other countries might take their initiatives to support their domestic semiconductor product capabilities. Product Managers and management should fully assess their corporate strategy to determine how they can operate globally with leadership product differentiation and comply with geo-based restrictions.

CONCLUSION

After the semiconductor products are manufactured, they must be assembled into the final consumer products such as PCs and smartphones. These consumer products are manufactured by the OEMs responsible for procuring and assembling the manufactured semiconductor products and other required components. Before OEMs access the semiconductor chips for product integration, semiconductor product managers must ensure the manufactured semiconductor wafers are cut, packaged, tested for functionality, inspected for quality, and assembled for easy integration by the OEMs. These services are offered by OSAT (outsourced semiconductor assembly and test) facilities and handle the physical encapsulation of semiconductor chips into packages to help OEMs easily integrate the semiconductor chips into the PC or smartphone motherboards using various packaging technologies.

OEMs receive semiconductor chip packages, such as SoCs, CPUs, GPUs, and memory chips, from semiconductor design companies like Intel, AMD, NVIDIA, and others through OSATs. Upon receiving the components, OEMs also perform quality and reliability checks to ensure the received packages meet the required standards. The packages are passed on to manufacturing using a systematic multi-step approach, as shown in the figure such as motherboard assembly, final product assembly and testing, operating system, driver and other software installation, final quality inspection, performance testing, and packaging before they are shipped to channel partners or the customers directly.

OEM channel partners such as Best Buy, Costco, Amazon, Walmart, and others are essential for expanding the reach, customization, and support of OEM products. They add significant value by tailoring solutions to customer needs, managing distribution, and providing localized expertise and support. Product managers must ensure the sales and marketing teams collaborate effectively with OEM and channel partners for technical support, product messaging and other marketing efforts required to generate awareness and help communicate the product's value to the consumer market.

CONCLUSION

The product performance management strategy should integrate various aspects of product management, performance analytics, and strategic planning to ensure that semiconductor products meet their performance, quality, and reliability targets. The performance management strategy also helps product managers to clearly differentiate and manage the product's capabilities as basic, differentiated, and augmented features tailored to the user segment needs, such as gamers and casual users in the PC industry. The ideal approach to performance management is combining the SoC and system-level performance management frameworks to efficiently manage the end-to-end performance of semiconductor products. Continuous monitoring and optimization using a unified framework help product managers quickly adapt to changing workloads and user requirements, ensuring sustained system performance over time. Using pre-silicon, post-silicon, microbenchmarks, synthetic, and real-world benchmarks, product managers can enable end-to-end semiconductor product performance management and profiling tools until the product reaches EOL.

A semiconductor product roadmap is a strategic tool that outlines the competitive product strategy plans for semiconductor products over a specific period with actionable objectives. It serves as a high-level guide for product development, helping align stakeholders, prioritize product features, communicate the product direction both internally and externally, and track progress. The guidance includes clear directions for innovation with objectives and deliverables to build value and trust with customers and partners.

The key aspect of the roadmap is that the KPIs should be compared to the prior generation SoCs and the competition to enforce continuous improvements to the SoCs and stay ahead of the competition. A product roadmap should also be flexible and adaptable to changes in market conditions, customer needs, and internal priorities. The roadmap should be regularly reviewed and revised based on new information, changing priorities, and lessons learned from previous launches.

Product managers should broadly communicate revised roadmap updates to ensure that all stakeholders are informed of the product direction and take input or feedback as necessary. To achieve the product roadmap KPIs, product managers should understand the underlying KPI dependencies such as process technology, microarchitecture, memory architecture, HW-SW and System co-design, programmability, competitive intelligence, projections, and product portfolio. The secret to strong roadmaps is to explore, improve, and exploit features, while performance analysis tools are the secret to strong product roadmap implementation.

AI continuously transforms semiconductor product management by enhancing efficiency, reducing costs, and enabling data-driven decision-making. From planning roadmaps to design, development, and manufacturing to EOL, AI can help develop powerful tools and algorithms to optimize every stage of the semiconductor product life cycle. Product managers can leverage AI tools in each semiconductor product life cycle phase for better control and data-driven decision-making. Additionally, the automated tools help improve and exploit the existing product implementation, fostering operational excellence.

Competitive semiconductor product management is a highly complex process that forces product managers to implement key decisions across various cycle stages. As product managers alone cannot fulfill these challenging decision-making aspects, it would be helpful to implement a rigorous framework such as competitive product strategy development frameworks, performance management framework, and roadmap definition framework to foster an automatic implementation of the process by the product manager teams creating a loop of effective process implementation.

The idea is to create a mechanism of competitive product management that continuously updates and works systematically to ensure long-term sustainable success. Following a strategic framework-based approach ensures teams do not miss any key aspect or deliverable and that the products continuously strive to win in the market. With this process,

CONCLUSION

product managers can foster successful organizational execution by making the right decisions and directing the teams to follow the lead and execute to meet the KPI targets.

The final and critical aspect of a product manager's role in the semiconductor industry is a customer-centric approach. The approach must define the use of technology to solve or improve the customer experience, not the other way around. The technology should only be implemented when it can create and capture value to the customers not because a new technology exists.

Next Steps: Reading Pointers

This book discusses competitive product management, providing specific details into technical aspects and product strategy, and briefly touches on pricing analysis.

Index

A

Advanced matrix extensions (AMX), 112, 113, 271
Advanced RISC machines (ARM), 98, 99
Advanced transistor technology, 160
AI, *see* Artificial intelligence (AI)
AIBO's buggy technology, 86
AI-driven technology capabilities, 28
AI-powered decision tree models, 302
AMD, 15, 192
  acquired Xilinx, 85
  Ryzen Pro 8000 series product offerings, 170
AMX, *see* Advanced matrix extensions (AMX)
Android, 10
Apple, 12, 15, 178, 191, 192
  ecosystem, 16, 17, 21, 255
  Intelligence, 32
  M3 Series SoC Configurations, 133
  PC SoC Launch Timelines from 2020 to 2024, 83
ARM, *see* Advanced RISC machines (ARM)
Artificial intelligence (AI), 1, 182
  AI use case, 302, 303
  chipsets, 9
  in competition, 304, 305
  generative, 299
  possibilities, 300
  in product development life cycle, 301, 302
  software frameworks, 305, 306
  transforms, 300–302
  use case, 302, 303
AVX512, 270

B

Ball grid array (BGA), 171
B2B, *see* Business to business (B2B)
B2C, *see* Business to customer (B2C)
Benchmarking tools, 121
Benchmarks
  and applications, 239
  characteristics, 253
  collaboration, 253
  customer experience, 251

INDEX

Benchmarks (*cont.*)
   development, 253
   microbenchmarks, 241–248
   performance evaluation, 239
   performance evaluation to meet and improve performance, 252
   performance of SoC designs, 238
   product managers, 238
   real-world, 250, 251
   real-world workloads, 251
   role for product managers, 239
   self-identify, 238
   synthetic, 248–250
   systematic and adaptive measurement methodology, 238
   tools and methodologies, 239
   types, 239, 240, 251
   user segments, 239
BGA, *see* Ball grid array (BGA)
BlackBerry, 64, 65, 85
Blockbuster, 10
Build-to-order (BTO) methodology, 291
Business to business (B2B), 13
Business to customer (B2C), 13

C

CAD, *see* Computer-aided design (CAD)
Central processing unit (CPU), 307, 308
   architecture, 96, 308
   clock frequency, 234
   cores, 309
   instructions per cycle (IPC), 234
   microbenchmarks, 242, 243
   performance positioning, 110
   single thread (ST) performance, 268, 269
Channel partners, 200
ChatGPT, 299, 302
Chemical/physical vapor deposition (CVD/PVD), 158
CHIPS Act of 2022, 35, 174, 310
   challenges, 190
   cutting-edge research, 186
   economic impacts, 188, 189
   fabrication facilities (fabs), 186
   JIT manufacturing, 192, 193
   Just-in-Time (JIT) manufacturing, 192, 193
   product managers and management, 190–192
   supply chain and manufacturing vulnerabilities, 186
   technological impacts, 186–188
   TSMC, 185
   United States' technology leadership, 186
CHIPS and Science Act, 35
CineBench GPU, 121
CISC, *see* Complex instruction set computer (CISC)
Client and Cloud Space, 4

INDEX

Cloud-client service flexibility, 3
Cloud services, 2
COGS, *see* Cost of goods sold (COGS)
Competition in Windows PC, 26–28
Competitive environment, 29, 30
Competitive environment assessment, 71
Competitive intelligence, 285, 286
Competitive product management, 5
    client semiconductor products, 5
    computing devices, 6
    research and development, 10
Competitive product strategy, 32
Competitive semiconductor product strategy
    adaptability, 79
    advantages, 67
    architectural improvement, 66
    competitive advantage, 62
        and market-driven product characteristics, 62
    competitor strategies, 63
    customer needs, 63, 64
    decision-making, 66
    development, 76
    development framework, 66–68
    differentiated competitive advantages, 79
    drive innovation with emerging technologies, 63
    execution stages, 87, 88
    information gathering, 63
    informed data-driven decisions, 65
    innovative features, 65
    and strategic differentiation, 63
    internal capabilities, 64
    ISVs in PC Industry, 80
    long-term product success, 63
    long-term product targets, 63
    market conditions change, 64
    market dynamics, 63, 79
    market needs, 79
    opportunities, 63
    performance and technological innovations, 62
    process technology needs, 66
    product competitive advantage, 63
    product-related decisions, 78
    product renewal plans, 81
    product roadmap, 65
    renewal plans and objectives, 78
    risk assessment, 63
    short-and long-term product roadmaps, 65
    short-term and long-term success, 77
    SoC in PC Industry, 80
    strategic decisions, 65
    strategic product positioning, 78
    sustainability, 78

INDEX

Competitive semiconductor product strategy (*cont.*)
    sustainable competitive advantage, 79
    systematic framework approach, 62
    value chain, 76
Competitor products, 286
Competitor SWOT analysis, 75, 76
Complex instruction set computer (CISC), 97
Computer-aided design (CAD), 52, 116
Compute unified design architecture (CUDA), 124, 279, 282, 284, 285
Computing technology industry, 3
Consumer products, 311
Copilot Runtime, 305
Cost of goods sold (COGS), 189
CPU, *see* Central processing unit (CPU)
CUDA, *see* Compute unified design architecture (CUDA)
Cutting-edge lithography techniques, 188
Cutting-edge process technology, 158
Cutting-edge technology, 191
CVD/PVD, *see* Chemical/physical vapor deposition (CVD/PVD)

D

Database management system, 207
Data-driven competitive landscape, 31
Data-driven decision-making, 302
DDR, *see* Double data rate (DDR)
Deep learning, 124
Dell Latitude, 94
Device-level performance management, 232
DFT and DFD approach, 228–231
DFT tests, 199
Disaggregated multi-die design, 92
Discrete GPU, 119
Discrete graphics, 119
Distributed ecosystem, 34
Distributed semiconductor product ecosystem, 22, 23
Diverse data sources, 299
Double data rate (DDR), 271
DRAM capacity, 107
DRAM modules, 198
Dynamic voltage and frequency scaling (DVFS), 209

E

Economic and social value, 18–22, 308
    competition, 2
    product, 18, 24, 43, 58
Ecosystem partner analysis, 70
Ecosystem partners, 292

EDA, *see* Electronic design automation (EDA)
EDA tools, 231
Electromagnetic compatibility (EMC) standards, 58
Electronic design automation (EDA), 52, 228
End of life (EOL), 222, 312
Engineering samples, 53
Enterprise businesses, 303
EOL, *see* End of life (EOL)
EOL management, 256
External industrial influencers, 73
External semiconductor industry, 72
Extreme ultraviolet (EUV) lithography, 137, 173, 188

F

Fabless semiconductor product companies, 171
Fabrication technologies and design methodologies, 9, 25
Fixed transistor technology, 142
FLOPS, 120, 121
FP16, 32, 128

G

GDDR memory, 118
Geekbench, 153, 237
Geekbench CPU, 108, 121
Generations, 263
Generative AI, 299
Generic CPU performance, 108
Generic product success criteria, 66
Generic progress tracking methodology, 62
GFLOPS, 117
Giga, 117
GitHub, 282
GlobalFoundries, 173, 175
Gmail application service, 3
Google ChromeOS, 12
Go-to-market strategy, 254, 255
Graphics processing unit (GPU), 307, 308
  accelerated graphics rendering, 114
  accelerator, 114
  design, 115
  market, 279
  microbenchmarks, 244, 245
  programmability, 123

H

Hardware and software solutions in PCs, 8
Hardware-software (HW-SW) co-design, 273–277
High-bandwidth memory (HBM), 271
High-tech employment, 189
HP EliteBook, 94

INDEX

HW-SW co-design/HW-guided quality of service, 266
Hybrid framework, 283

I

iMac, 19
Independent software vendors (ISVs) applications, 14, 206, 214
Instruction set architecture (ISA), 97–101, 269, 270, 308
Integrated graphics in SoCs, 119
Intel, 25, 26, 58, 187, 192, 310
Intel Core i3, 12
Intel Core i5, 12
Intel Core i7, 12
Intel designs and manufactures, 174, 176, 177
Intellectual property (IP), 181
Intel Meteor Lake processors, 93
Intel PC SoC Launch Timelines from 2021 to 2023[2], 82
Intel's IDM 2.0 strategy, 174
Internal analysis, 70
iPadOS, 12
IP, see Intellectual property (IP)
IP power management, 145, 146
i5/Ryzen5, 95
i7/Ryzen 7, 95
i9/Ryzen 9, 95

ISA, see Instruction set architecture (ISA)
ISVs, see Independent software vendors (ISVs)

J

Just-in-Time (JIT) and distribution, 291

K

Key performance indicators (KPIs), 44, 309, 312, 313
  defined, 260, 261
  GPU power management, 123
  NPU, 129
KPIs, see Key performance indicators (KPIs)

L

Land grid array (LGA), 171
Large language models (LLMs), 271, 302
Lenovo ThinkPad, 94
LGA, see Land grid array (LGA)
LLMs, see Large language models (LLMs)
Logic board, 198
Low power double data rate memory (LPDDR), 271

M

MacBook Pro, 94
macOS, 12
MACs (multiply-accumulate), 246
MAD (multiply-add)
  operations, 246
Market analysis, 70, 71, 76
Market dynamics, 34
Market segment share (MSS), 15
McAfee, 7
MCM, *see* Multi-chip
  modules (MCM)
Media Block, 131
MediaTek, 119, 123
Metal oxide semiconductor field
  effect transistors
  (MOSFET), 138
Memory architecture, 270–273
Memory hierarchy, 106, 107,
  118, 119
Microarchitecture, 268–273, 287
Microbenchmarks
  advantages, 242
  architecture of hardware IP, 241
  CPU, 242, 243
  divide and conquer
    method, 241
  GPU, 244, 245
  media blocks, 247
  memory controllers, 247
  NPUs, 246, 247
  performance characteristics, 241
  product managers, 241
  and profilers, 247
  profiler tools, 241
  specialized tests, 241
  storage controllers, 247
Microsoft, 12
  Copilot+ PCs capabilities, 32
  DirectX, 125
  Surface Pro, 94
  Windows, 12
  Windows phone, 5
Monolithic die design, 166, 167
Monolithic SoC, 92
Monolithic SoC design, 310
Moore's law, 164, 310
MOSFET transistors, *see* Metal
  oxide semiconductor field
  effect transistors (MOSFET)
Motherboard, 198
M3 Series SoCs, 132
MSI Stealth, 94
MSS, *see* Market segment
  share (MSS)
Multi-chip modules (MCM), 267
  design, 92
  method, 310
Multi-die, 167

N

Netflix, 10
Neural processing unit (NPU),
  307, 308
  architecture, 125–127, 129, 130
  microbenchmarks, 246, 247

INDEX

NPU, see Neural processing unit (NPU)
NVIDIA, 15, 26, 178, 191, 192, 271, 282-284, 294, 295, 304
  discrete GPU design, 119
  GeForce RTX GPU Launch, 82
NVLink, 271

O

ONNX Runtime, 305
OpenCL, 282
Open ecosystems, 34
OpenGL, 282
Open source and proprietary GPU programming frameworks, 125
Open source pre-trained model generation, 304
Open source programming frameworks, 281-285
Open universal scene description (OpenUSD), 303
Operating system software, 6
Operating voltage and frequency, 142, 143
Original equipment manufacturers (OEMs), 177, 308, 311
  channel partners, 200
  consumer products, 195
  drivers, 199
  final product assembly and testing, 198, 199
  motherboard assembly, 198
  operating system, 199
  OSAT facilities, 195
  packages, 200
  PC devices, 94
  performance testing, 199
  product manufacturing flow, 196, 197
  quality and reliability checks, 197
  quality inspection, 199
  semiconductor chip packages, 197
  semiconductor product design to deployment flow, 195, 196
  semiconductor product developmental flow, 195
  software installation, 199
  and supply chain, 291
  tuning, 199
  warehouse, 310
Outsourced semiconductor assembly (OSAT), 162, 171-173, 194, 195, 311

P

PCB, see Printed circuit board (PCB)
PC ecosystems, 12
PC industry, 307
PC market segmentation, 71
PC SoC KPIs, 132
Performance analysis tools, 295, 296

INDEX

Performance management, 204
    KPIs, 204
    and measurement, 204, 205
    product strategy (*see* Product performance management strategy)
    semiconductor industry, 205
    strategy, 312
    systematic and strategic, 205
Performance measurement, 203
Performance per dollar, 179–181
Performance per watt, 152–155
Peripheral component interconnect express (PCIe) data speed, 271
PESTEL analysis, 73, 76
Pin grid array (PGA), 171
Porter's Five Forces framework, 74, 75
POST, *see* Power-on self-test (POST)
Power gating methods, 309
Power management, 134–137, 309
    from IP to device level, 149–152
Power-on self-test (POST), 198
Pre-silicon and post-silicon performance measurements, 233
    bring up measurements, 226
    characteristic measurement analysis, 223
    design and development phases, 232
    design specifications and architecture variables, 223
    device-level performance management, 232
    DFT and DFD approach, 228–231
    EDA tools, 231
    emulation and prototype measurements, 226
    formal verification measurements, 225
    functional testing measurements, 227
    and management, 224
    performance testing measurements, 227
    power and thermal Analysis measurements, 226
    product managers, 224
    simulation measurements, 224
    simulation synthesis and timing analysis data, 224
    static timing analysis (STA) measurements, 225
    stress and reliability testing measurements, 227
    yield analysis measurements, 228
Printed circuit board (PCB), 198
Process node differentiation, 176
Procyon 3DMarks, 237
Product management
    competitiveness, 307
    decision phases, 307
    mechanism, 313

INDEX

Product managers, 292, 307–309, 311–314
  advantages and disadvantages, 309
  AI-driven dynamic pricing algorithms, 301
  features, 293
  framework approach, 292
  and management, 310
  power, 309
  role, 308
  role in customer-centric approach, 314
  roles and responsibilities, 49, 50, 55–57
  social and economic value, 308
Product performance management strategy
  advantages, 218
  continuous learning, 218
  database management system, 207
  design phase, 220
  design specifications, 222
  device-level features, 220
  EOL, 222
  framework, 222
  gamers, 206
  go-to-market strategy, 254, 255
  implementing, 207
  life cycles, 219
  managing and monitoring, 218
  managing/improving performance and power, 220
  market positioning, 206
  and measurements, 219, 222
  performance analytics, 206
  performance characteristics, 207
  pre-silicon and post-silicon, 220, 222–232
  product KPIs, 219
  product managers, 206, 220
  product revisions, 207
  significance, 218
  skills and technologies, 221
  SoC, 232–238
  SoC level, 207–212
  stages in, 221
  stock exchange server, 207
  strategic planning, 206
  support and EOL management, 256
  system-level, 214–218
Product portfolio, 288–291
Product Release Qualification (PRQ), 54
Product roadmap KPIs, 257
  competitive intelligence, 285, 286
  dependencies, 265, 266
  design and microarchitecture, 268–273
  HW-SW co-design, 273–277
  process technology, 266, 267

product portfolio, 288–291
programmability and developer tools, 279–285
projections, 287, 288
semiconductor manufacturing technology, 266
SoC features, 266
system co-design, 277–279
Programmability and developer tools
building strengths, 281
CUDA, 279
drivers and APIs, 279
GPU market, 279
layers of end-to-end semiconductor devices, 280
open source and proprietary frameworks, 281–285
product roadmap, 281
semiconductor products, 279
Programmability framework, 304
Programmable frameworks, 305
Projections, 287, 288
Proprietary programming frameworks, 281–285
PRQ, *see* Product Release Qualification (PRQ)
Puget Bench, 153

Q

Qualcomm, 178
Qualcomm's Snapdragon X Elite CPU, 101

Quality management systems, 58

R

Radeon Open Compute (ROCm), 122, 281
Raymond, Lee R., 4
Ray tracing cores, 116
Ray tracing features, 293
RDNA3, 128
Real-world benchmarks, 250, 251
Reduced instruction set computer (RISC), 97
RISC V CPUs, 101
Risk mitigation model, 56
Roadmap planning, 29
Roadmaps KPIs, 261, 262
ROCm, *see* Radeon Open Compute (ROCm)

S

Samsung, 58, 174, 187, 192, 310
Samsung Galaxy, 94
Scalable matrix extensions (SME), 101
Security in semiconductor manufacturing, 181–183
Semiconductor competitive environment assessments, 72
Semiconductor design methodology, 51, 52

INDEX

Semiconductor industry, competition, 1
Semiconductor lithography, 158
Semiconductor manufacturing
   advanced process technologies, 160
   clock frequency and power efficiency, 159
   industry, 173
   IP scalability, 178
   leaders, 173–175
   monolithic and disaggregated design, 166
   multi-level metallization designs, 159
   muti-die chip, 165
   nonfunctional dies, 162
   pricing methodology, 175
   purification of silicon, 158
   signal propagation time, 159
   specialized skills and methodology, 157
   SWOT analysis, 161
   tape-out and masks, 161
   technology innovation, 163
Semiconductor product management, 16
   AI, 306
   life cycle, 308
      closed ecosystem, 38
      competitive analysis, 42
      competitive and improve user experience, 40
      contributors, 44
      demand generation, 45
      design and development cycles, 50, 51
      ecosystem partners, 41
      electronic device manufacturing, 37
      electronic devices, 59
      end of life, 59
      existing competition, 46, 47
      fabless design companies, 38
      go-to-market plans and planning productlaunch, 58
      hardware with augmented features, 39
      high-volume manufacturing, 57
      innovative features, 40
      maintenance and support, 59
      market, and product launch plans, 41
      market awareness, 45
      network connection, 40
      new product, 47–49
      performance degradation, 39
      planning phase, 43–45
      product plan, 44
      software applications, 37
      stages, 42
      technical feasibility, 44
      validation complexity, 39
Semiconductor product managers, 255

Semiconductor product roadmaps
  defining, 260, 261, 292
  guidance, 260
  KPIs, 261, 262, 265–296
  organized, 263, 264
  secret to strong, 292–296
Semiconductor products, 1
Semiconductor SoCs
  architecture of, 308
  packages, 196
  segments, 288
Shader cores, 116
Silicon, 8
Silicon technology, 160
Single instruction multiple data units (SIMD), 113, 121, 126, 132
SKUs i3/Ryzen 3, 95
Smartphones, 1
SME, *see* Scalable matrix extensions (SME)
SoC, *see* System on chip (SoC)
SoC architecture
  components, 93
  CPU AI, 112–114
  CPU KPIs, 108–112
  customer segments, 94
  data type support, 114
  integrated circuit, 92
  integration, 131, 133
  logical assumptions, 169
  microarchitecture, 102–105
  power supply and delivery management, 147, 148
  types, 168, 169
  unified IP design methodology across product lines, 94
Social value, 17, 18
SoC-level performance management strategy
  categories, 208
  categorization, 211
  characterization framework, 212, 213
  consumer and commercial PC user segments, 208
  design companies, 209
  DVFS, 209
  framework, 211
  PPA, 208–210
  product feature categories, 212
  scalability, 209
  semiconductor IP, 208
  targets, 211
  TDP, 208
  voltage scaling, 209
SoC system performance measurements
  architecture section, 235
  benchmarks, 237–253
  clock frequency, 234
  CPU IPC, 234
  features and characteristics, 234
  functional operation, 232
  hierarchy, 233
  key performance contributors and indicators, 234
  KPIs, 235, 236

INDEX

Benchmarks (*cont.*)
   launch phase, 233
   market positioning, 233
   methodology, 234
   metrics, 236
   operates efficiently, 232
   parameters, 234
   pre-silicon and post-silicon, 233
   pre-silicon and post-silicon design parameters, 234
   product development life cycle, 232
   quality of semiconductor, 232
   specifications, 232
   standardization, 236
   technology industry, 237
Software, 9
   applications, 10
   manageability and asset management IT infrastructure, 11
Sony's AIBO (AI RoBot), 86
SPECrate, 153
Strategic analysis in competitive strategy development framework, 69
Strategic innovations and investments, 85
Strategic product positioning, 78, 79
Strategic risk identification and mitigation plans, 86
Strategic roadmap objectives, 83, 84

Strategic sustainability and product renewal plans, 81, 82
Supervised machine learning models, 301
Supply chain and OEMs, 291
Strengths, weaknesses, opportunities, and threats (SWOT) analysis, 30, 31, 33, 34, 70, 191, 304
Synthetic benchmarks, 248–250
System co-design, 277–279
System hardware and software organization, 6
System-level performance management strategy, 214–218
System on chip (SoC), 39, 206, 307, 309, 312
   architecture (*see* SoC architecture)
   packages, 198
   product management, 5
SWOT analysis, *see* Strengths, weaknesses, opportunities, and threats (SWOT) analysis

T

Taiwan Semiconductor Manufacturing Company (TSMC), 161, 175, 176, 185, 187, 266, 267, 310
Tape-in, 52

INDEX

Tape-out, 53
Tensor cores, 116
TensorRT runtime, 304
Tera, 117
TFLOPS of GPU on PC SoCs, 122
Thermal design power (TDP), 143–145, 208
3D Wildlife, 121
TOPS, *see* Trillion operations per second (TOPS)
TOPs/FLOPs, 309
Total addressable market (TAM), 38
Transistor technology, 8, 9, 159, 160, 188
Transistor threshold voltage, 138–141
Trillion operations per second (TOPS), 127
TSMC, *see* Taiwan Semiconductor Manufacturing Company (TSMC)

U

Unsupervised machine learning models, 301

V

Value chain and skill set analysis, 70
VCache, 107

Visual identifiers, 229
Voltage to leakage dependencies, 140

W

Wafer fabrication, 162
Wafer pricing plus pricing, 177
Waste electrical and electronic equipment (WEEE), 58
Wave matrix multiply accumulate (WMMA), 271
WEEE, *see* (*see* Waste electrical and electronic equipment (WEEE))
Windows PC ecosystem, 13
Windows PC ecosystem economic value distribution, 24, 25
WMMA, *see* (*see* Wave matrix multiply accumulate (WMMA))
WWDC, 274

X

x86 architecture, 97, 99, 100
Xilinx, 85

Y, Z

Yahoo dismissed Google, 10

GPSR Compliance

The European Union's (EU) General Product Safety Regulation (GPSR) is a set of rules that requires consumer products to be safe and our obligations to ensure this.

If you have any concerns about our products, you can contact us on

ProductSafety@springernature.com

In case Publisher is established outside the EU, the EU authorized representative is:

Springer Nature Customer Service Center GmbH
Europaplatz 3
69115 Heidelberg, Germany

www.ingramcontent.com/pod-product-compliance
Lightning Source LLC
LaVergne TN
LVHW010335260326
834688LV00036B/724